Objects of Devotion

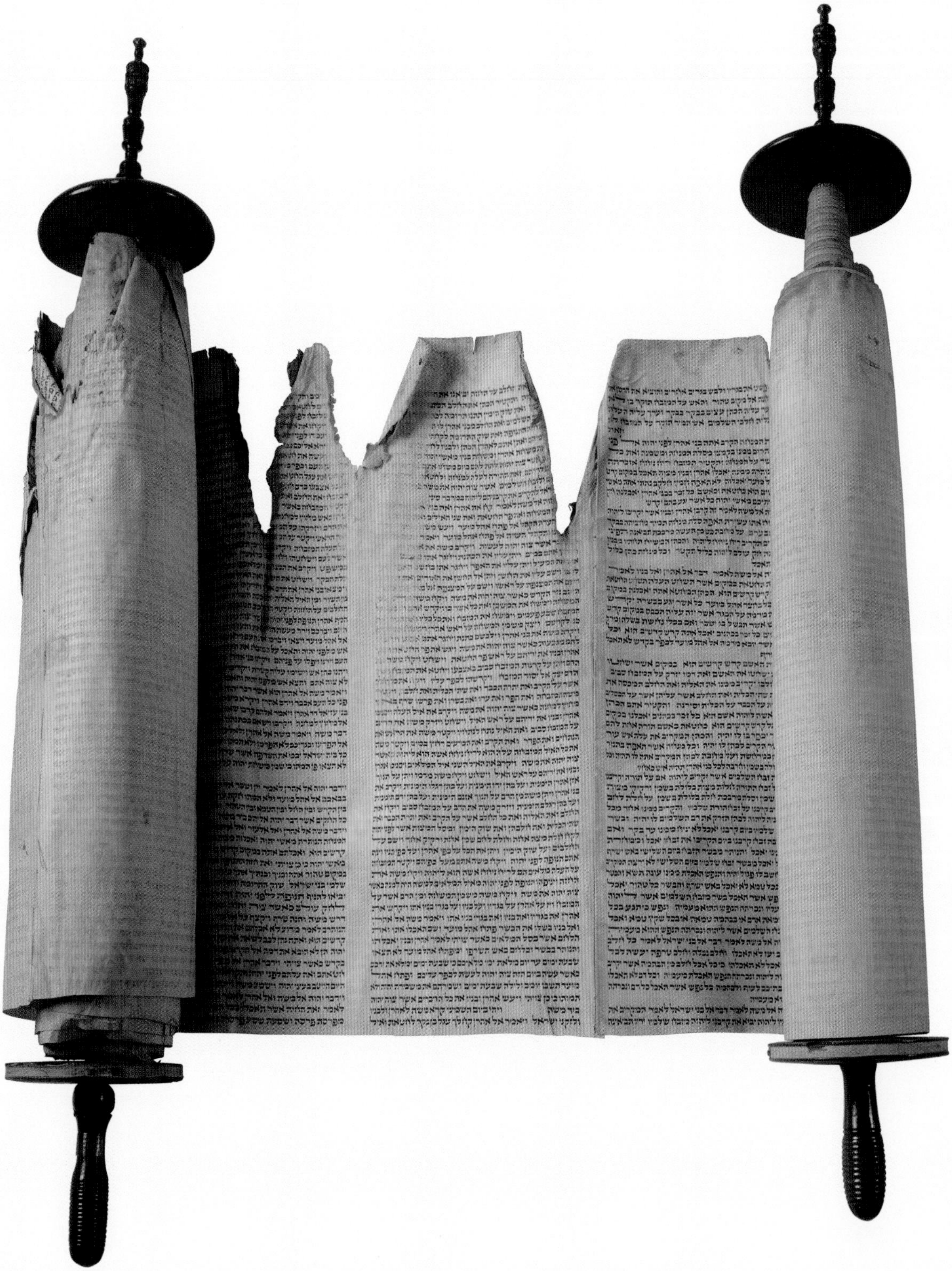

Objects of Devotion

Religion in Early America

Peter Manseau

Smithsonian Books
Washington, DC

Contents

Foreword

IT HAS OFTEN BEEN SAID that religion is a subject best avoided in polite conversation. Few other topics have inspired such fierce devotion or kindled such heated debate. Yet one cannot go very far in the discussion of American history without encountering the influence of religious communities, spiritual traditions, and individuals motivated by the many faiths that have called the United States home. Religion in all its variety is a vital part of the past we share.

In this publication and its accompanying exhibition, we are pleased to present religion in early America as seen through some of the objects with which it was practiced, the people who used them, and a number of significant documents that have expressed, challenged, and transformed American beliefs.

In the stories told throughout this book, religion is rarely walled off or kept separate from other aspects of life but rather is a dimension that informs many others. Consequently, some of the objects shown here are easily identifiable as religious, while others are not. A silver chalice that Governor John Winthrop brought to the Massachusetts Bay Colony in 1630, for example, was later given as a gift to First Church in Boston, where Puritan settlers used it for the sacrament of Communion. A compass sundial owned by Winthrop's contemporary Roger Williams, meanwhile, does not so loudly proclaim its role in American religious history, though it was equally significant. Both objects reveal the ways in which the sacred and the secular have interacted in American history. The cup bears the ornament of a sea monster, suggesting that it was a common drinking vessel put to liturgical use. The compass sundial, used after Williams was exiled from Massachusetts for his heretical views, played a role in the creation of Providence Plantation, the American colony where religious freedom first took root. *Objects of Devotion* seeks to put such objects into dialogue with one another, demonstrating that religion was as complex and dynamic in early America as it is today.

This book and the *Religion in Early America* exhibition, on which it is based, are only the beginning of a renewed engagement with the role of religion in American history by the museum. In the years ahead, we will offer concerts, lectures, theatrical presentations, and educational programs that will expand our exploration of religion in America from our earliest history to the present and into the future.

We hope you will join us as we make this a conversation not to be avoided but encouraged and enjoyed.

John L. Gray,
Elizabeth MacMillan Director,
National Museum of American History

J. Carwitham, *A South East View of the Great Town of Boston in New England in America,* circa 1730–60. Print. From *The American Revolution in Drawings and Prints: A Checklist of 1765– 1790 Graphics in the Library of Congress* (Washington, DC: U.S. Government Printing Office, 1975), no. 496.

Introduction

FOR DECADES, AN OLD, RUGGED CROSS lay hidden in the nation's capital. A few short miles from the White House, the Capitol Building, and the Smithsonian Institution, its two crudely welded beams of weathered iron, inscribed in English and Latin, were packed away in a nineteenth-century tower on the campus of Georgetown University, where understanding of the object's significance had faded with time.

Once forgotten even by archivists, this cross is, in fact, a vital piece of American history. It is believed to have been made by members of the first Catholic expedition to the English colonies, which traveled to Maryland in 1634 in two ships called the *Ark* and the *Dove*. Until then, settlement of the regions that would soon become home to the thirteen colonies had been overwhelmingly Protestant. These new settlers hoped to create a safe haven for religious difference in an age when theological disputes were often settled with violence.

The voyage itself—made by Catholics and Protestants packed together in tight quarters for four months—might be seen as an extreme experiment in what is today called interreligious dialogue. At the time, all involved understood their journey to be attended by even greater risk than the usual ocean crossing. Before they arrived, the Catholic passengers were given strict instructions on how to behave. "In their voyage to Mary Land," they were told, they should "be very careful to preserve unity & peace amongst all the passengers on Shipboard" and "suffer no scandal nor offence to be given to any of the Protestants . . . and that for that end, they [should] cause all Acts of Roman Catholic Religion to be done as privately as may be."

When these settlers performed the earliest Catholic liturgies in English North America soon after landing, the cross they used was made of rough-hewn timber, and it was large enough to suggest that they quickly became less concerned about worshipping "privately" than they had been while plying the Atlantic. Although this wooden cross has been lost to history, the more durable iron model they later fashioned somehow survived.

In 1862, 228 years after their landing, someone hoping to preserve the object's significance wrote on the vertical bar, "This cross is said to have been brought by the first settlers from England to St. Mary's." On the horizontal bar, another inscription reads, "Ad perpetuam rei memoriam" (For the eternal memory of the event).

Yet human memory is rarely eternal, at least not without frequent reminders. At some unknown moment in the last quarter of the nineteenth century or the first quarter of the twentieth, information about the cross's history became sufficiently scarce that it was packed away in storage at Georgetown, where it might never have been seen again. Crafted of metal and thus mostly immune to the ravages of time, it was not in danger of sharing the fate of the wooden cross that came before it, but →

Iron cross made by the first English Catholics in Maryland, mid-seventeenth century (detail). According to legend, it was made of materials taken from the *Ark* and the *Dove*, the ships that had brought Catholic settlers to America in 1634. The inscription on the horizontal bar translates as "For the eternal memory of the event."

1

like so much of the material culture of the American past, it faced a form of oblivion nearly as permanent: forgetting.

Late in the twentieth century, however, a Georgetown University professor rediscovered the cross by literally stumbling upon it in the storeroom of an administration building. Well aware of his church's struggle for acceptance throughout American history—a struggle similar to that undertaken by so many religious communities from the colonial era until today—Rev. G. Ronald Murphy, a Jesuit professor of German literature, immediately realized the importance of what he had found. Noting its use in some of the earliest liturgies held by Catholics "on English-speaking American soil," Professor Murphy stated that "the cross . . . represents the freedom of religion upon which this country was built."

Though the idea of this freedom is well known around the world, its construction was not without complications. Some might even argue that it remains a work in progress. To see an object that helped lay its foundation is to be reminded that freedom of religion is not just an idea but something welded together by the hands, the work, and the lives of previous generations. To be in its presence is also to discover that an object such as this old, rugged cross is not merely a piece of the past. It is part of an ongoing story of belief and believers, the places that brought them together, and the objects that both shaped and came to symbolize the complex system of relationships that together are known as religion.

When the current leader of the Roman Catholic Church, Pope Francis, visited the United States for the first time, in 2015, the centuries-old religious object previously packed away in a storeroom was taken from its newfound place of honor, in Dahlgren Chapel at the heart of Georgetown University, for use in the papal Mass in Washington, DC. Once hidden from view, it again stood for America's rich religious history. At times forgotten, the cross was now displayed for the world to see.

✵　✵　✵

There is perhaps no narrative more vital to the history of the United States than that of the role religion has played, variously as stimulus and complication, in the nation's exploration, establishment, and expansion. Regardless of one's own beliefs, the cultural significance of religion remains relevant to all. It is an inescapable fact of America's past, present, and future.

It has often been said that the United States is one of the "most religious" nations on earth. If this is so, it is not merely because it is today home to more Christians than any other country, or because the diversity of faiths within its borders is greater than that in any other corner of the globe. It is, rather, among the most religious of nations because a unique combination of religious freedom, religious diversity, and religious growth has created throughout the centuries a particularly fruitful—and at times volatile—environment for both interaction among spiritual traditions and the birth of new beliefs and practices.

Religion in Early America is the first exhibit at the Smithsonian Institution's National Museum of American History to tell the story of religion in the United

States through the material culture of the diverse spiritual pursuits at large when the nation was young. With objects drawn from every part of American life and every region of the country as it came into being, the exhibition explores the great variety of religious traditions vying for adherents, acceptance, and a prominent place in the public square during the colonial period and the early republic, roughly from the 1630s to the 1840s.

Interior of the First Baptist Meetinghouse, Providence, Rhode Island, circa 1933. Photograph by George J. Vaillancourt. The church, built in 1774–75, was designed by Joseph Brown following English models.

The original thirteen states were home to approximately three thousand churches and more than a dozen Christian denominations, including Anglicans, Baptists, Catholics, Congregationalists, Lutherans, Methodists, Presbyterians, and Quakers. Christianity, however, has never been the whole story. Those who held various Christian creeds lived from the beginning alongside other traditions: Judaism was practiced from Charleston, South Carolina, to Philadelphia, Pennsylvania, and Newport, Rhode Island. Islam and a dozen or more African religions were brought by the enslaved and practiced in secret as solace and protest. Native American rituals survived against the odds, often through the adaptive blending of new beliefs with old ones. Some homegrown movements such as Mormonism prospered beyond all expectation, while others flared brightly but then quickly faded away. These faiths were soon joined by others, giving the United States a reputation throughout the world as a nation where, in theory if not always in practice, all are free to believe and worship as they choose, both individually and in communities of their own making.

Rather than being achieved through fiat, this freedom was wrought through struggle and negotiation. While some early statesmen proposed the use of taxes to support churches as safeguards of morality and social order, for example, others argued that preferential treatment for one group would put all others in jeopardy. Proponents of Enlightenment ideals emphatically declared religion a personal matter but maintained that each citizen's freedom necessarily must not extend so far as to infringe on the freedom of another. Among the founders were those who believed government should remain neutral in matters of faith while insisting that the people who make up government would be foolish to act as if religion did not exist. Crafting the religion clauses of the First Amendment, James Madison anticipated the spirit of Thomas Jefferson's proposed "wall of separation" between church and state but left the height and porousness of this wall open to interpretation.

Yet even this centuries-long epic of compromise does not fully capture the interaction of faiths within a society at once thoroughly secular and endlessly diverse in matters of belief. Though government has certainly played a role in American religious life, from the beginning the direction of spiritual transformation in this country has far more often been bottom-up than top-down. →

Methodist Camp Meeting,
1836. Lithograph.

Flowerings of religious devotion known as Great Awakenings redrew the nation's spiritual landscape in the 1730s and again from the 1790s to the 1840s. Led by charismatic preachers including George Whitefield, Jonathan Edwards, and Charles Finney, these movements encouraged emotional exuberance in prayer and dramatic conversions at camp meetings and tent revivals. More restrained modes of worship fell away as Americans sought heightened religious experiences in newly formed denominations such as Methodism, which had no churches in the middle of the eighteenth century but nearly twenty thousand one hundred years later.

Through this lens, the story of religion in America might primarily be seen as concerning the movement of ideas, but it is also about the various means by which those ideas were transported. From the massive church bells of bustling urban centers to the makeshift pulpits that the traveling preachers of the Great Awakenings used to deliver open-air sermons across the expanse of a mostly rural nation, the medium has often been inseparable from the message in American religion. Religious communication frequently served both sacred and civic functions. While its primary audience was often a single congregation, at other times it drew much larger communities together.

Meanwhile, sacred texts of all varieties found eager readerships in sanctuaries, personal libraries, and the increasingly crowded public square. The creation of such works was at once a reflection of communal religious concerns, an opportunity for individual spiritual expression, and a contribution to the material record of the era.

The Bible especially has had a remarkable influence in the United States. According to two preeminent scholars of the religion clauses of the U.S. Constitution, John Witte and Joel Nichols, it was "by far the most widely used and commonly cited text in the American founding era." Though codified centuries before Columbus set sail, the Bible has arguably come into its own in America, where more editions of the Jewish and Christian sacred books have been published than anywhere else. The examples of biblical texts throughout this book suggest a few of the many roles it has played in the lives of Americans and the development of communities from which the nation emerged. The Bible in America is not one book but many. From colonial primers that used the stories of scripture to teach reading skills to children, through the first texts printed in the New World, to the thick tome on which George Washington took his first oath of office, no other single book has meant so much to so many.

The story told in the *Religion in Early America* exhibit is not merely about individual experiences with religious traditions, however. Nor does it concern only shifts in church membership or the dissemination of ideas. It is also a story of mass migrations and the widespread societal changes they wrought: the turbulent interactions of longtime residents and new arrivals, each challenging and transforming the distinctive mores of the country's many regional cultures.

From the arrival of the Pilgrims in Massachusetts in 1620, for example, religion in New England was shaped by the tension between traditions brought across the ocean and spiritual developments born of new experiences in a new land. Early efforts to enforce uniformity of belief and practice eventually gave way to an ever-expanding "spiritual marketplace" of Anglicans and Baptists, Quakers and Shakers, Congregationalists and Unitarians, as well as the resilient traditions of the region's original inhabitants. The Pilgrims were only one chapter of a story that soon included new worlds of faith. While the first English settlements in Massachusetts were intended to be theologically uniform, almost immediately differences of opinion became a part of the American religious experience. Dissenters left to establish colonies of their own, while members of new denominations arrived and soon brought about changes from within, creating a region known for both piety and diversity.

Meanwhile, at the crossroads of the colonies and the young United States, the Mid-Atlantic became the site of ongoing struggles for two kinds of liberty: freedom of worship and the abolition of slavery. Throughout the colonial era and the early republic, successive reconsiderations of the meaning of religious tolerance shaped the region. Jews made a home in New Amsterdam despite the colonial governor Peter Stuyvesant's reluctance to host them. Under the leadership of the Calvert and Carroll families, Catholics established Maryland as their only safe haven in English North America. Formerly enslaved men and women founded churches of their own in Pennsylvania, which, thanks to William Penn and waves of German immigrants who saw in his colony a hope of freedoms that their own nation lacked, had long served as a refuge for those wanting to practice religion as they pleased.

Finally, the frontier spirit and wide-open spaces of the southern colonies fostered an explosion of religious devotion, which continued throughout the years of the early republic. While not exclusively a rural phenomenon, the Second Great Awakening encouraged an eminently portable, emotionally driven form of faith ideally suited to an expanding country. Born in the so-called Burned-Over District of upstate New York, the movement exploded in the South, with its variety of cultures and high degree of religious hybridity and syncretism. Evangelical revivals brought the faithful out of their churches and into fields and forests, while the non-Christian beliefs and practices of the enslaved managed both to endure out of sight and, through adaption, to add new dimensions to Christian worship. Through it all, the influence of the established Anglican Church sought to impose religious norms even →

as it inspired forceful reactions in the form of dissenters willing to risk fines and imprisonment in defense of conscience.

Of course, American religious life did not end at the national borders. Outside the territory of the English colonies and the early republic, lands then in Spanish and French control developed distinctive religious cultures that would soon bring even greater diversity to the young United States. Blending Roman Catholic beliefs with Native American aesthetics and techniques, the carved and painted religious statues known as santos became a particularly vibrant art form in Puerto Rico. As the conception of which lands should be part of America spread west—and the slave trade continued throughout the Caribbean—the spiritual traditions found just beyond U.S. territory became even more influential.

Drawn from all these regions and from radically different moments spanning from the middle of the seventeenth century to the middle of the nineteenth, the objects assembled for *Religion in Early America* paint a picture of the many ways religious ideas have remade the country. Seen individually, each object—such as the iron cross found at Georgetown—says something in particular about the influence of religious diversity, freedom, and growth in a young nation rapidly expanding both its borders and its beliefs. Taken together, the objects also suggest the importance of the work of museums in preserving the past and conveying its stories. Religion in America cannot be understood merely through the history of ideas; it must also be understood through the history of things—the objects of devotion around which Americans of every generation have organized their communities and collaboratively built their nation.

To view objects within a museum space, and in books such as this one, is inevitably to consider the relationships among them. Arranged in display cases, they seem gathered as if in conversation—a conversation to which museum visitors are invited as well. As you study the images of the objects that follow, it is worth turning the pages between centuries and regions to see the ways in which religious traditions, the people who followed them, and the things that helped inform, maintain, and create the distinctions among diverse faiths likewise converse across the ages, sometimes in agreement, often in argument.

Some of the objects collected here might have been used side by side, such as strings of wampum beads from the Native American tribes of New England and the Algonquian Bible completed by John Eliot. Each is a marker of cultures in transition, transformed through interaction with new understandings of the world.

Other objects have unexpectedly intertwined histories, such as the saddlebags of the former slave-owning preacher Freeborn Garrettson and the hymnal prepared by the formerly enslaved minister Richard Allen. A sermon delivered by Garrettson—perhaps from notes held in the leather bags shown on page 98—helped Allen win his freedom. In this case, one object played a role in the creation of another.

Still other objects never could have come into contact, but they have much in common despite their signs of apparent difference. The Communion cup owned by one of the best-known early Americans, Governor John Winthrop of

Massachusetts, and the polished beads used for protection by an enslaved man or woman whose name has been lost to history are objects whose owners could not have been more different, yet perhaps each was brought across the Atlantic and treasured as a symbol of the divine, and they are joined here as expressions of the American experience.

In the gathering of the objects and documents that fill this book and the exhibit cases of *Religion in Early America*, care has been taken to include items drawn from many different peoples and traditions that can claim the name "American." Their materiality is a reminder of their commonality, the complementary nature of the diverse lives that together are our common history. While the question of who should be enumerated as citizens has often been fraught, considering both the counted and the uncounted through the material culture they have left behind allows us to contend anew with the reality of the past.

At the same time, it can never be forgotten that telling stories of religious experiences based on objects that endure across the centuries risks privileging certain kinds of experiences over others. By design or by circumstance, many faiths in American history have found their power in the ephemeral, or in varieties of materiality whose sacred quality is believed to be diminished by precisely the kind of display that museums and books such as this require. Because of this, and in order to provide a view of the men and women who created and made use of the objects shown here and a look at the places where these objects would have been found, a sampling of representative people and houses of worship provides further context throughout the pages that follow. While some are well known and historically significant, others are less so but are included in order not to overlook those who lived their faiths quietly and mostly unnoticed, as a great number of Americans have always done.

Paten, eighteenth century. Silver. This small plate for the Eucharist was used by Archbishop John Carroll, the first Roman Catholic prelate in America.

The interplay of communal and individual identities was one of the most vital, and at times volatile, aspects of religious life in the colonies and the nascent United States. The question of whether belief should be a wholly personal matter or something subject to public discussion began in churches and among people of faith, and it continues to enliven current debates among the religious and the nonreligious alike. As the display of religious items both personal and communal makes clear, objects of devotion are often where the private and the public meet.

In the United States, the influence of religion has long reached beyond home and church to virtually every facet of life, from commerce to defense, politics to media, education to entertainment. The touchstones of our common culture—America's music, literature, arts, and even its sports—are impossible to imagine without the distinctive blend of deep faith and irreverent doubt that has marked American attitudes toward religion since colonial times. From the First Great Awakening's contributions to the American Revolution to the influence of the Second Great Awakening on such social reform movements as abolitionism and women's suffrage, we remain the nation that religion in our early history has made. ◆

New England

The popular image of the dour Puritan—dressed in black, resigned to a life of hardship, eager to pass judgment, and suspicious of all manner of enjoyment—suggests only part of the story of religion in the northern English colonies and the states they would become. Though many of the settlers of Plymouth Plantation and the Massachusetts Bay Colony came to New England in the hope of creating a religiously homogenous society in which they could worship as they saw fit, spiritual life in America proved to be vastly more complicated. Theological disputes turned so bitter that they often threatened the very survival of villages and the churches that were the centers of civic life. The "strange opinions" of some religious rabble-rousers challenged the idea of theological uniformity, the establishment of which many of those who had fled England in search of their own religious freedom took for granted as their right.

The varieties of religious experience in New England were not limited to disagreements among Christians. From the very beginning, European settlers lived within a complex of spiritual influences, including the traditions of the Native peoples of the region; beliefs and practices brought by enslaved laborers from Africa, South America, and the Caribbean; and constantly kindling innovative expressions of devotion.

Thomas Cole, *New England Scenery,* 1839. Oil on canvas. Mr. and Mrs. Samuel M. Nickerson Collection, 1900.558, The Art Institute of Chicago

✳ The Bay Psalm Book

Title page, Bay Psalm
Book, 1640.

WHEN THE ENGLISH PROTESTANTS known as the Pilgrims and the Puritans arrived in Massachusetts in the 1620s and 1630s, each in their own way sought a fresh start in their lives and their faith. While the former were separatists who had fully split from the Church of England and the latter hoped that stricter religious practices might purify their church from within, both groups regarded America as a "New Jerusalem" where they might build a revitalized community of faith.

Despite such ambitions, many of the trappings of their worship, which they had brought from the other side of the Atlantic, remained unchanged for some time. While they continued to use the same versions of scripture in their communal worship for a decade after arriving in New England, many began to believe their new land might require new words of praise.

The Book of Psalms was at the time the primary source of sung devotion during church services. The idea of creating their own renderings of these biblical songs emerged among the colonists of Massachusetts in the 1630s. Believing that existing editions of the works traditionally understood to have been written by King David gave them only paraphrases of his poetry, in which alterations of his original meaning were frequent and unnecessary, they hoped to find a way to move closer to the source.

There were by then significant scholarly resources available in New England, in the form of ministers well versed in the languages of the Bible. Divines such as John Cotton (page 25), Richard Mather, Thomas Welde, and John Eliot (page 13) saw the need not only to translate the ancient Hebrew songs anew, but also to print the result on American soil.

The Bay Psalm Book, also known as *The Whole Booke of Psalmes Faithfully Translated into English Metre*, is the product of that ambitious undertaking, completed in 1640. Within a generation of the original English settlement of the region, 1,700 copies were printed in Cambridge, Massachusetts. Though often called the first book printed in the English colonies, it was not, in fact, the first title to roll off the Puritan printing press. (That distinction belongs to "Oath of a Freeman," a loyalty vow required of all men of the colony not enslaved or indentured.) The Bay Psalm Book was, however, America's first hymnal.

Much like carving homes out of the wilderness, it was a fully communal effort. Thirty scholar-translators worked from existing English paraphrases as well as the original biblical text, dividing the 150 psalms equally among themselves. French-milled paper and an English-made printing press and ink were shipped from London, accompanied by an indentured laborer trained in operating the equipment. The press's owner, Rev. Joseph Glover, died during the ocean passage, making his widow, Elizabeth, this country's earliest purveyor of print media. →

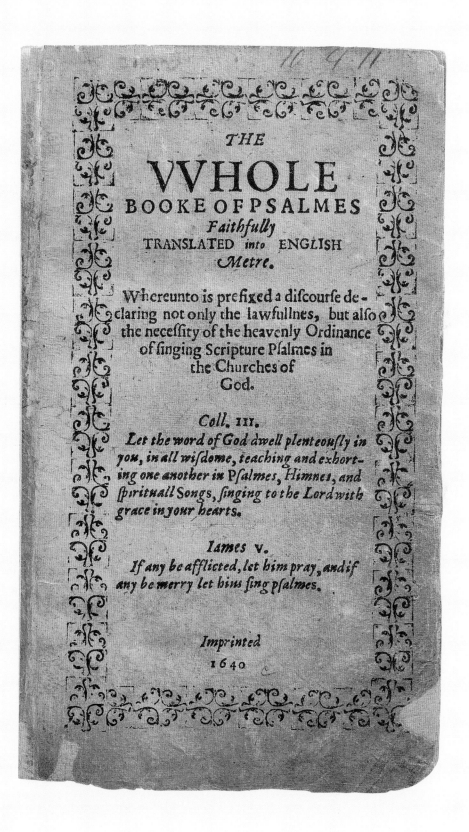

THE
VVHOLE
BOOKE OF PSALMES
Faithfully
TRANSLATED *into* ENGLISH
Metre.

Whereunto is prefixed a discourse declaring not only the lawfullnes, but also
the necessity of the heavenly Ordinance
of singing Scripture Psalmes in
the Churches of
God.

Coll. III.

*Let the word of God dwell plenteously in
you, in all wisdome, teaching and exhort-
ing one another in Psalmes, Himnes, and
spirituall Songs, singing to the Lord with
grace in your hearts.*

Iames V.

*If any be afflicted, let him pray, and if
any be merry let him sing psalmes.*

Imprinted
1640

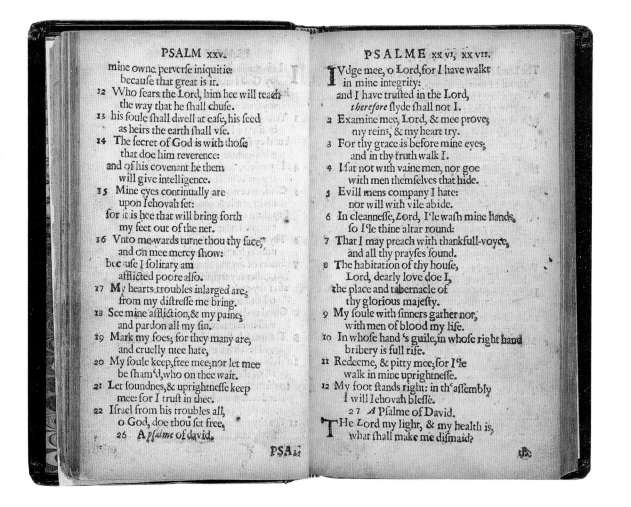

PSALM xxv.

mine owne perverse iniquitie:
  because that great is it.
12 Who fears the Lord, him hee will teach
   the way that he shall chuse.
13 his soule shall dwell at ease, his seed
   as heirs the earth shall vse.
14 The secret of God is with those
   that doe him reverence:
   and of his covenant he them
   will give intelligence.
15 Mine eyes continually are
   upon Iehovah set:
   for it is hee that will bring forth
   my feet out of the net.
16 Vnto me-wards turne thou thy face,
   and on mee mercy show:
   bee-ause I solitary am
   afflicted poore also.
17 My hearts troubles inlarged are,
   from my distresse me bring.
18 See mine affliction,& my paine,
   and pardon all my sin.
19 Mark my foes; for they many are,
   and cruelly mee hate,
20 My soule keep,free mee;nor let mee
   be sham'd,who on thee wait.
21 Let soundnes,& uprightnesse keep
   mee: for I trust in thee.
22 Israel from his troubles all,
   o God, doe thou set free.
   26 A psalme of david.

PSAL.

PSALME xxvi, xxvii.

I Vdge mee, o Lord,for I have walkt
  in mine integrity:
  and I have trusted in the Lord,
  therefore slyde shall not I.
2 Examine mee, Lord, & mee prove,
  my reins, & my heart try.
3 For thy grace is before mine eyes,
  and in thy truth walk I.
4 I sat not with vaine men, nor goe
  with men themselves that hide.
5 Evill mens company I hate:
  nor will with vile abide.
6 In cleannesse, Lord, I'le wash mine hands,
  so I'le thine altar round:
7 That I may preach with thankfull-voyce,
  and all thy prayses sound.
8 The habitation of thy house,
  Lord, dearly love doe I,
  the place and tabernacle of
  thy glorious majesty.
9 My soule with sinners gather nor,
  with men of blood my life.
10 In whose hand's guile,in whose right hand
   bribery is full rife.
11 Redeeme, & pitty mee;for I'le
   walk in mine uprightnesse.
12 My foot stands right: in th'assembly
   I will Iehovah blesse.
   27 A Psalme of David.
T He Lord my light, & my health is,
  what shall make me dismaid?

Interior pages, Bay Psalm Book. Psalms were sung by Puritans as their primary mode of worship and were the only music allowed to them.

Despite the enormity of their achievement, the book's creators were humble about what they had accomplished. "If therefore the verses are not always so smooth and elegant as some may desire or expect, let them consider that God's altar needs not our polishings," they wrote in the preface, "for we have respected rather a plain translation than to smooth our verses with the sweetness of any paraphrase, and so have attended conscience rather than elegance, fidelity rather than poetry, in translating the Hebrew words into the English language."

While the Bay Psalm Book was widely distributed, only eleven copies are known to have survived until today. It was, after all, intended to be used. Though it was the result of scholarly effort theretofore unknown in America, the book was created primarily, in the words of its makers, "so we may sing in Zion the Lord's songs of praise according to His own will, until He takes us from hence, and wipes away all our tears, and bids us enter into our Master's joy to sing eternal Halleluiahs."

In a society where attendance at worship services was compulsory, every copy of the Bay Psalm Book was likely held and handled as often as public prayers were spoken. Its pages were turned by men, women, and children, some of whom had been born in England, some on American soil. Its verses were sung by those who knew the tunes by heart; its rhythms echoed through their days. ◆

John Eliot's Algonquian Bible

THIRTY YEARS AFTER he had joined the scholarly effort that led to the creation of the Bay Psalm Book (page 10), the Rev. John Eliot took on an even more ambitious translation project: a rendering of the Christian scripture into the Algonquian language of the Wampanoag people. His work ultimately led to the first publication of a Bible in America.

From the beginning of the English settlement of Massachusetts Bay, the conversion of the region's Native inhabitants was stated as a reason for the colony's existence. Governor John Winthrop (page 21) had sworn that he would "draw the natives of this country to the knowledge of the true God." Such efforts, however, seemed far from a priority as the hardships of colonial life accumulated.

Eliot arrived in Boston in 1631 and almost immediately made evangelism his life's work. Offered a prestigious post at Winthrop's First Church (page 20), he chose instead to work on the outskirts of the settlement in Roxbury and Dorchester, from which he was better able to make contact with those he believed were most in need of his Gospel message.

Within five years of his arrival, Eliot made his first, mostly futile efforts to preach to the Native peoples. "When I first attempted it, they gave no heed unto it," he wrote, "but were weary, and rather despised what I said." Sometime later, however, he heard that some of his original audience had developed an interest in "English fashions" and a desire to "live after their manner." He wrote: "When I heard, my heart moved with in mee, abhorring that wee should sit still and let that work alone, and hoping that this motion of them was of the Lord, and that this mind in them was a preparative to imbrace the Law and Word of God; and therefore I told them that they and wee were already one. . . . I told them that if they would learn to know God, I would teach them."

But first, Eliot knew, he himself had to learn. The key to evangelism, he came to believe, was not forcing Native Americans to bend to "English fashions" but rather bending scripture to meet them, using the language of his audience and remaking the Bible so that they could understand it.

To accomplish this, he needed first to learn a new language, a process that involved, he said, "some paines and teaching." With the help of Wampanoag converts, including →

John Chester Buttre, engraving after J. A. Oertel, *Eliot, the First Missionary among the Indians,* 1856, published by Marian Johnson & Co., New York.

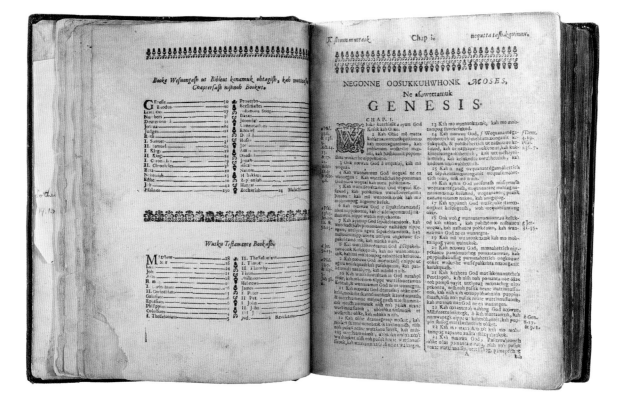

John Eliot's translation of scripture into the Algonquian language, the first Bible published in English North America.

John Sassamon and a young man trained in printing operations called John Printer, Eliot published *The Holy Bible Containing the Old Testament and the New; Translated into the Indian Language* in 1663.

In a sense, the true audience for Eliot's Algonquian Bible may not have been those who spoke the language. The Algonquian language was purely oral, with no system of writing, so the book was largely incomprehensible to those for whom it was supposedly intended. For his Bible to be of any use, Eliot had not only to learn to speak in the manner of the Wampanoag tribe, but also to provide instruction on how the written form was to be read. Toward this end, he published the *Primer of the Massachusetts Indian Language*, to be used alongside the sacred text. "I told [them] I would come to their Wigwams, and teach them, their wives and children, which they seemed very glad of," he said.

While a thousand copies of Eliot's Bible were printed for distribution throughout New England—mainly to the settlements of converted Indians called "praying towns"—it is unknown how many were actively used. The book was perhaps of greater interest back home in England, where significant funds had been collected for its production. English supporters of evangelization received it as proof of the possibility of converting the peoples of the Americas to Christianity.

Though perhaps little read on either side of the Atlantic, Eliot's Bible was the first of uncountable editions of scripture that would be produced in America. It appeared eighty years before the next full edition, in German, was published in 1743, and more than a century before the first U.S. English Bible was published in 1782. ◆

❋ *Wampum*

WAMPUM IS PERHAPS the most commonly misunderstood emblem of Native American life. Popular history has often depicted these garlands of polished shell (page 16) merely as a form of premodern money. For a quarter century in Massachusetts (1637–61), it was even recognized as legal tender and accepted for the payment of taxes. Yet obsession with its usefulness for trading has often obscured its true value to the cultures that created it.

In the mid-seventeenth century, New England colonists assigned a rate of exchange for wampum of four beads to a penny. Strings of these white and black beads might also be bartered for other goods prized in the early colonial period, such as deer, bear, and beaver skins. As trade grew between colonists and various East Coast Native American nations, the quahog and periwinkle shells that were the raw material of wampum became scarce, while forgery of strings by Europeans increased. Its cash value plummeting, wampum soon faded as a preferred currency for intercultural commerce.

While most colonial considerations of wampum and its worth largely focused on its numismatic role, in fact this was not its only—or even its primary—function. It also had religious significance. Before it was a form of cash, it was a priceless ritual object used to mark sacred occasions or record communal memories. Its spiritual uses rather than its economic weight added solemnity to its presentation during negotiations with the colonies and the young United States. From the beginning, interactions between English settlers and Native Americans included exchanges of religious ideas.

"Indian religion," the scholar George Snyderman once noted, "was subject to constant change from within and without. Beliefs and ceremonies changed as new needs became evident, and acceptance of beliefs and utilization of ceremonies varied from band to band." Within a system of spiritual beliefs and practices in which, as Snyderman further observed, "the willingness and ability to adopt and remold content, function, and ceremonials" was always evident, the use of wampum as a religious signifier remained flexible but constant. There were few ceremonies that did not employ strings of beads to some degree. Often crafted from pure white shells, "message strings" were used to announce the coming of an important ritual; "confession strings," meanwhile, were of more varied hues and were used to acknowledge wrongdoing or conflict, and in hopes of its resolution.

As a memory-keeping device, wampum also served as something akin to scripture. It was used to tell the sacred history of a people. As such, it played an important role in rituals of birth, death, marriage, and the bestowal of authority. Understanding its significance, European settlers sometimes sought to use it to their advantage. In at least one case, Jesuits persuaded a group within the Iroquois →

Wampum, 1700s. While
they often served as a form
of currency, the strings of
shell made by the Native
American tribes of
New England also had
many religious uses.

people to create a wampum belt promising that they would embrace Christianity and leave their traditional beliefs and practices behind.

The word *wampum* comes from *wampumpeage*, which in the Algonquian language means "white strings"—a simply descriptive name that obscures the gathered beads' cultural significance. As a nineteenth-century account described them, these white strings were "the universal bonds of nations and individuals, the inviolable and sacred pledges of word and deed. No promise was binding unless confirmed by gifts of wampum. . . . They cemented friendships, confirmed alliances, sealed treaties, and effectually effaced the memory of injuries."

No mere raw materials, wampum beads were fashioned through a painstaking process. First, shells had to be gathered in great numbers and their smooth inner sections removed from their rough outer surfaces. Each piece was then carefully pierced with a stone drill and finally shaped and shined on a polishing stone.

Along with drawing out beautiful white, black, and purple shades in the shells, such accumulated human effort made wampum ideal for moments of healing, mourning, negotiation, and reconciliation. It was given to the spirits of the dead to aid their journey to the next world. It was considered so sacred and essential to the act of ratifying treaties between peoples that it was naturally used when Native Americans negotiated agreements with Europeans.

At a meeting of Iroquois and English in 1756, for example, a "prodigious large belt" was displayed. As recorded in the papers of Sir William Johnson, a British official who commanded Iroquois and colonial militia forces during the French and Indian War, a leader called Red Head of the Onondaga people, one of the Six Nations of the Iroquois, urged the colonists to understand its significance. "Look with all attention on this belt and remember the solemn and mutual engagements we entered into," he said. "Be assured we look upon them as sound and shall on our part punctually perform them as long as we remain a people."

Wampum maintained this ritual significance for a short time after the birth of the republic. In 1794, President George Washington marked a treaty with the Six Nations of the Iroquois with the creation of a six-foot-long belt of wampum shells arranged in a pattern showing thirteen forms, symbolizing the original states, holding hands with two forms representing the Mohawk and the Seneca, both prominent members of the Iroquois league. All the figures were arranged around a depiction of a longhouse, the traditional dwelling that was also a symbol of the beliefs and traditions of the people. Article 1 of the treaty begins as hopefully as the wampum belt's image of cooperation: "Peace and friendship are hereby firmly established, and shall be perpetual, between the United States and the Six Nations."

The symbolic importance of wampum in diplomatic settings was such that when first English colonists and then representatives of the American government accepted it as a sign of agreement and later broke their word, this was an unfathomable turn of events. Sadly, as this pattern came to be expected, wampum's meaning nearly disappeared. Its transformation from a largely religious and political device before European arrival to an economic instrument afterward was a significant cultural change that rippled through American history. ◆

✳ *The Winthrop Cup*

AS THE FIRST GOVERNOR of the Massachusetts Bay Colony, John Winthrop (page 21) borrowed a phrase from Christian scripture when he said his settlement should be "a city upon a hill," serving as a model for others to follow. Aboard the *Arbella*, the flagship of the fleet that transported early Puritan settlers from England in 1630, he offered a sermon that famously used this phrase, while also warning his followers what would happen if they failed to keep the promises they had made to one another and to God. "The Lord will surely break out in wrath against us," he said, "and be revenged of such a people, and make us know the price of the breach of such a covenant."

The key to unlocking Winthrop's understanding of what would allow this "city" to prosper is the idea of the covenant, the central theme in the religious and social organization of the group of reform-minded Christians we have come to know as the Puritans. Used in the broadest sense, the label *Puritan* in the American context applies to both the separatists of William Bradford's Plymouth Colony, who had arrived on the *Mayflower* ten years before, and the colonists of Massachusetts Bay, who believed no less than Bradford's Pilgrims that the Anglican Church was corrupt but hoped it could be transformed without formal schism.

According to their covenantal theology, the relationship between God and humanity was based on a series of promises and obligations, contracts made in scripture that continued to outline the responsibility of Christians to uphold divine law. This responsibility was not limited to religious practice but had bearing on all aspects of life, including economics and governance. Equally important, the covenant that the Puritans had with one another stressed their shared reliance on God and the community they would create together.

"For this end, we must be knit together, in this work, as one man," Winthrop preached. "We must entertain each other in brotherly affection. We must be willing to abridge ourselves of our superfluities, for the supply of others' necessities. We must uphold a familiar commerce together in all meekness, gentleness, patience and liberality. We must delight in each other; make others' conditions our own; rejoice together, mourn together, labor and suffer together, always having before our eyes our commission and community in the work, as members of the same body."

Symbolizing this complex of relationships, Winthrop's Communion cup traveled with him aboard the *Arbella*, and he later gave it to Boston's First Church (page 20), which he helped to found in 1630, for use in its monthly ritual Communion meal. The Lord's Supper, as the Puritans called it, was as orderly as they hoped their society would be. As the nineteenth-century *History of the First Church in Boston, 1630–1880*, describes it: "The ministers and ruling elders sat at the table, the rest in their seats or upon forms [benches]." With Winthrop's cup at the center, the meal was →

Winthrop cup, 1610. Governor John Winthrop and members of Boston's First Church used this silver Communion cup.

First Church of Boston, established in 1630. This was the center of social, intellectual, and religious life for the colonists of Massachusetts Bay.

society in miniature: all the church members played their respective parts according to the covenant they believed they had with God and one another.

The cup bears the 1610 date of its London manufacture, and an inscription on its lip states that it was a "gift of Governor Jn Winthrop" to Boston's First Church. Possibly employed for secular purposes before it found its liturgical use, it bears ornamentation entwining the common motif of leaves and fruits with sea monsters. Suggesting as it does trouble lurking beneath still waters, this latter detail might be seen as accidentally prescient. Despite Winthrop's assumption that residents of his "city upon a hill" would be religiously like-minded, theological disagreements beset it from the start. But his decision to exile dissenters such as Anne Hutchinson (page 25) only delayed the colony's eventual and perhaps inevitable, though grudging, acceptance of religious difference.

First Church in Boston, which has owned the Winthrop cup since the colonial era, itself eventually become an example of the diversity that has thrived in America. Formally established by Puritans even before Boston itself, the church emerged in the nineteenth century as the spiritual center of the eclectic transcendentalist movement and as an early home to both Unitarianism and religious humanism. It doubtless would have surprised the defender of Massachusetts's Puritan orthodoxy to know that the church he cofounded would one day give rise to the likes of Ralph Waldo Emerson, whose father was a First Church pastor and who is often credited with introducing to the United States Hindu literature and the religious ideas of the East (page 73).

As First Church nears the end of its fourth century, it serves a thriving Unitarian Universalist community, and its Winthrop cup, on regular display at the Museum of Fine Arts in Boston, is venerated now as both an object of devotion and a striking work of art that provides a view into another time. ◆

✳ John Winthrop

THOUGH HE IS REMEMBERED most for a sermon that came to define the American experiment for many (page 19), John Winthrop's formal training was not as a minister but as a lawyer. He spent his early adulthood as the lord of the manor of his family's estate in Suffolk, on England's east coast. His experiences managing agriculture and wrangling over legal disputes there would serve him well in New England.

Winthrop was elected the governor of the planned Massachusetts Colony in 1629 and sailed for America aboard the *Arbella* six months later. Over the next twenty years, he not only served continuously as the governor or a member of the court, but also kept a journal (page 22) that provides intimate views first of the colonists' ocean passage and then of life in the handful of towns the English settlers had begun to build.

In the first few entries written after his arrival in Massachusetts, Winthrop describes events ranging from religious observances ("We kept a day of thanksgiving in all the plantations") through early diplomacy with the Native population ("In the morning, the sagamore [chief] of Agawam and one of his men came aboard our ship and stayed with us all day") to personal tragedy ("My son Henry Winthrop was drowned at Salem").

Throughout the trials of life in Massachusetts, Winthrop's style of governance remained informed by the religious devotion that had led him to leave his homeland. "Let us choose life that we, and our seed, may live by obeying His voice and cleaving to Him," he preached, "for He is our life and our prosperity."

In making this choice to live in a place where he might practice his faith as he saw fit, however, Winthrop saw no room for dissent. He dealt harshly with those who disagreed with his vision for the colony, sending dissenters into exile. By the time of his death in 1649, his authority had been challenged on both religious and civil fronts, but his vision of America as a place where society might be remade endured for generations. →

Portrait of John Winthrop, circa 1630–31. Oil on canvas.

Easter monday

Ridinge at the Cowes, neere the Ile of wight, in the
Arbella, a shipp of 350: tu wherof Capt Peter
Milborne was master, & being manned w
52 seamen, & 28: peeces of ordinance, the winde comming
to the N: & by W: the day before, it was resolved vpon good
grownd aboute vs, m^r Cradock the late gour, & the
masters of the 2 shipps wth the Lady Arbella
of the Ambrose, & m^r his Assistant abord
of the Iewell, & m^r the. Barger master of the
of the Talbot, (viz: 3: shipps and the by vs the Eagle,
the mayflower, the Whale the Thornewell, her whale
then Successe, & her royall being filled at the
& not weley, & vpon goon Conference it was agreed
that (in regard it was vncertaine, when the rest
of fleet wold be ready) that the 4: shipps should
vndert togither, the rest to be ledden, the Talbott
vice Ad: the Ambr: viceadm: & the Eagle a R^a
& according Artic of Consort were drawn &
deliured to the said shipps & masters. wherupon
Cradock tooke leave of vs, & a^d shipp gave
a farewell wth 4: or 5: shott. at
aboute 10: of the Clock we weigh anchor, & se
farther wth the winde at N: & came to an anchor againe
ouer ag Yarmouth, & the Talbott weigh likewise
came & anch: by vs. heere we mett wth a shipp of

George H. Boughton, *Pilgrims Going to Church, Plymouth, Mass.*, 1867. Oil on canvas.

Winthrop's words still echo through history. Shortly before he took he took his oath of office in 1961, President John F. Kennedy remarked:

> I have been guided by the standard John Winthrop set before his shipmates on the flagship *Arbella* three hundred and thirty-one years ago, as they, too, faced the task of building a new government on a perilous frontier.
>
> "We must always consider," he said, "that we shall be as a city upon a hill—the eyes of all people are upon us."

President Ronald Reagan similarly made Winthrop's "city" a recurring theme of his political life. Thirty-eight years after Kennedy, he used them to close his farewell address as he prepared to leave office at the end of his second term. "The past few days when I've been at that window upstairs," he said from the Oval Office, "I've thought a bit of the 'shining city upon a hill.' The phrase comes from John Winthrop, who wrote it to describe the America he imagined. What he imagined was important because he was an early Pilgrim, an early freedom man. He journeyed here on what today we'd call a little wooden boat; and like the other Pilgrims, he was looking for a home that would be free."

As he was preparing to run for the presidency, Barack Obama also turned to Winthrop for inspiration. "It was right here, in the waters around us, where the American experiment began," he said in a commencement address at the University of Massachusetts in Boston. "As the earliest settlers arrived on the shores of Boston and Salem and Plymouth, they dreamed of building a City upon a Hill. And the world watched, waiting to see if this improbable idea called America would succeed."

Even as we approach the four hundredth year since Winthrop quoted the Gospel to describe the experiment he and his fellow settlers were about to begin, we have likely not heard the last of that "city upon a hill." Though its meaning has changed over time, it remains a phrase that resonates, because it enshrines the past while suggesting possibilities for the future. ◆

First page of John Winthrop's journal, 1630–49. Winthrop was not only the governor of Massachusetts Bay, but also its unofficial historian. The journal he kept provides a view of daily life among the Puritans.

✳ Anne Hutchinson

JOHN WINTHROP'S VISION of a "city upon a hill" (page 19) suggests a community with shared beliefs serving as a wall of protection, yet in reality, Puritan New England faced a crisis of religious difference at its start. This crisis was made flesh in the person of Anne Hutchinson. As Winthrop himself said, she was "a woman of a ready wit and bold spirit." To his chagrin, she used that wit to argue in favor of her right to interpret scripture.

In 1634, Hutchinson arrived in Boston at the age of forty-three, along with her husband and ten of the sixteen children she would ultimately bear. The family began their lives in New England widely respected and considered godly by all. Hutchinson had come from England to be close to the preacher John Cotton, who had become her spiritual mentor in the county of Lincolnshire before leaving to take up a position in the Puritan colony. Aligned with Cotton, the Hutchinsons were at the center of Boston society.

Yet within a few years of her arrival, Hutchinson became the focal point of the so-called antinomian controversy. This dispute over how and why individuals might consider themselves saved led inevitably to the question of who should be allowed to voice their opinions concerning the matter. Winthrop held that it was beyond the role of women to speak of such things. Through regular lectures offered in her home, Hutchinson begged to differ, and many others took her side.

As Winthrop framed the cause of the controversy, Hutchinson's lectures began as recitations of sermons delivered by sanctioned divines. But then they took a turn. "After she had repeated the sermon," he wrote, "she would make her comment upon it" and "vent her mischievous opinions as she pleased."

For her crimes, Hutchinson was brought to trial at the General Court at Newton, the highest authority in Massachusetts Bay Colony. Conducting the interrogation of this one woman were Governor Winthrop as the chair of the court, the deputy governor, and ten assistants. After Winthrop's lengthy preamble accusing her of having "troubled the peace of the commonwealth and the churches here" and of having held instructive gatherings in her home, an act "not tolerable nor comely in the sight of God nor fitting for your sex," Hutchinson responded simply that her conscience had brought her to preach.

Expelled from Massachusetts Bay as a danger to the colony, Anne Hutchinson traveled to New Netherland, where members of her family were waiting for her. When many of the Hutchinsons, including the matriarch, were killed in an Indian attack a few years later, her Puritan opponents said that she had gotten what was coming to her. Her exile and death, however, did not put an end to her message of the right of those without official authority to express religious insights. ◆

Anne Hutchinson Preaching in Her House in Boston, 1901. Insisting she had the authority to interpret scripture, Hutchinson was at the center of the first theological rift in Puritan Massachusetts. From *Harper's Monthly* 102 (February 1901): 356.

✳ *Roger Williams's Compass Sundial*

THE NOTION THAT AMERICA might be the "promised land" was born with the Pilgrims, who saw themselves as similar to the ancient Israelites in their desire to escape oppression and find the good life that God intended for them. Yet Massachusetts in 1631 offered sickness and death far more often than milk and honey.

In February of that year, at a time when "the poorer sort of people," as Governor John Winthrop wrote, "were much afflicted with the scurvy, and many died," another ship dropped anchor in Boston's harbor. This ship, called the *Lyon*, carried a cargo of lemon juice to help those afflicted, as well as a twenty-eight-year-old preacher by the name of Roger Williams, who offered far stronger medicine.

Winthrop pronounced Williams a pious man not long after the latter came ashore, but the governor of neighboring Plymouth was more accurate when he said that this new arrival was "a man godly and zealous . . . but very unsettled in judgment."

A separatist from the Church of England, Williams refused to associate with Winthrop's First Church of Boston (page 20), preferring the more austere community that had been established in Salem. Even there, though, he ran into trouble by questioning the role of religion in civil government. Called before the General

Compass sundial. Exiled from Massachusetts, Roger Williams traveled south in 1635 into the land that would become Rhode Island with the aid of this tool.

Court in 1635, Williams was found to be "erroneous, and very dangerous." Showing "a great contempt of authority," he was driven from the colony. He avoided deportation back to England only by slipping off into the unexplored regions of southern New England.

Leaving Massachusetts, Roger Williams set off on his own errand in the wilderness, specifically in the woodlands south and west of the arm of Cape Cod, where he lived for a time among the Narragansett Indians in the region that would become Rhode Island. To find his way through lands largely unsettled by the English, he used the compass sundial shown opposite. Manufactured in England and likely carried with him when he crossed the Atlantic, Williams's compass sundial is round, with a screw-top design. Measuring just two and a half inches across and less than an inch thick, it is a remarkably portable piece of technology, etched with fine engravings and featuring a folding sun vane. The central image on its removal cover, a skull atop a winged hourglass, was a popular memento mori of the day, a reminder that death awaits all. While such a device might be seen as a hopeful symbol of search and discovery, the motif shown here was also often carved on gravestones.

Led by his compass sundial, Williams eventually located a site where he could begin a colony of his own. In 1637, he drew up a contract (page 28) between himself and its former inhabitants and purchased the land that would become the city of Providence.

During his time among the Narragansett, Williams not only oriented himself geographically, but also attempted to make sense of Native peoples' place in his theologically informed understanding of history while taking their own beliefs into account. Like many religiously educated men of his day, he came to believe that they were distant relations of the Lost Tribes of Israel. Williams wrote:

> First, others (and myselfe) have conceived some of their words to hold affinitie with the Hebrew.
> Secondly, they constantly anoint their heads as the Jewes did.
> Thirdly, they give Dowries for their wives as the Jewes did.
> Fourthly, (and which I have not so observed amongst other nations as amongst the Jewes, and these) they constantly separate their women (during the time of their monthly sicknesse) in a little house alone by themselves foure or five dayes, and hold it an Irreligious thing for either Father or Husband or any Male to come neere them.

Despite his eagerness to find biblical connections to the Narragansett, Williams was content to let Native beliefs speak for themselves. To better understand their customs and to share his observations of them with other colonists, he wrote a →

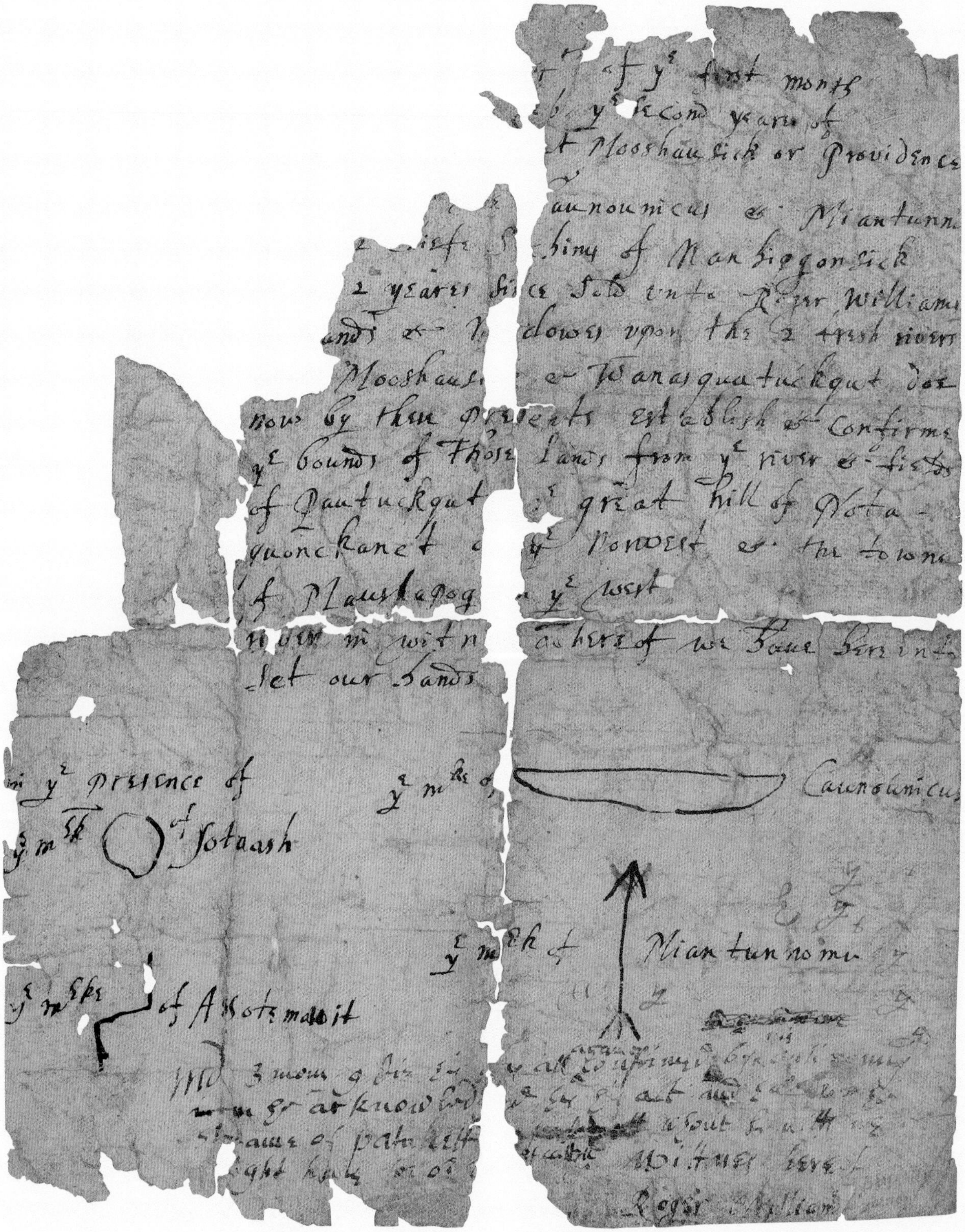

[illegible] of yᵉ first month
[illegible] yᵉ second yeare of
[illegible] at Mooshausick or Providence

[illegible] Caunounicus & Miantunn[illegible]
[illegible] chiefe Sachims of Nanhiggonsick
[illegible] 2 yeares since sold unto Roger Williams
[illegible] ands & Meadowes upon the 2 fresh rivers
Mooshaus[illegible] & Wanasquatuckqut doe
now by these presents establish & confirme
yᵉ bounds of those lands from yᵉ river & fields
of Pautuckqut [illegible] great hill of Nota-
quonckanet [illegible] Norwest & the towne
of Maushapog [illegible] yᵉ west
[illegible] witn[illegible] whereof we have hereunto
set our hands

In yᵉ presence of
yᵉ mke of Sotaash

yᵉ mke of Assotemawit

yᵉ mke of Caunounicus

yᵉ mke of Miantunnomu

[illegible] confirmed [illegible] acknowledged [illegible]
streames of Pawtuckett [illegible]
[illegible] Witnes here[illegible]
Roger Williams

handbook for use by English settlers hoping to communicate with their neighbors. Published in 1643, "A Key into the Language of America" stated its intention in its impressively verbose subtitle: "An Help to the Language of the Natives in That Part of America, Called New-England: Together, with Briefe Observations of the Customes, Manners and Worships, &c. of the Aforesaid Natives, in Peace and Warre, in Life and Death. On All Which Are Added Spirituall Observations, Generall and Particular by the Authour, of Chiefe and Speciall Use (upon All Occasions,) to All the English Inhabiting Those Parts; yet Pleasant and Profitable to the View of All Men."

The chapter headings alone in this combination grammar, dictionary, and anthropological essay provide a view of the categories with which colonists sought to understand the peoples whom their settlements would soon supplant. Williams devoted several pages each to the subjects "Salutation," "Eating and Entertainment," "Sleepe and Lodging," "Numbers," "Relations of Consanguinitie and Affinitie, or Blood and Marriage," "Family and the Business of the House," "Persons and Parts of the Body," "Fowle," "Fish and Fishing," "Earth and the Fruits Thereof," and dozens of other topics.

Williams recognized that the Narragansett had a religion all their own (he had made an effort to count their gods, for example, and came up with a list of thirty-seven), as well as their own religiously informed understanding of human origins. "From Adam and Noah that they spring, it is granted on all hands," he wrote of his hosts. "But . . . they say themselves, that they have sprung and growne up in that very place, like the very trees of the wildernesse." "They will generally confesse that God made all," he continued. "Although they deny not that [the] Englishmans God made English men, and the Heavens and Earth there, yet their Gods made them, and the Heaven, and the Earth where they dwell."

Such willingness to take note of Narragansett accounts of how the land he now inhabited had come to be inevitably influenced Williams's approach to making some of that land his own. He negotiated treaties with local chiefs and created a contract outlining the boundaries of the colony he would build. The deed he wrote acknowledged that he and his followers had "made covenant of peaceable neighborhood with all the Sachems and natives round about us."

Williams's experience of being rejected in Massachusetts but welcomed by the Narragansett helped make Rhode Island an early herald of American religious liberty, a promised land after all. A testimony to the importance of his legacy of searching and discovery, Williams's compass sundial is now in the permanent collection of the Rhode Island Historical Society. ◆

Roger Williams's 1637 contract for the purchase of the land that would become the city of Providence, Rhode Island.

✳ *The First Baptist Church in America*

First Baptist Church in America, Providence, Rhode Island, built in 1775 and originally founded by the followers of Roger Williams.

THE CITY OVER WHICH the First Baptist Church in America watches had its origins in exile. Forced from Massachusetts for his religious views, Roger Williams (page 26) fled south into territory inhabited by the Narragansett tribe. After surviving a winter without the relative comforts of an English settlement, he purchased land from the tribal chiefs and established a settlement of his own. In thanks for the divine protection he believed he had received, he called his town Providence.

As those who shared his beliefs began to follow him south, Williams offered to lead them in worship in his home. In time, these believers became affiliated with another group of English separatist Christians, known as Baptists, so called because they held that Christians must accept the faith as adults and be re-baptized even if they had received the sacrament as children.

Tracing their history to 1638, when Williams began leading worship, the Baptists of Providence built their first meeting-house in 1700, a single room not larger than twenty feet wide and as many deep. After they outgrew this first building, they constructed another twice the size nearby, but this also soon proved to be too small. The grand church shown here was built in 1775. Small but telling details reveal that it was born on the eve of the Revolution. Not long after rebels in Boston famously threw boxes of tea into the harbor the previous year, British authorities shut down Massachusetts ports with the Coercive Acts. Skilled shipwrights and carpenters in search of work traveled south to Providence, where they lent their talents to the church whose construction was then in progress, filling it with tightly made and finely crafted woodwork more often seen in seafaring vessels. It was not just the workmanship that made the church shipshape. When a crystal chandelier was installed in 1792, it hung high above the pews thanks to a collection of cannonballs used as counterweights. Taken from warships, they found a new, peaceful purpose assisting in the illumination of the sanctuary.

Though the church today continues to trace its history to Roger Williams, a single building or denomination apparently could not contain its founder's journey. Within months of organizing the first Baptist congregation in America, he had moved on, announcing that he did not believe any church could measure up to the ideals of the faith. ◆

✴ *Touro Synagogue*

IN 1658, just twenty years after the earliest beginnings of the First Baptist Church in America, the first Jews arrived in the city of Newport, some thirty miles to the south. Within a generation, they were acknowledged by the General Assembly of Rhode Island, which granted the full protection of the law to these "resident strangers."

The oldest synagogue in America, Touro Synagogue traces its lineage to merchants who arrived in the trade hub of Newport from the English island of Barbados late in the seventeenth century. Within a hundred years, the Jewish congregation, which had been meeting in private homes, had grown large enough that it needed its own house of worship, whose construction began in 1759.

When the building was completed less than five years later, it was dedicated with a ceremony that attracted not only the growing Jewish community, but also Christian religious leaders from around New England. Among the most prominent was Ezra Stiles, a minister and future president of Yale University. As the pastor →

Postcard depicting Touro Synagogue, Newport, Rhode Island, the oldest house of Jewish worship in America, completed in 1763.

of the nearby Second Congregational Church, he noted in his diary that he had "been acquainted with six rabbies" and regularly corresponded with one of them in Hebrew. In 1781, when a non-Jewish Newport resident applied to use the synagogue for a Christian service, Stiles "express'd much concern and amazement at the application" and promised the synagogue member Moses Mendes Seixas that "all that lay in his power shou'd be done to remove any unfavorable impressions that a refusal might create amongst his congregation."

Such high-placed support no doubt helped inspire the confidence that this same synagogue member displayed when he wrote a letter that further secured his congregation's place in American history a few years later. When George Washington visited Newport as the newly elected first president of the United States, Seixas wrote him a letter of welcome from "the children of the Stock of Abraham" that praised the new nation for having "a Government which to bigotry gives no sanction, to persecution no assistance."

Washington's reply, written to "the Hebrew Congregation in Newport" (pages 34–35) on August 18, 1790, provides perhaps his most famous statement on religious freedom: "It is now no more that toleration is spoken of, as if it were by the indulgence of one class of people, that another enjoyed the exercise of their inherent natural rights. For happily the Government of the United States, which gives to bigotry no sanction, to persecution no assistance, requires only that they who live under its protection should demean themselves as good citizens, in giving it on all occasions their effectual support." ◆

Gilbert Stuart, *George Washington*, 1796. Oil on canvas.

To the Hebrew Congregation in Newport Rhode Island.

Gentlemen.

While I receive, with much satisfaction, your Address replete with expressions of affection and esteem; I rejoice in the opportunity of assuring you, that I shall always retain a grateful remembrance of the cordial welcome I experienced in my visit to Newport, from all classes of citizens.

The reflection on the days of difficulty and danger which are past is rendered the more sweet, from a consciousness that they are succeeded by days of uncommon prosperity and security. If we have wisdom to make the best use of the advantages with which we are now favored, we cannot fail, under the just administration of a good Government, to become a great and a happy people.

The Citizens of the United States of America have a right to applaud themselves for having given to mankind examples of an enlarged and liberal policy: a policy worthy of imitation. All possess alike liberty of conscience and immunities of citizenship. It is now no more that toleration is spoken of, as if it was by the indulgence of one class of people, that another enjoyed the exercise of their inherent natural rights. For happily the

the Government of the United States, which gives to bigotry no sanction, to persecution no assistance, requires only that they who live under its protection, should demean themselves as good citizens, in giving it on all occasions their effectual support.

It would be inconsistent with the frankness of my character not to avow that I am pleased with your favorable opinion of my administration, and fervent wishes for my felicity. May the Children of the Stock of Abraham, who dwell in this land, continue to merit and enjoy the good will of the other Inhabitants; while every one shall sit in safety under his own vine and figtree, and there shall be none to make him afraid. May the father of all mercies scatter light and not darkness in our paths, and make us all in our several vocations useful here, and in his own due time and way everlastingly happy.

G. Washington

✳ *Tituba*

THE WOMAN KNOWN as Tituba in the court records of colonial Massachusetts was likely an Arawak Indian of South American birth. She had been purchased as a slave by a young man named Samuel Parris, a merchant-turned-minister whose church and family would soon play a role in one of the most notorious chapters in American religious history.

According to popular accounts of the ten months of madness now known as the Salem witch trials, the root cause of the allegations of demonic influence that overtook several New England towns in 1692 was the unfortunate collision of the mischief of children and the vendettas of adults. After several young girls began complaining of mysterious maladies, neighbors used the opportunity to cast blame upon one another, often with malicious intent. Yet the spark that lit this fire was the often forgotten fact that the world of the Puritans was not as religiously uniform as is often supposed.

Not long before the troubles began, Tituba had arrived in Massachusetts from Barbados, a place where African, Caribbean, and European cultures clashed and remade one another. During her time there, it is likely that Tituba learned a variety of folk traditions used for healing and divination, which she then brought with her to New England.

Puritan religious writers knew of and feared such practices. "Some young persons through a vain curiosity to know their future condition, have tampered with the Devils tools," the minister John Hale wrote in 1697. Yet despite the risks believed to be involved, when two girls in the Parris household fell ill, a neighboring woman asked Tituba to intercede. Specifically, she asked the enslaved Tituba to prepare a "witchcake," a biscuit that was made by mixing rye flour with urine, which was then fed to a dog to complete a spell intended to improve the children's condition and locate the source of their torment.

Though popular histories often suggest that the outsider Tituba alone brought supposedly magical practices to Salem, the baking of witchcakes has deep English roots. A recipe found in a *Treatise of Witchcraft* published in London in 1616 records the advice given by a "Wisard" to the father of a daughter believed to be bewitched: "Make a cake with flower from the Bakers, & to mix the same instead of other liquor, with her own water, and bake it on the harth, wherof the one halfe was to be applyed and laid to the region of the heart, the other halfe to the back directly opposite."

When Rev. Parris discovered that this practice had been performed in his own home, he delivered a sermon warning of diabolical influence in the village. "By these means," he preached, "the Devil hath been raised amongst us, and his rage is vehement and terrible." A few days later, Tituba was arrested for the crime of witchcraft.

According to Elaine Breslaw, a scholar of the intersection of magic, belief, and medicine in early America, Tituba's actions were a kind of spiritual rebellion. Enslaved though she was, she believed her skills and traditions could make a difference, and she acted outside religious norms on behalf of those who could not. She continued to provide a counterpoint to Puritan religious authority throughout her trial, during which she insisted on telling her side of the story.

Unlike twenty of the dozens accused, Tituba managed to escape with her life. In many ways, the society that had put her on trial was not so lucky. The excesses of the trials of the supposed witches, as well as the regret of those who had been involved in executing so many of their neighbors, put a crack in the foundation of Puritanism that would never be repaired. ◆

Court document from the 1692 events now known as the Salem witch trials, recording the names of Tituba and others among the accused.

✳ Cotton Mather

FAR AND AWAY the most famous clergyman of his day, Cotton Mather is now perhaps best remembered for his role in the Salem witch trials. Some trace the roots of the colonial obsession with diabolical influence to his book *Memorable Providences, Relating to Witchcrafts and Possessions*.

Peter Pelham, *Portrait of Cotton Mather*, 1728. Mezzotint.

Yet Mather was not the Puritan scold jumping at shadows that we might suppose. He was, in fact, a figure of great learning and broad interests, who late in life considered himself as much a man of science as of faith. Born into a family of ministers that was nearly religious royalty in seventeenth-century New England, Cotton was the son of Increase Mather, the pastor of Boston's North Church and the president of Harvard College, and a grandson of the influential Puritan divines Richard Mather and John Cotton.

Like his forebears, Cotton Mather lived in a difficult time in colonial Massachusetts. A recurring smallpox epidemic regularly emptied church pews while decimating the population. The majority of the Puritan clergy regarded such catastrophes as divine punishment. But in the 1720s, Mather broke ranks. He proposed that the citizens of Boston could avoid future epidemics not only by repenting of their sins, but also by proactively combatting the illness. Having read of the process of inoculation in European medical journals, he also discovered that many of the city's African-born slaves had used the technique. "I don't know why 'tis more unlawful to learn of Africans, how to help against the Poison of the Small Pox," he wrote, "than it is to learn of our Indians, how to help against the Poison of a Rattle-Snake."

Though it was considered blasphemy to suggest that the will of God could be changed, Mather wrote in favor of inoculation in the press. Supported by the groundbreaking doctor Zabdiel Boylston, who had performed the first successful surgeries on American soil, he eventually succeeded in convincing many of his fellow ministers that science and faith could coexist.

Mather's most towering achievement, however, was his writing, which set a standard for output by a prominent public intellectual rarely matched in American history. He was the author of more than four hundred books and pamphlets, including *Magnalia Christi Americana: The Ecclesiastical History of New England from Its First Planting in 1620, until the Year of Our Lord 1698*. As suggested by the meaning of his book's title (*The Glorious Works of Christ in America*), Mather sought to combine the story of his faith with the saga of settling a new land, as many ministers who followed in his footsteps would also hope to do. ◆

❋ Children's Letter Books

RELIGION INFORMED every stage of life in early America, beginning with childhood. From the establishment of the first schools in New England in the seventeenth century, moral lessons and scriptural allusions were an essential part of education.

Before the public-school movement of the mid-nineteenth century, the role of religious communities in the education of children was largely taken for granted. Churches founded and administered schools, and the same men who preached as ministers on the Sabbath often served as teachers during the week. At a time when there was often little distinction between secular instruction and spiritual development, letter books such as the one shown here used biblical tales to teach basic reading skills.

The most popular reading book of the colonial era was *The New England Primer*, first published in 1690. To introduce children to their ABCs, it used pedagogical styles ranging from the scriptural ("In Adam's Fall, we sinned all") through the threatening ("The idle Fool is whipped at school") to the astronomical ("The Moon shines bright in time of night"). The two million copies of this book sold in the eighteenth century suggest an explosion of interest in both religion and education.

In wide use throughout the 1700s, *The New England Primer* maintained its Puritan leanings even as the religious makeup of the country shifted with the spiritual earthquake of the First Great Awakening, the major transformation of American Protantism that occurred in the third and fourth decades of the eighteenth century. In churches and open-air meetings, worship styles had expanded to include emotionally driven testimony of spiritual experiences and the dynamic preaching of orators who now sought to engage rather than merely declaim to congregations, but in the classroom the moral lessons used for instruction seemed little changed from those deemed necessary during the hardest days of early colonial experience.

After reading pages on the alphabet and the Lord's Prayer, for example, a child learning from *The New England Primer* would stumble upon a few bleak verses called "Uncertainty of Life":

> I in the burying place may see
> Graves shorter there than I;
> From death's arrest no age is free
> Young children, too, may die.
> My God, may such an awful sight
> Awakening be to me!
> O that by early grace I might
> For death prepared be! →

"Suffer the little children to come unto me."

THE

HISTORY

OF

LITTLE JOHN MERRY

WRITTEN BY HIS FATHER.

———

Revised by the Committee of Publication of the American Sunday-school Union.

———

PHILADELPHIA:
AMERICAN SUNDAY-SCHOOL UNION,
1122 CHESTNUT STREET.

Interior pages from
*The History of Little
John Merry.*

The next section, "On Life and Death," puts matters even more succinctly:

Life and the grave two different lessons give;
Life shows us how to die, death how to live.

Even the primer's vocabulary lessons seem cut from darkest Puritan cloth. Its section on words of five syllables, for example, includes ten examples, five of which are "A-bom-in-a-tion," "Ed-i-fi-ca-tion," "Hu-mil-i-a-tion," "Mor-ti-fi-ca-tion," and "Pu-ri-fi-ca-tion." The book ends with sections called "A Dialogue between Christ, a Youth and the Devil" and "Lessons for Children," the first of which is "They that fear God least, have the greatest reason to fear him."

Despite its peculiarities, *The New England Primer* remained the most popular schoolbook in America until Noah Webster's *Blue-Backed Speller* (1758) replaced it late in the eighteenth century. Webster's approach was comparatively secular (his book begins with a section called "Analysis of Sounds in the English Language"), but even the great lexicographer did not leave religious and moral instruction entirely behind. Within his primer's "Lessons of easy words, to teach children to read, and to know their duty," the first sentence given is "No man may put off the law of God."

The 1846 children's book shown here, *The History of Little John Merry*, displays a later version of the same pedagogical technique. In addition to an illustrated alphabet full of biblical allusions, it features an easy-reading story about a pious little boy who died at six years old. "He was always a very delicate child, and we often feared he would not live to be a man," the book begins. "He was, from an early age, much more attentive to what was said to him on religious subjects than other children."

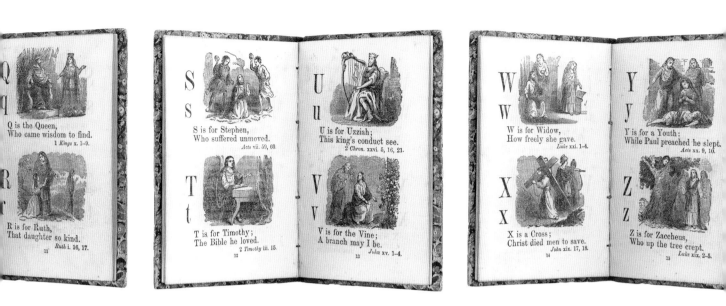

Though little John's story is told mainly to tug at the heartstrings, it does not shy away from reinforcing rules that less godly children might have ignored. "On seeing a boy playing one Sunday, though naturally very modest," it continues, "[John] went up to him and reproved him, telling him how wicked it was to play on the Sabbath."

Like *The New England Primer*, *The History of Little John Merry* then offers a bit of verse before moving on to the ABCs, as if to remind its young readers of what is at stake in such lessons.

Children die, though e'er so young;
Infants bid the world adieu;
As my life may not be long,
May I keep its end in view.

Heavenly Father, grant that I
May the name of Jesus love.
That if shortly I should die,
I may go to him above. ◆

❊ Jonathan Edwards

AMERICAN HIGH SCHOOL students have long been taught to associate the name Jonathan Edwards with eight words: "Sinners in the Hands of an Angry God." A sermon by that title which he delivered in Northampton, Massachusetts, and Enfield, Connecticut, in 1741 has served for generations as shorthand for fire-and-brimstone preaching. "There is no want of power in God to cast wicked men into hell at any moment," Edwards told his frightened congregations. "He is not only able to cast wicked men into hell, but he can most easily do it."

Yet Edwards was more to American religious history than a reliable source of doom and gloom. He preached as often on love and beauty as on eternal damnation, and the tension between these themes is a key to understanding the man whom many historians have considered both a significant philosopher and "the most brilliant of all American theologians."

A major figure of the Great Awakening that spread across the English colonies in the 1730s and 1740s, Edwards was a child of Puritan New England, yet also well versed in the searching ethos of the Enlightenment. His preaching drew not only on Calvinist theology, but also on the works of John Locke and Isaac Newton. As the historian George Marsden noted, "Edwards came of age at a time and place that would give him an acute sense of the juxtaposition of old and new outlooks."

Born in Connecticut at the dawn of the eighteenth century into a family known for its clergymen, Jonathan Edwards studied Hebrew, Greek, and Latin at home before entering Yale College when he was not yet thirteen years old. Before he was twenty, he was preaching from the pulpit of a church in New York City, and a few years later he joined his grandfather as a pastor of the Congregational Church in Northampton.

He distinguished himself not with a flamboyant preaching style but with his thoroughness and the depth of thought evident in every sermon. While "Sinners in the Hands of an Angry God" told his audiences what they should fear, other sermons, such as "Love, the Sum of All Virtues," told them to what they should aspire. "If men have a sincere love to their neighbours, it will dispose them to all acts of justice towards those neighbours," he preached, "for real love and friendship always dispose us to give those we love their due, and never to wrong them."

Martin Marty, a leading scholar of religion in the United States, once suggested that a "Mt. Rushmore of Protestant American shapers" would include twentieth-century figures such as Billy Graham and Martin Luther King Jr., with Edwards alone standing for the nation's spiritual prehistory. ◆

Portrait of the Puritan preacher Jonathan Edwards. From G. H. Hollister, *The History of Connecticut, from the First Settlement of the Colony to the Adoption of the Present Constitution* (New Haven, CT: Durrie and Peck, 1855).

✳ *Phillis Wheatley*

Portrait of Phillis Wheatley from *Poems on Various Subjects, Religious and Moral,* 1773. Wheatley, one of the most celebrated poets in early America, had a facility with words that helped convince her owners to release her from slavery.

IN HER BRIEF LIFE, Phillis Wheatley survived being taken from her home in West Africa and brought to New England; learned to read English and Latin; studied astronomy, ancient history, and modern geography; and became the first African American woman to publish a book of poems—all before she died at the age of thirty-one.

Enslaved when she was just eight years old, she lost, along with her freedom, the name she had been given at birth. In 1761, she arrived in Boston aboard a ship called the *Phillis*, and the man who bought her, the tailor John Wheatley, apparently liked the name of the vessel so much that he decided to use it when addressing the child he had acquired as a gift for his wife. Though she was brought into the Wheatley household as a slave, Phillis soon began to learn alongside the family's children. As a teenager, with her education encouraged, she wrote her first poems, which usually reflected her newfound Christian faith.

With the spiritual revival of the Great Awakening in the air, seventeen-year-old Phillis composed a memorial poem to the preacher George Whitefield (page 152), whose emotive open-air sermons had signaled a new moment in the religious life of the colonies:

> Thy pray'rs, great saint, and thine incessant cries
> Have pierc'd the bosom of thy native skies.
> Thou, moon, hast seen, and all the stars of light,
> How he has wrestled with his God by night.
> He pray'd that grace in ev'ry heart might dwell,
> He long'd to see America excel.

"On the Death of the Rev. Mr. George Whitefield" was published in Boston, New York, Philadelphia, and London, and it made Phillis Wheatley's name widely known on both sides of the ocean.

She traveled to England soon afterward and saw a collection of her verse published there in 1773. Around this time, the Wheatleys died, and the young writer was given her freedom. Despite having been stolen from her family and her homeland, she never spoke ill of those who had enslaved her. One of her poems, "On Being Brought from Africa to America," went as far as to express gratitude that they had exposed her to Christianity:

> 'Twas mercy brought me from my Pagan land,
> Taught my benighted soul to understand
> That there's a God, that there's a Saviour too:
> Once I redemption neither sought nor knew.

Of course, she also knew that her experience of slavery was far different from that of most enslaved men, women, and children. For decades following her untimely death in 1784, abolitionists often republished her words and used them as a counterpoint to any argument about differences in ability between races.

"There is as much mental and moral beauty in her verses," one writer for the antislavery newspaper the *Liberator* wrote in 1836, "as can be found in the verses of a whole score of poets that might be mentioned, who were not colored persons, but whose poems have every hue." ◆

❋ Revere and Son Church Bell

Bronze bell, Revere and Son, 1802. In the early years of the nineteenth century, Paul Revere emerged as a prominent maker of church bells. This one was installed in the Meeting House of the Unitarian Universalist Congregation of Castine, Maine, in 1804 and was moved to Steven's Mill in Andover, Massachusetts, in 1831.

CHURCH BELLS PROVIDED the iconic sounds of early America, not only summoning the faithful to worship, but also serving as a communication system that could function at the great distances of the mostly rural nation.

For several decades after the Revolution, Paul Revere was better known for his bells than for his midnight ride, which did not become the stuff of legend until Henry Wadsworth Longfellow wrote about it in the middle of the nineteenth century. Revere first established his reputation in Boston as a metalsmith, creating fine examples of liturgical silver, many of which may still be found in the city's historic churches. The patriot broadened his business to include a bell foundry in 1792, when the congregation to which he belonged, the New Brick Church, required a replacement bell for its tower. The existing bell had developed a crack, which limited its use to the announcement of nearby fires. When the expense and logistics of shipping the bell to England for repair became too much for the church members to bear, Revere volunteered to forge a new bell.

Though a novice maker of bells at the time, Revere had a long history with their use. He had served as a bell ringer beginning at the age of thirteen, when he and a few friends had taken on the responsibility of signaling times of worship, moments of celebration, and causes for alarm to their city. Standing at the base of the bell tower, the boys would grip its thick ropes and allow their weight to rock the resonant bronze high above them, filling the church and the streets around it with a deep and melodious sound.

Between 1792 and his death in 1818, Revere was personally involved in making more than one hundred bells. His family-run foundry, Revere and Son, would ultimately cast 398, with the last bell sold in 1828. "Bell-making remained a high-tech trade in Revere's time," the historian Robert Martello has written. As all the earlier large bells in the United States had been made in Europe, Revere mastered the necessary principles of metallurgy and acoustics through a combination of trial and error and correspondence with experts overseas.

The public's opinions of his earliest efforts were mixed. The bell for the New Brick Church was not only his first, but also the first large bell fashioned by anyone in Boston. Excitement over this development in the industrial capabilities of the young nation did not save the budding bell smith from negative reviews, however. "The sound is not clear and prolonged," a critic complained, "from the lips to the crown shrill." Yet despite any deficiencies in the quality of its toll, Revere's first bell served a crucial communal function for centuries. As the years passed and the religious foundations of the city shifted, it hung above Congregational, Unitarian, and Methodist churches, and today it rings out over Saint James Episcopal Church in Cambridge, Massachusetts. →

Naturally, the allure of Revere bells was tied up in stories of their maker's role in the Revolution. "Mr. Revere has not yet learned to give sweetness and clearness to the tone of his bells. He has no ear and perhaps knows nothing of the laws of sound," wrote Rev. William Bentley of the Second Congregational Church in Salem, Massachusetts. Like many others, however, he made a point of purchasing a bell from Revere rather than an imported model. He did so, he explained, out of patriotism rather than admiration for Revere's skill as a bell maker.

One of Revere's largest bells is still in use in Boston's King's Chapel. Faced with an existing bell beyond repair, Revere and Son melted it down and used the salvaged material to fashion an impressively substantial statement of the foundry's skill. The new bell weighed 2,437 pounds, twice the weight of most bells in use at the time. The positive effects that its 1814 hanging had on the community were greeted with verse by the local press:

The Chapel Church,
left in the lurch,
must surely fall.
For church and people
and bell and steeple
are crazy all.

The church still lives,
the priest survives
with mind the same;
Revere refounds,
the bell resounds,
and all is well again.

CHURCH BELLS.

PAUL REVERE & SON,
No. 13, Lynn Street, North End, BOSTON,

HAVE conftantly for fale, CHURCH and ACADEMY BELLS, of all fizes, which they will warrant equal to any made in Europe, or this country. From perfonal information obtained in Europe, and twenty years experience, they are affured they can give fatisfaction, and will fell, on as good terms, as they can be imported for, or obtained in this country.
Boften, May 7, 1807.   (79, 6m.)

Revere and Son
advertisement, 1804.

Overshadowed by the dramatic tales of his exploits in the cause of liberty as a younger man, the work that Revere came to as a bell maker later in life may have contributed even more significantly to American history. While church bells had rung throughout the colonies before the Revolution, Revere's efforts at his Boston foundry provided an example to his fellow citizens of an industry long associated with European skills and craftsmanship that could prosper in the United States.

The 1802 Revere and Son bell shown on page 49 hung for three decades in a Unitarian church in Castine, Maine, and then for more than a century at Steven's Mill in Andover, Massachusetts, before joining the collection of the American Textile History Museum in 1961 and then the permanent holdings of the National Museum of American History in 2016. Originally crafted to summon the faithful to worship, the bell later sounded the call to workers to report to their shifts during the Industrial Revolution. It remains a symbol of both the changes and the continuities in the communal life of the nation. ◆

The Shakers

Left Shaker worship, after a work by John Warner Barber, 1856. Lithograph. Known for the distinctive style of movement they used during worship, the Shakers embraced an originally pejorative name as their own. Printed and published by D. W. Kellogg & Co.

Below Advertisement for Shaker remedies, nineteenth century. While famed for their piety, the Shakers were also successful entrepreneurs, becoming pioneers in marketing through their sale of seeds and herbal medicines.

LED TO AMERICA by Mother Ann Lee (1736–84), the United Society of Believers in Christ's Second Appearing was a religious community influential throughout the eighteenth and nineteenth centuries. Called Shakers for their ecstatic worship style, they embraced industry and commerce to further their cause, becoming known for their craftsmanship, mail-order seeds, herbal remedies—and, perhaps most of all, their celibacy.

As both an apocalyptic sect anticipating the world-ending return of Jesus Christ and a living community shaped by practical concerns, the Shakers represent a creative tension present throughout American religious history. Even as they swore off procreation in preparation for the end times, the Shakers built vibrant communities famous for their artistry and attention to detail. Among the innovations credited to the Shakers are the flat broom, various herbal remedies, and the first commercially produced washing machine. →

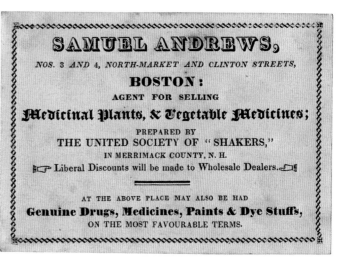

Phares Fulton Goist,
*View of Sabbathday Lake,
Maine*, 1879.

With origins among the Quakers of northwest England early in the eighteenth century (page 85), the group mocked as "Shaking Quakers" embraced the epithet as their most commonly used name (as the similarly derided Methodists and Dunkers did around the same time).

According to Shaker lore, Mother Ann Lee had been inspired by a vision when she left Liverpool for New York with a group of eight followers in the spring of 1774. Her reasons were likely as practical as they were spiritual, however. Like other Shakers, she had been subjected to vicious persecution in England, including from her own family. She later told her followers:

> One of my brothers, being greatly enraged, said he was determined to over-come me. So he brought a staff, about the size of a large broom handle; and came to me while I was sitting in my chair, and singing by the power of God. He spoke to me, but I felt no liberty to answer. "Will you not answer me," said he. He then beat me over my face and nose with his staff till one end of it was very much splintered. But I sensibly felt, and saw, the bright rays of the glory of God pass between my face and his staff, which shielded off the blows, so that I did but just feel them. He continued beating till he was so far spent that he had to stop, and call for drink.

Such experiences were likely related to the ascendency of women as Shaker leaders in the 1760s. Lee herself had been married when she had arrived in the United States, but her husband had left her in New York. She had not been sorry to see him go. "When the man is gone," she said, "the right of government belongs to women."

The dissolution of her marriage coincided with the beginning of remarkable growth for the Shaker community. First buying property in upstate New York, Lee attracted converts so quickly that the Shakers eventually had eighteen communities and four thousand members spread out across the early republic from Kentucky to Maine.

Many, no doubt, were drawn by descriptions of the Shakers' unique style of devotion, which often took the form of dance. A visitor recorded his impression of this peculiar ritual: "At half past seven P.M. on the dancing days, all the members retired to their separate rooms, where they sat in solemn silence, just gazing at the stove, until the silver tones of the small tea-bell gave the signal for them to assemble in the large hall. Thither they proceeded in perfect order and solemn silence." After an elder gave a short sermon, the dancing began in earnest:

> First they formed a procession and marched around the room in double-quick time, while four brothers and sisters stood in the center singing for them. After marching in this manner until they got a little warm, they commenced dancing, and continued it until they were pretty well tired.
>
> During the dance the sisters kept on one side, and the brothers on the other, and not a word was spoken by any of them. After they appeared to have had enough of this exercise, the Elder gave the signal to stop, when immediately each one took his or her place in an oblong circle formed around the room, and all waited to see if anyone had received a "gift," that is, an inspiration to do something odd. Then two of the sisters would commence whirling round like a top, with their eyes shut; and continued this motion for about fifteen minutes; when they suddenly stopped and resumed their places, as steady as if they had never stirred.

Yet even a community that placed dancing at the center of its devotional life apparently could not compete with the exploding spiritual marketplace of the nineteenth century. The Second Great Awakening, a period of increased religious devotion that altered the American religious landscape from the 1790s through the 1840s, opened a new universe of spiritual options, many of which promised greater freedom than the tightly regulated communities inspired by Ann Lee. No doubt hampered by celibacy and the sect's austere lifestyle, Shaker membership began to fall by the third quarter of the nineteenth century and never recovered.

※ ※ ※

Several Shaker villages remain active today as education foundations, but only one is still home to members of the United Society of Believers in Christ's Second Appearing. Established in 1782, Sabbathday Lake is a working farm on the outskirts of the town of New Gloucester, Maine. While not the first or the largest of Shaker settlements, it prospered well into the twentieth century, in part thanks to the entrepreneurial spirit of its community and to its proximity to the Poland Springs Resort, a popular spot for those seeking the allegedly curative qualities of its underground waters. In an unlikely collaboration, the lavish resort became a frequent site of commerce for the plain-living religious group.

In fact, the creation of Poland Springs had involved Shakers as well. In the late eighteenth century, a man named Jabez Ricker had owned a farm near a Shaker establishment some fifty miles to the south, in the town of Alfred. Hoping to →

Spinning wheel,
nineteenth century. Many
Shaker communities
manufactured spinning
wheels both for their own
use and for sale.

Shaker Meeting House,
established in 1794,
Sabbathday Lake, Maine.

expand, the Shakers of Alfred had offered Ricker land from their northern outpost in exchange for some of his. Ricker moved north and soon discovered that the tract of land he had acquired from the Sabbathday Lake Shakers included a remarkable natural spring. After his grandson Hiram claimed that the water on the property cured his dyspepsia, the family soon began sharing it, then selling it. The constant influx of guests to the hotel that the Ricker family built near the spot of the miracle cure drew the Shakers on multiple trips each week for fifty years to sell their produce, clothing, and woodcrafts. The products were not as simple as one might expect. In 1824, Sabbathday Lake community members developed an elaborate method, using zinc chloride and heat, to make fabric both waterproof and permanently wrinkle free.

By 1850, the community owned nearly two thousand acres and twenty-six large buildings, many of which are still standing and continue to be used by the group's two active members, the last of the Shakers. As their average age is sixty-nine, the future of the community is uncertain, but its legacy will live on in the form of educational and historical programs.

Today as in the early nineteenth century, the Sabbathday Lake Shakers make crafts for sale and arrange to have their produce brought to market. Business is not what it used to be—when their products included everything from their iconic furniture through medicines and herbal remedies to personal items such as the eyeglass case and spinning wheel pictured here—but it is still done according to Mother Ann Lee's dictate to work and pray "as if you had a thousand years to live, and as if you were going to die tomorrow." ◆

Eyeglass case, nineteenth century. Along with the furniture for which they are best known, the Shakers fashioned and sold small personal items.

✳ *Edward Bass's Book of Common Prayer*

Portrait of Edward Bass, eighteenth century. Oil on canvas. Bass was the first Episcopal bishop of Massachusetts.

SAINT PAUL'S EPISCOPAL CHURCH in Newburyport, Massachusetts, kept its doors open during the Revolution despite the fraught relationship between the Anglican faith and New England's patriotic mood. The church's rector at the time, Edward Bass, remained loyal to the crown in the early days of the war but later crossed out benedictions for the king in his prayer book and inserted blessings for Congress, as seen in the image on page 58.

Bass likely decided to edit the text not solely for reasons of newfound patriotism. "When the late rebellion commenced," he later wrote, "I preserved as firm and unshaken a loyalty to his Majesty & attachment to the British Government as was consistent with my remaining in the country."

Elsewhere in New England, rectors of Anglican churches had become concerned that they "could not with safety perform the service of the Church for the future." Since "the Continental Congress had declared the American Provinces free and independent States," Rev. Samuel Parker of Boston's Trinity Church wrote, he was often interrupted "reading the prayers in the Liturgy of the Church for the king, and had received many threats and menaces that he would be interrupted and insulted in future if the prayers for the king should be again read in the church." If changes were not made, he feared, "some damage would accrue."

At nearby Christ Church in Cambridge, it already had. The rector had fled for his life when the Continental Army had taken over the building. According to a nineteenth-century account, "the organ-pipes were melted into bullets, and the sacred edifice was defaced by the inconsiderate soldiers." It was an unfortunate end to a church where precisely the liturgical changes that Bass later made had been considered as early as 1775. On the last day of that year, a service attended by General George Washington had been "one of the earliest incidents to show that in the minds of the wisest churchmen the Prayer-Book services were no longer identified with loyalty to the English government." Suspicion of the Church of England ran deep, however, and a few altered words did not always offer protection.

Nor, in the aftermath of the war, did it seem that any decision was clearly the right one. In 1784, Bass was still defending himself from both sides. Writing to his superiors in the church, he argued that there were extenuating circumstances involved:

> The articles against me which have come to my knowledge are that being a Chaplain in one of his Majesty's Regiments I endeavoured to seduce the soldiers from their allegiance . . . that I read the Declaration of Independence in my Church . . . that I preached a sermon exhorting my Hearers to contribute liberally towards cloathing the rebel Army, and that I observed the Fasts appointed by the Congress.

> All these Charges I absolutely deny except the last, for I do not, nor ever did deny that I did generally open my Church on those Fasts, tho' not in consequence of the Orders or commands of an rebel Powers . . . but in order to preserve the Church from destruction, such was the spirit or Frenzy of People in general at that time. →

Title page, Book of Common Prayer, 1766 ed. This was the primary worship text used by members of the Church of England. With a few changes, the book continued to be used in the United States after the Revolution.

Marked page in Edward Bass's Book of Common Prayer. During the Revolution, words of worship invoking the name of King George were often changed by hand.

While some Anglican clergymen fled the country in the wake of the Revolution, many others, such as Bass, remained. Doing so, they demonstrated at once the resilience of Americans' religious ties even in the face of political upheaval and the flexibility those ties would need if they were going to endure in a new nation shaped by religious diversity beyond what the colonies had known. With the official split of the Episcopal Church of America from the Church of England five years after the war ended, minsters like Bass who were caught in the middle finally had room to breathe.

With Bass's elevation to the episcopacy of the new Episcopal Church in 1789, Saint Paul's in Newburyport became known as the Bishop's Church, because it was the home of the first Episcopal bishop in Massachusetts. It displayed this status atop its steeple with a wooden miter (opposite), the traditional headgear worn by ecclesiastical leaders, carved by the local woodworker Joseph Wilson in 1800. The miter was the most understated of the works created by Wilson, who was often in the employ of Richard Dexter, a wealthy eccentric "notorious for his extravagancies and foolish exhibitions." For Dexter, Wilson went on to carve a menagerie of famous figures, from Washington, Jefferson, and Adams to Indian chiefs, generals, and philosophers, plus statues of Fame and Liberty personified as goddesses. Wilson's humble church-top miter survived them all. ◆

Wooden miter created by Joseph Wilson, 1800, and displayed atop the steeple of Saint Paul's Episcopal Church in Newburyport, Massachusetts, to indicate the church was home to the state's first Episcopal bishop.

✳ *Lucretia Mott's Bonnet*

THE QUAKER MINISTER Lucretia Coffin Mott (1793–1880) was an educator, abolitionist, and pioneer of women's rights. She led efforts to avoid the use of goods produced by the labor of enslaved men and women and organized the 1848 Seneca Falls Convention with the suffragist Elizabeth Cady Stanton.

Born in Nantucket, Massachusetts, Lucretia Coffin could trace her family history back to the earliest colonial arrivals. She was called a "spitfire" in her youth and maintained something of that reputation all her life. After training as a teacher at a Quaker school in New York, she married her fellow educator James Mott in Philadelphia, where they became known for taking in fugitive slaves. Over time, she came to an awareness that helping individuals was not enough. Even in the North, she realized, nearly all society and commerce were implicated in the sinful sale and ownership of human flesh. In her later years, she recalled the birth of her awareness that removing oneself from complicity with the slave trade required effort and risk.

"About the year 1825, feeling called to the gospel of Christ, and submitting to this call, and feeling all the peace attendant on submission, I strove to live in obedience to manifest duty," she wrote. "Going one day to our meeting, in a disposition to do that to which I might feel myself called, most unexpectedly to myself the duty was impressed upon my mind to abstain from the products of slave labor."

Despite the abolitionist stance of many of in her circle, her insistence that more must be done on a daily and personal basis alienated friends and relations. Breaking with those who did not agree "was like parting with the right hand, or the right eye," she remembered. "But when I left the meeting I yielded to the obligation, and then, for nearly forty years, whatever I did was under the conviction, that it was wrong to partake of the products of slave labor."

This was a conviction she shared with anyone and everyone with whom she came into contact. For her children's birthday parties, she made candies with sugar she knew to be untainted by forced labor and passed them out in bags containing verses:

Take this, my friend, you need not fear to eat.
No slave hath toiled to cultivate this sweet.

Her zeal for the abolitionist cause led her to tour extensively to speak on the evils of slavery. During these travels, Mott often clashed with abolitionists who believed that women should not have a prominent role in the movement. When Mott announced her intention to serve as a delegate to an abolitionist conference in London despite its stated policy of seating only men, critics expressed outrage. →

The editor of a Pittsburgh abolitionist newspaper wrote:

> We know this lady well, and for kindness, hospitality, benevolence, and purity of life, she had no superior, but in morals she is an ultraist of the most ultra stamp—in religion a latitudinarian in the widest sense, and we should not be surprised if she should so far forget the true dignity of womanhood in her intractable zeal for what she terms "principle," as to attempt to take her seat as a delegate in the "World's Anti-Slavery Convention." If she does, and mutual distrust, heart-burnings, and confusion result from such a step, upon her and her advisors will rest the tremendous onus of putting back the day of the slave's redemption, and sacrificing mercy and righteousness to an insane caprice.

The resistance she encountered expanded her activism from just antislavery concerns to a broader advocacy for equality. Though she was a Christian ordained as a minister by the Society of Friends, she liked to refer to her positions on social ills as "heretical." "The early Friends were agitators, disturbers of the peace," she said. It was the duty of those following in their footsteps, she insisted, "to stand out in our heresy." Her willingness to speak uncomfortable truths made her among the most famous women of her day, sharing rostrums with such icons as Sojourner Truth. The Seneca Falls Convention, which she co-organized, is credited with launching the women's rights movement. Even earlier than that, Mott had led a women's meeting advocating "that it was time that woman should move in the sphere Providence assigned her, & no longer rest satisfied in the limits [within] which corrupt custom & a perverted application of the Scriptures had placed her."

Mott often wore the dark bonnet shown at left, along with a distinctive cloak that must have fully engulfed her. Always petite, she was said to have weighed only seventy-six pounds near the end of her life. Even a heavy cloak could barely contain her outsize spirit, however. Her daughter Mariana Hopper once said, "I must tell you how mother came in from the roadside. Under that deceiving cloak of hers, which is supposed to be merely a covering for her little wire threads of legs, she carried eggs by the dozen, chickens and 'a little sweet piece of pickled pork,' mince pies, the vegetables of the season. She concealed how much of the way she had walked from the station or how broad a trail of dropped eggs she left behind her."

When, at the age of eighty, she learned that President Ulysses Grant was staying not far from her home, she put on the bonnet she was known for and announced that she was going to see him. Grant had recently ordered the removal of Indians from a California reservation, and the spitfire Lucretia Mott, as ever, had something to say. ◆

☀ *Old Round Church*

LIKE MANY MEETINGHOUSES built in the colonial era and the early republic, the Old Round Church in Richmond, Vermont, has served both religious and civic functions throughout its long life. Unlike most, however, it was born as an experiment in interreligious cooperation.

Early in the nineteenth century, several Protestant denominations in this small riverside village were in need of a house of worship, yet none of them had sufficient numbers to build one. These assorted Baptists, Universalists, Congregationalists, →

Old Round Church, Richmond, Vermont, opened in 1814, one of only a few standing churches built in this once-popular style.

and Methodists each wondered how they could gather the resources necessary to construct a church of their own.

The problem they all faced separately found a collective solution when Isaac Gleason, a wealthy local businessman who had donated land for the town's public common, decided to gift the competing denominations a small tract on the south side of the Winooski River on which they might build together. Thus, like a religious version of the national motto, *E pluribus unum*, or "Out of many, one," a new structure formally known as Union Church opened for worship in 1814.

To pay for the construction of this sixteen-sided structure, Baptists, Universalists, Congregationalists, and Methodists purchased pews, raising more than two thousand dollars. The church they built is the only surviving example of the polygon design that, local legend has it, was intended to have no deep corners, which might serve as hiding places for the devil.

Legend further maintains that, as a press report once put it, "seventeen men participated in its erection, each of the sixteen building one side and the seventeenth adding the belfry." Yet while the labors of many certainly were required, it is known that the construction was managed by one man, the blacksmith and carpenter William Rhodes, who was likely inspired by octangular churches he had seen elsewhere in New England during his youth.

Thanks to the practical hopefulness that brought them together, the various denominations succeeded for years in the logistical marvel of finding time for each community of believers to pray as they saw fit. It is not known what inspired their initial separation, but eventually the theologically diverse groups involved in constructing a shared church built other places where they could worship. After hosting both religious and civic events at the start, the Old Round Church was employed exclusively for the latter by the late nineteenth century.

"It has not been occupied as a church for years," a report stated in 1882, "and is now used for town purposes," as it still is today. Though it was no longer a place where multiple religious perspectives made their home, the reporter did not mention whether the devil had yet found his way into its corners. ◆

✳ *Abington Congregational Church*

ABINGTON CONGREGATIONAL CHURCH, the oldest standing religious building in Connecticut, is a small peg-and-beam church completed in 1751. It is located in the village of Abington in the town of Pomfret, in the northeastern corner of the state. The diversity of its earliest community can seem surprising today but was in fact fairly common at the time. Records dating back to its founding include English, Native American, and African American men, women, and child congregants.

Like many structures of its era, it is a simple building without much ornamentation. Its original dimensions were forty-eight by thirty-nine feet, and it was expanded only slightly over time. However, in its very ordinariness it stands as a tribute to the unheralded individuals who have worshipped there, and to the challenges they have faced.

The church's marriage and death records, for example, serve as accounts of mortality and celebration as experienced by the community. In most years, the church lost on average one or two members a month. Many of the deceased were in their seventies or eighties. But far more were children, who at times died young enough that they were buried without a name. In one particularly trying fortnight in 1787, three infants died of unnamed causes. The life-ending maladies that were recorded in other instances included "hooping cough," dropsy, "supposed worms," consumption, "plague in the bowels," "convultion fits," and "bilious fever." Taken together, such records provide a view into the lives of those who turned to the church for not only solace but a means of remembrance.

While the march of death through the village of Abington perhaps seemed relentless at times, so too was the march of life. In many years the church averaged equal numbers of weddings and funerals. It still survives as a small but active Congregational church. ◆

Abington Congregational Church, completed in 1751, the oldest standing house of worship in Connecticut.

Thomas Jefferson's Letter to the Danbury Baptist Association

DESPITE THE FIRST AMENDMENT'S prohibition of established religion at the federal level, the majority of U.S. citizens in the early republic lived in the shadow of official churches supported by the states. The privileged status of the Congregational Church in Connecticut led the Baptist Association of the town of Danbury to send a letter to the newly elected president, Thomas Jefferson, in the hope of receiving assurances that the rights of religious minorities would not be threatened locally. They wrote:

> Our sentiments are uniformly on the side of religious liberty, that Religion is at all times and places a matter between God and individuals, that no man ought to suffer in name, person, or effects on account of his religious opinions, that the legitimate power of civil government extends no further than to punish the man who works ill to his neighbor. But sir, our constitution of government is not specific. . . . Sir, we are sensible that the President of the United States is not the National Legislator and also sensible that the national government cannot destroy the laws of each State, but our hopes are strong that the sentiments of our beloved President, which have had such genial effect already, like the radiant beams of the sun, will shine and prevail through all these States—and all the world—until hierarchy and tyranny be destroyed from the earth.

This letter prompted perhaps the best-known expression of religious liberty in American history. The principle that religion and government should not directly influence each other is stated most plainly in Jefferson's famous phrase "wall of eternal separation between church and state." Despite their significance, these words are found not in any official document but only in this short letter of January 1, 1802, which he sent to the Baptists in Danbury (page 68). Jefferson wrote it to assure an anxious religious minority that the federal government would not meddle in matters he thought should be left between believers and their God.

While Jefferson was often reluctant to broadcast his personal beliefs, his devotion to the necessity of defending religious difference was well known. The one book he published in his lifetime, *Notes on the State of Virginia*, includes a section on religion that captures the purpose and possibilities of matters of the spirit as he understood them.

In his estimation, the various religions of the world interact in ways at once contentious and transformative. "Difference of opinion," he noted, "is advantageous in religion." Competing denominations will inevitably try to influence one another, he believed, and government's role in this process is simply to stay out of the way, avoiding any appearance of favoring one religious perspective over another. →

Rembrandt Peale, *Portrait of Thomas Jefferson*, 1800. Oil on canvas.

To mess^{rs}. Nehemiah Dodge, Ephraim Robbins, & Stephen S. Nelson a committee of the Danbury Baptist association in the state of Connecticut.

Gentlemen

The affectionate sentiments of esteem & approbation which you are so good as to express towards me, on behalf of the Danbury Baptist association, give me the highest satisfaction. my duties dictate a faithful & zealous pursuit of the interests of my constituents, and in proportion as they are persuaded of my fidelity to those duties, the discharge of them becomes more & more pleasing.

Believing with you that religion is a matter which lies solely between man & his god, that he owes account to none other for his faith or his worship, that the legitimate powers of government reach actions only and not opinions, I contemplate with sovereign reverence that act of the whole American people which declared that their legislature should make no law respecting an establishment of religion, or prohibiting the free exercise thereof, thus building a wall of eternal separation between church and state. Congress thus inhibited from acts respecting religion, and the Executive authorised only to execute their acts, I have refrained from prescribing even those occasional performances of devotion practised indeed by the Executive of another nation as the legal head of his church, but subject here, as religious exercises only to the voluntary regulations and discipline of each respective sect. confining myself therefore to the duties of my station, which are merely temporal, be assured that your religious rights shall never be infringed by any act of mine, and that I shall see with friendly dispositions the progress of those sentiments which tend to restore to man all his natural rights, convinced he has no natural right in opposition to his social duties.

I reciprocate your kind prayers for the protection and blessing of the common father and creator of man, and tender you for yourselves and the Danbury Baptist association, assurances of my high respect & esteem.

Th Jefferson
Jan. 1. 1802.

20593

Thomas Jefferson, draft of letter to the Danbury Baptist Association, January 1, 1802. Jefferson's letter has become one of the most influential texts addressing American religious liberty.

Elsewhere in his letter to the Danbury Baptists, Jefferson summed up this idea in a phrase less famous than his "wall of separation" but equally important. "The legitimate powers of government," he wrote, "reach actions only, and not opinions." That the American people saw fit to enshrine this as law within the Constitution's First Amendment, Jefferson suggested, was worthy of "sovereign reverence."

The draft of Jefferson's letter shown here demonstrates that his conception of religious liberty was no less a work in progress for him than it was for the nation as a whole.

While in the final version of the letter sent to Danbury, he affirmed the Baptist Association's opinions that "religion is a matter which lies solely between Man & his God" and that "he owes account to none other for his faith or his worship," in his initial effort to respond to their query, he also included a curious qualification. "Confining myself therefore to the duties of my station, which are merely temporal," he wrote, "be assured that your religious rights shall never be infringed by any act of mine." As one implication of this statement might be that others who would hold his office in the future perhaps might feel differently, Jefferson redacted this suggestion, which could have raised more questions than he had intended to answer. Though removed from the letter, it would turn out to be far more prescient than he could have known, for the meaning of religious liberty has remained open to interpretation and debate by every American generation.

Yet perhaps the most surprising line in Jefferson's famous letter is its understated closing. This iconic statement ensuring the separation between church and state closes with the president offering prayers. ◆

❋ John Adams's Letters to Thomas Jefferson

JOHN ADAMS was among the most conventionally religious of the founding fathers. In the journal he kept throughout his life, he frequently pondered the place of faith in society and individual experience. "What is the proper Business of Mankind in this Life?" he wrote in 1756 at the age of twenty-one. "Habits of Contemplating the Deity and his transcendent Excellences, and correspondent Habits of complacency in and Dependence upon him, Habits of Reverence and Gratitude, to God, and Habits of Love and Compassion to our fellow men and Habits of Temperance, Recollection and self Government will afford us a real and substantial Pleasure."

Such diary devotions were personal and heartfelt, but for Adams, religiosity was not merely a private affair. His 1780 draft of the Massachusetts Constitution, for example, makes it clear that he believed religious participation was a communal responsibility: "It is the duty of all men in society, publicly, and at stated seasons, to worship the SUPREME BEING, the great Creator and Preserver of the universe," he wrote. "And no subject shall be hurt, molested, or restrained, in his person, liberty, or estate, for worshipping GOD in the manner most agreeable to the dictates of his own conscience; or for his religious profession or sentiments; provided he doth not disturb the public peace, or obstruct others in their religious worship."

Despite such unambiguous statements in support of freedom of conscience, the churchgoing Adams occasionally allowed his faith to be used to cast a negative light on his less devout rivals. He ran an aggressively religious campaign for the presidency in the election of 1800, during which his supporters suggested that the choice between him and his opponent, Thomas Jefferson, was that of "God—and a Religious President; or . . . Jefferson—and No God."

Yet the second president was not beyond questioning the less than favorable consequences that religion sometimes brings. Late in life, he and Jefferson enjoyed a lengthy correspondence, in which they

Portrait of John Adams, after Gilbert Stuart, circa 1815. Oil on canvas.

covered theological matters with the candor of two men who by then had spent decades considering what the role of religion in the life of the new nation should be.

In a letter of April 19, 1817, Adams briefly laments the excesses of religion but ultimately concludes that society cannot function without it. (The two men ungenerously mentioned as fanatical—"Bryant or Cleverly"—were, respectively, a parson in his family's boyhood parish and a Latin teacher from his school days whom he remembers, earlier in the same letter, as "eternally disputing about government and religion.")

> Twenty times, in the course of my late Reading, have I been upon the point of breaking out, "This would be the best of all possible Worlds, if there were no Religion in it."!!! But in this exclamation, I should have been as fanatical as Bryant or Cleverly. Without Religion this World would be Something not fit to be mentioned in polite Company, I mean Hell. So far from believing in the total and universal depravity of human Nature; I believe there is no Individual totally depraved. The most abandoned Scoundrel that ever existed, never Yet Wholly extinguished his Conscience, and while Conscience remains there is some Religion.

In his reply, Jefferson suggested that when it came to discussing spiritual matters, they must first settle on the meaning of their terms:

> If, by religion, we are to understand Sectarian dogmas, in which no two of them agree, then your exclamation on that hypothesis is just, that this would be the best of all possible worlds, if there were no religion in it. But if the moral precepts, innate in man, and made a part of his physical constitution, as necessary for a social being, if the sublime doctrines of philanthropism, and deism taught us by Jesus of Nazareth in which all agree, constitute true religion, then, without it, this would be, as you again say, something not fit to be named, even indeed a Hell.

The two founding statesmen continued their correspondence on matters political and religious until shortly before their deaths, which came on the same day, July 4, 1826. Elsewhere in their letters, Jefferson was willing to grant to Adams that there could be some communal benefit to spiritual practices, and that Christianity provided moral instruction useful to the kind of society they hoped to build. He remained adamant, however, that the teachings of Jesus ought to be considered separately from many traditions that those teachings had spawned.

"In extracting the pure principles which he taught," Jefferson wrote to Adams in 1813, "we should have to strip off the artificial vestments in which they have been →

muffled by priests, who have travestied them into various forms, as instruments of riches and power to them."

Jefferson went on to describe a pastime that would become an obsession during his later years: reading scripture with an eye toward extracting from it only those passages that provided a direct connection to the man he considered an inadvertent founder of the faith—a man who, in Jefferson's estimation, never wanted to be thought of as God.

"We must reduce our volume to the simple evangelists, select, even from them, the very words only of Jesus," he wrote. "There will be found remaining the most sublime and benevolent code of morals which has ever been offered to man. I have performed this operation for my own use [page 163] by cutting verse by verse out of the printed book, and arranging, the matter which is evidently his, and which is as easily distinguishable as diamonds in a dunghill."

If the self-described "church-going animal" Adams was scandalized by this project, he did not say so. Instead he told Jefferson that he felt their young nation had much to do in order to make it safe for such experimental religious thinking, writing:

> There exists I believe throughout the whole Christian world a law which makes it blasphemy to deny or to doubt the divine inspiration of all the books of the old and new Testaments from Genesis to Revelations. In most countries of Europe it is punished by fire at the stake, or the rack or the wheel: in England itself it is punished by boring through the tongue with a red hot poker: in America it is not much better, even in our Massachusetts which I believe upon the whole is as temperate and moderate in religious zeal as most of the States. A law was made in the latter end of the last century repealing the cruel punishments of the former laws but substituting fine and imprisonment upon all those blasphemers upon any book of the old Testament or new.

"I think such laws a great embarrassment, great obstructions to the improvement of the human mind," Adams told his old friend and rival. "Books that cannot bear examination certainly ought not to be established as divine inspiration by penal laws." ◆

✳ Mary Moody Emerson

WHEN MARY MOODY EMERSON, a descendent of Puritan preachers, arrived for a short stay at a parsonage in Byfield, Massachusetts, in 1822, she did not expect to have a meeting that would transform American literature.

Emerson was by then in her midforties and stubbornly unmarried, known as a person unbound by social expectations. Traveling alone on what she called a pilgrimage, she had an autonomy rare for a woman of the time. She was also, many of her contemporaries said, an undeniable genius. In her youth she had been formed by the works of authors ranging from John Milton to Jonathan Edwards, Plato to John Locke, and of course her Bible. A devout Christian, she was nonetheless open to unorthodox influences.

Also visiting the parsonage at the time was a man recently returned from India. After listening to a presentation on religion in that region, Emerson was so taken by what she had heard that she wrote a letter to her nephew, a young poet then studying at Harvard by the name of Ralph Waldo Emerson.

"My Dear Waldo," she wrote, "I have been fortunate this week to find a Visitor here from India, well versed in its literature and theology." The visitor had gifted her with several images of the Hindu god Vishnu, she added, and in each there was something that reminded her of her own Christian faith as she understood it. Sending these illustrations to her nephew, she noted, "There was a strong resemblance to the xtian facts."

Thanks in part to his aunt's influence, Ralph Waldo Emerson, a founder of the transcendentalist movement in American poetry, became the first man of letters in the United States to take a sustained interest in the part of the world then broadly called "the East." As he began his career as the preeminent public intellectual of the age, Emerson acquired a library of books related to Hinduism, including a copy of the Bhagavad Gita (page 74), which his friend Henry David Thoreau later borrowed and took with him during his sojourn in the New England woods that led to the writing of *Walden*. "The pure Walden water," Thoreau wrote, "is mingled with the sacred water of the Ganges."

Other writers engaged in the creation of America's poetic vernacular drank from these same waters. A Hindu epic, the *Ramayana*, inspired one of Henry Wadsworth Longfellow's most beguiling poems, "King Trisanku." Herman Melville likewise drew on Hindu mythology while writing *Moby-Dick*, in which he compares the whale at the heart of his great American novel to Vishnu, the same image of the divine that Mary Moody Emerson had shared with her soon-to-be-famous nephew. →

Death portrait of Mary Moody Emerson, 1863. Tintype. This is the only known image of Ralph Waldo Emerson's influential aunt.

Henry David Thoreau's Bhagavad Gita, circa 1855, one of the many books of Hindu literature in Ralph Waldo Emerson's library.

A. Bronson Alcott
from H. D. Thoreau

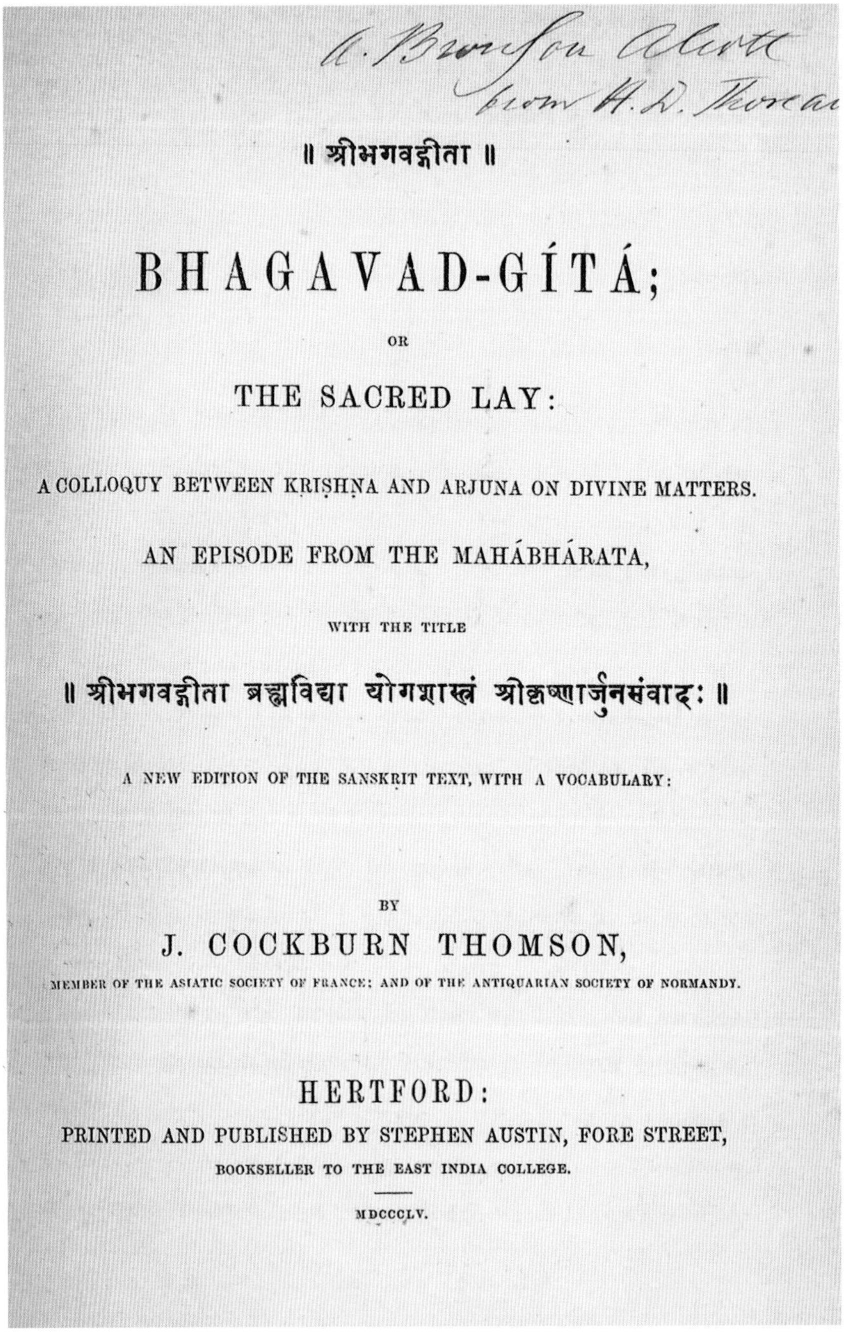

॥ श्रीभगवद्गीता ॥

BHAGAVAD-GÍTÁ;

OR

THE SACRED LAY:

A COLLOQUY BETWEEN KṚISHṆA AND ARJUNA ON DIVINE MATTERS.

AN EPISODE FROM THE MAHÁBHÁRATA,

WITH THE TITLE

॥ श्रीभगवद्गीता ब्रह्मविद्या योगशास्त्रं श्रीकृष्णार्जुनसंवादः ॥

A NEW EDITION OF THE SANSKṚIT TEXT, WITH A VOCABULARY:

BY

J. COCKBURN THOMSON,

MEMBER OF THE ASIATIC SOCIETY OF FRANCE; AND OF THE ANTIQUARIAN SOCIETY OF NORMANDY.

HERTFORD:

PRINTED AND PUBLISHED BY STEPHEN AUSTIN, FORE STREET,

BOOKSELLER TO THE EAST INDIA COLLEGE.

MDCCCLV.

Significant numbers of emigrants from India would not begin to arrive in this country until the following century. Yet this sharing of religious ideas within a single family transformed American literature and prepared the ground for the arrival of Hindu practices decades later. ◆

✳ Olde Meeting House

THE OLDEST CHURCH in New Hampshire, the Olde Meeting House stands stolidly beside a cemetery in the tiny town of Danville, its tall, rectangular windows arrayed like shadows of the headstones below.

A simple, mostly unadorned structure built in 1755, it is significant not only for its age, but also for the evidence it provides of the importance of church buildings to the formal establishment of villages in colonial America. This meeting-house was constructed as a center of both civic and religious life and also to provide justification for the incorporation of a new town as the population surrounding it increased. Shortly after the church was completed, more than two hundred local people signed a petition to separate from a neighboring town.

Olde Meeting House, Danville, built starting in 1755, the oldest standing house of worship in New Hampshire.

Built with the collaboration of twenty-seven families, it was given to the town of Danville in 1760 both as a house of worship and for meetings of the local government. Still unfinished when it was opened to the public, the church raised funds for its completion through the auction of sixteen pews, whose use on Sundays was sold for more than one hundred pounds apiece.

Along with pews for those well off enough to pay such prices for the privilege of worship, the meetinghouse included benches for enslaved workers and indentured servants. Church services continued for nearly eighty years, during which time regular pew auctions raised funds for building improvements and for medical care that helped the congregation survive a smallpox epidemic that ravaged the region in 1782 and took the life of Rev. John Page, the only minister the meetinghouse had known.

In 1832, religious functions at the Olde Meeting House largely came to an end. Afterward, the building was used primarily for town meetings, but it remained a hub of local life for a reason that might have surprised all those pious souls who had spent hundreds of pounds and dollars purchasing their church seats: by the middle of the nineteenth century, the pews had been removed to make way for dancing. ◆

The Mid-Atlantic

While early New England was guided in theory—if not always in practice—by a single, dominant religious perspective, the colonies of the Mid-Atlantic region had diversity built in from the start. The earliest groups of settlers in Delaware were Lutherans from Holland and Sweden. Quakers arrived in Pennsylvania after William Penn cleared the way, and other believers who had been persecuted in Europe soon journeyed to New York and Maryland, including Catholics, Presbyterians, and Jews. By the eighteenth century, so many religious groups had made the region home that none was able to claim a clear majority or social dominance.

Such diversity made the Mid-Atlantic a natural breeding ground for the ideas of religious liberty that would eventually become the law of the land. Although such laws and declarations as Maryland's 1649 Act Concerning Religion and New York's 1657 Flushing Remonstrance did not protect everyone, they provided early standards for how religious difference might be addressed in American public life.

While some feared that freedom of religion might mean the end of religion's broad social influence, it had the opposite effect throughout the Mid-Atlantic and across the country. A generation before the Revolution, the First Great Awakening brought traditional religious authority into question and transformed American life by allowing new forms of religious expression to multiply. Nowhere was this more true than in the middle of the nascent nation, where regions such as New York's Burned-Over District were said to have been ignited by spiritual flames of revival.

Arch Street, with the Second Presbyterian Church, Philadelphia. From *The City of Philadelphia as It Appeared in the Year 1800* (Philadelphia: William Birch & Son, 1800), plate 5.

✳ First Dutch Reformed Congregation of New York

Millstones from the 1626 gristmill that hosted some of the earliest Christian and Jewish worship services in New York. The stones are now housed at Congregation Shearith Israel.

RELIGIOUS PLURALISM IN AMERICA has from the beginning been mostly a practical matter. Forced by circumstance to live and work side by side, early European colonists occasionally found it inevitable that they would worship in close proximity—sometimes even in the same building.

Never was this more true than at a site that may have hosted the first organized worship in the colonial outpost of New Amsterdam. In 1626, the Dutch founders of New Netherland built a horse mill on the island of Manhattan, which became not only the unlikely location of the first Dutch Reformed church in the future United States, but also the first institutional home for Jewish prayers.

In a room above the milling operation that was spacious enough for a small congregation, many colonists gathered on the Sabbath to hear scripture read aloud and to partake of the Christian ritual known as the Lord's Supper. Laymen led the services until the Rev. Jonas Michaelius arrived in 1628. The faithful numbered fifty, a combination of Dutch settlers and Huguenots from Belgium and France. Michaelius preached mainly in Dutch but regularly offered special services for the colony's French-speaking Protestants.

Within five years of the minister's arrival, the Dutch Reformed congregation had built a church of their own. The mill did not remain without a religious use for long, however. When a group of Jews from Brazil arrived in New Amsterdam in 1654 (page 91), they were at first not permitted to establish a house of worship. Following the lead of their Dutch neighbors, they began to meet in the upper rooms of the mill. In time it fell into disuse and a more permanent structure for Jewish services was built on the site, but the millstones—apparently too large to be conveniently discarded—remained.

As a nineteenth-century history notes, "When the old mill disappeared may never be known, but in the years that followed, the Jewish congregation extended the borders of its property so as to include its site. Grandfathers and great-grandfathers of present officers of the congregation indulged in boyish pranks over these old, abandoned millstones, as a relief from the tedious succession of Sabbath-day services in the synagogue."

In 1833, when the Jewish congregation moved away from the location that had come to be known as Mill Street, the millstones found yet another purpose: they became paving stones for a fast-growing city. Today these unlikely relics of religious pluralism in early America are displayed in the synagogue whose congregation traces its roots to the long-forgotten mill: Shearith Israel, on New York's Upper West Side. Once coarse enough to grind wheat into flour, they have been worn smooth by cart wheels, horse hooves and New Yorkers of all faiths. ◆

✳ *Iron Cross from the* Ark *and the* Dove

The *Ark* and the *Dove*, the ships that brought the first English Catholics to America in 1634, two years after the creation of the Province of Maryland.

THE PROVINCE OF MARYLAND was founded as a safe haven for Catholics in the largely Protestant English colonies of North America. King Charles I granted its founders, the Catholic convert George Calvert and his son Cecil, a charter for a colony where English followers of Rome could live in peace. Though this peace proved fleeting and Catholics became a persecuted minority within a generation, their experiences helped shape the struggle for religious freedom in America.

The first ships full of those who wished to take advantage of the protection promised in Maryland, the *Ark* and the *Dove*, arrived in 1634. Instructions to these earliest arrivals listed coexistence among religious factions as a requirement of the colony, but it was clear from the start who was considered responsible for avoiding conflict. To ensure that "no scandal nor offence . . . be given" to Protestant settlers, Cecil Calvert, commonly known as Lord Baltimore, told his fellow Catholics that they must perform acts related to their faith "as privately as may be." Moreover, so as not to incite any disagreements that could be catastrophic for a new settlement, they were instructed "to be silent upon all occasions of discourse concerning matters of Religion."

Though they shared a creed with the colony's founder, Catholic arrivals to Maryland were told in no uncertain terms that their faith should be kept out of sight for the sake of preserving the peace. This is not exactly what happened. On landing at Saint Mary's City in southeastern Maryland, the Catholics aboard the *Ark* and the *Dove* hewed a large cross from local timber and held an open-air Mass in its shadow.

Maryland's very first Catholic cross is lost to history, perhaps repurposed by colonists as firewood or building material. Yet further acts of colonial recycling soon yielded a more enduring symbol of the earliest Roman Catholics in the English-controlled portions of North America. According to legend, iron taken from the *Ark* and the *Dove* was melted down and refashioned into a cross that traveled with Calvert's original followers as they founded settlements throughout the colony.

The recorded history of this cross begins with the Jesuit Mission of Saint Francis Xavier at Warwick, Maryland, in the northeastern corner of the colony. Commonly known as Old Bohemia, it was the earliest permanent Catholic foundation in English American territory outside the Jesuit establishments in lower Maryland.

The Jesuits chose Old Bohemia as a hub of their missionary outreach in the region for practical reasons. Despite promises of protection for Catholics in the colony, persecution was common. Old Bohemia's remote location kept it somewhat insulated from the negative attention of Protestants. It was not very far, however, from the religiously tolerant city of Philadelphia, then the largest population center in the colonies.

The Old Bohemia mission was founded by the Jesuit priest Thomas Mansell. Born in 1669 in Oxfordshire, England, he had entered the Society of Jesus in 1686 and was eventually sent to Maryland. By 1704 he had arrived at the mission, by way of Saint Mary's, perhaps bringing this cross along with him. Thereafter it served as a focal point of the faith of nearby Catholics.

The tradition that the cross came directly from the ships that had brought the first representatives of the Catholic faith to the colony was reinforced by the remark of a nineteenth-century historian that "it certainly looks ancient enough to have been brought over by the Pilgrims who came in the *Ark* and *Dove*." By 1862, this story of the cross's origins was well enough known that the vertical bar was inscribed with the words "This cross is said to have been brought by the first settlers from England to St. Mary's." The crossbar, meanwhile, holds words in Latin that call for the perpetual remembrance of those first arrivals: "Ad perpetuam rei memoria" (For the eternal memory of the event). Other theories include the possibility that the cross was, according to the American Catholic Historical Society, "hammered from horse-shoes contributed by the first settlers of Maryland."

After many years of use, the cross found its way into the archives of Georgetown University, where it was eventually forgotten, not to be rediscovered until late in the twentieth century. No matter how it had gotten there or where it came from originally, the cross served generations of Catholics as a reminder of the transformations required for their faith to endure in America. ◆

Iron cross made by the first English Catholics in Maryland, mid-seventeenth century. Legend claims it was made of materials from the *Ark* and the *Dove*.

G. C. Heinsch del.

✳ Andrew White

THE JESUIT PRIEST who likely performed the first Catholic liturgy in Maryland, Father Andrew White, also became one of the earliest chroniclers of religion in the region. He was not interested only in the beliefs of those he had come to serve, however. He also reported on the customs and beliefs of the local Yaocomico and Piscataway peoples in great detail.

"Upon the whole, they cultivate generous minds," he wrote. "Whatever kindness you may confer, they repay. They determine nothing rashly, or when actuated by a sudden impulse of mind, but with reflection; so that when any thing of moment is, at any time, proposed, they are for a time silent in a thoughtful manner; then they answer briefly, Yes or No, and are very firm of their purpose."

Born in London in 1579, White lived in France, Spain, and Belgium before traveling to Lord Baltimore's colony at the age of fifty-four. As a Catholic in England, he had endured arrest and risked the death penalty for attempting to spread his faith. Late in life, he found America a challenge all its own.

"They are possessed with a wonderful desire of civilization," he noted of the Yaocomico, but "ignorance of their language renders it still doubtful for me to state what views they entertain concerning religion." What he knew of Native American religious practices was limited to what he could glean from observation and interpretation. "These few things we have learned at different times: They recognise one God of heaven, whom they call 'Our God'; nevertheless, they pay him no external worship, but by every means in their power, endeavor to appease a certain evil spirit which they call Okee, that he may not hurt them. They worship corn and fire, as I am informed, as Gods wonderfully beneficent to the human race."

With his interest piqued, White went to view native rituals for himself. At a place he called a "temple," he saw a ceremony in which children formed a ring around a large fire, with adults standing behind them. An elder threw deer fat into the flames, causing the gathering place to fill with smoke. All assembled then began to move rhythmically, while the boys and girls sang in what White found to be "an agreeable voice."

The Jesuit White recorded all this sympathetically. Though he would have liked to see the original inhabitants of America converted to Christianity and wrote hymns in the Piscataway language toward this end, this was not his first priority. A persecuted minority themselves, English Catholics in America were far more concerned with their own spiritual survival than with that of strangers. They had good reason to be. Protestants took control of the colonies' only safe haven for Catholics in 1645, setting the stage for decades of fighting over the place of religious difference in Maryland. As the homes of prosperous Catholics were looted, White awaited punishment. The "Apostle of Maryland," as he is often known, was sent back to England in chains. ◆

G. G. Heinsch, *Andrew White*, 1655. Engraving. The Jesuit Andrew White, one of three priests on the 1634 *Ark* and *Dove* journey to America, provided spiritual guidance to Maryland's Catholics. From *Mathias Tanner, Societas Jesu apostolorum imitatrix* (Prague: Typis Universitatis Carolo-Ferdinandeae, 1694).

✳ Old Swedes Church

Old Swedes Church, Wilmington, Delaware, consecrated in 1699. Old Swedes may be the oldest church in the United States still used for worship.

WHEN SWEDISH AND DUTCH immigrants arrived in the Mid-Atlantic region in the 1630s, the Dutch largely went north to establish New Amsterdam, while the Swedes remained in the Delaware Valley. Existing for less than half a century, the colony of New Sweden included settlements along the shores of the Delaware River and stretched into territories that would become the states of Delaware, New Jersey, and Pennsylvania.

Swedish fur traders and farmers built several Lutheran churches throughout the region, beginning in 1662 with a small chapel in the vicinity of the current town of New Castle and continuing in 1667 with another chapel south of the Christiana River. These churches, made of wood in the Swedish architectural style, fell into disuse when the church shown at left, constructed with local granite and brick, was consecrated in 1699. All three Lutheran churches hosted worship services entirely in the Swedish language.

As a nineteenth-century account of Swedish efforts in America explains, a steady supply of clergy had to be made available to keep these churches afloat. "From 1696 to 1786 the Swedish Government sent to the churches on the Delaware no less than twenty-four (24) Clergymen, generally giving them an outfit, and paying the expenses of their voyage from Sweden to America," Israel Acrelius noted in his *History of New Sweden*. Many of these ministers planned to return home "after many years of faithful labor," hoping to be granted "pastorates of the most desirable character" in recompense for the hardships they had endured. Others, however, intended to remain, and made efforts to communicate with the peoples whom they encountered.

While the Englishman John Eliot was translating the Bible into Algonquian (page 13), the Swedish priest Johan Campanius was at work rendering Martin Luther's Small Catechism into the Lenape/Delaware language. His *Dialogues and Vocabularies of the Language of the Delawares* likewise attempted to adapt Christianity to better speak to the needs of life in America. In a version of the Lord's Prayer, he proposed substituting "venison and corn" for "daily bread."

Today, Old Swedes Church claims to be "the oldest church in the United States standing as originally built and still in use as a house of worship." Known as Holy Trinity Church, it has been home to an Episcopal parish since 1791. An indication of the challenges that its members have faced throughout its long history can be seen in a message set into a wall: "Lux lucet in tenebris oriens ex alto" (The light shining in the darkness arises from on high). ◆

✳ *William Penn*

DURING THE ENGLISH CIVIL WAR of the mid-seventeenth century, the Royal Navy admiral William Penn remained loyal to the monarchy and was rewarded with a promise of property in the New World. He died before he could collect, but a son who shared his name was soon able to claim the promised land. "My God will Make it the Seed of a Nation," the younger William Penn said.

Penn was granted the land that would become Pennsylvania and Delaware in 1681, eleven years after his father's death. He was then thirty-eight years old and had been a Quaker for his entire adult life. Though his father had not shared his convictions, the younger Penn transformed the debt owed to his family into a legacy of religious freedom.

Portrait of William Penn, shown (with hands spread) speaking to members of the Lenape tribe in Edward Hicks's *The Peaceable Kingdom* (detail), 1826. Oil on canvas.

Founded by George Fox in the 1650s, Quakerism grew out of dissatisfaction with the Church of England and offered to individual believers the possibility of direct experiences of God. This was naturally an affront to Anglican clergymen, who referred to followers of Fox as Quakers because, as Fox himself later said, he admonished them to "tremble at the word of the Lord."

Penn was arrested for attending Quaker meetings at the age of twenty-two and soon began writing spirited defenses of the movement, as well as harsh critiques of those who sought to destroy it. As the persecution in England continued, he proposed an exodus of Quakers to America. Because the established settlements there would offer no safe haven—New England and Virginia were no more hospitable to those of his convictions than England was—the only solution was a colony of their own.

In 1682, Penn arrived in the province that King Charles had named Pennsylvania, "Penn's woods," in honor not of William himself but of his father, the admiral. He established the city of Philadelphia and then traveled through the lands of the Lenape tribe. He became known for dealing fairly with those who had lived on the land before he and other Europeans had arrived, and he created treaties that endured longer than many other such agreements.

Penn also took care to set out the rules by which his own people would live, including an explicit statement that the kinds of religious persecution which →

Quakers had endured would not be found in the settlements under his supervision.
His 1682 "Frame of Government of Pennsylvania" further describes the guiding
principle of this so-called Holy Experiment:

> All persons living in this province, who confess and acknowledge the one
> Almighty and eternal God, to be the Creator, Upholder and Ruler of the
> world; and that hold themselves obliged in conscience to live peaceably and
> justly in civil society, shall, in no ways, be molested or prejudiced for their
> religious persuasion, or practice, in matters of faith and worship, nor shall
> they be compelled, at any time, to frequent or maintain any religious worship,
> place or ministry whatever.

While he limited such protections to those "who confess and acknowledge the one
Almighty and eternal God," Penn's declaration showed that Pennsylvania would be
not only "the Seed of a Nation," but also the seed of an idea that this nation, like no
other, would embrace. ◆

✳ *George Washington Inaugural Bible*

WHEN PRESIDENT-ELECT George Washington stepped forward at New York City's Federal Hall to be sworn in on April 30, 1789, a large Bible on a crimson cushion awaited his oath-swearing hand. The iconic nature of the scene, and the fodder it would later provide for debates over the first president's faith and the separation of church and state, might lead one to believe that the book's presence was long planned for this purpose. Yet the use of a thick tome of scripture for an added note of ritual had been devised only hours before. As the Constitution does not require the presence of a sacred text when the oath is made, the book that was ever after known as the Washington Inaugural Bible (page 88) entered history almost by accident.

George Washington's first inauguration, April 30, 1789.

While the name of the person who first suggested a Bible should be used at Federal Hall that day is lost to history, legend maintains that it was the master of ceremonies for the inaugural parade, Jacob Morton, who provided the book when it was deemed necessary. Morton was a Freemason, a member of the fraternal organization with roots in stonemasonry guilds of medieval France, as was Washington himself. As the time for taking the oath of office approached, Morton offered to retrieve a Bible from the nearby Saint John's Lodge No. 1 of the Ancient York Masons. →

King James Bible used during the first presidential inauguration of George Washington, on April 30, 1789.

When the 1767 King James Version arrived, it was placed on a table covered in velvet on a balcony overlooking the corner of Wall and Broad streets.

The Bible may have been a late addition to the ceremony, but Washington fully embraced it. After taking the oath of office, the new president leaned forward to the pages, which had been opened at random, and kissed a single verse: "Zebulun shall dwell at the haven of the sea; and he shall be for an haven of ships; and his border shall be unto Zidon" (Genesis 49:13).

A page was later inserted into this Bible to record not only its significance in American history, but also the role the Freemasons had played on that auspicious day. The date was noted according to a system used for ceremonial and commemorative proceedings of Freemasonry, with "A.L." for *Anno Lucis*—"In the year of the light"—indicating the number of years since the biblical creation of the world, which at the time was often believed to have been in 4000 BCE.

> On this sacred volume, on the 30th day of April, A.L. 5789, in the City of New York, was administered to George Washington, the first president of the United States of America, the oath to support the Constitution of the United States. This important ceremony was performed by the Most Worshipful Grand Master of Free and Accepted Masons of the State of New York, the Honorable Robert R. Livingston, Chancellor of the State.

The page continued:

Fame stretched her wings and with her trumpet blew.
Great Washington is near. What praise is due?
What title shall he have? She paused, and said
"Not one—his name alone strikes every title dead."

Accidental or not, the tradition of using a Bible to administer the presidential oath has endured throughout American history. The custom of noting the text to which the book was open did not begin until 1837, when Martin Van Buren chose Proverbs 3:17: "Her ways are ways of pleasantness, and all her paths are peace."

In some cases, several passages have become associated with the same president. While the Bible used in 1861 for Abraham Lincoln's first inauguration was opened at random during his second, in 1865, near the end of the Civil War, he is said to have placed his hand variously on Matthew 7:1 ("Judge not, that ye be not judged"), Matthew 18:7 ("Woe to the man by whom the offence cometh!"), and Revelation 16:7 ("Even so, Lord God Almighty, true and righteous are thy judgments"). Some accounts also note that he kissed the page containing Isaiah 5:27–28, a passage appropriately concerned with remaining resolute during conflict:

None shall be weary nor stumble among them; none shall slumber nor sleep; neither shall the girdle of their loins be loosed, nor the latchet of their shoes be broken.
　Whose arrows are sharp, and all their bows best, their horses' hoofs shall be counted like flint, their wheels like a whirlwind.

The Washington Inaugural Bible was also used in the inaugurations of Warren G. Harding (Micah 6:8: "He hath shewed thee, O man, what is good; and what doth the Lord require of thee, but to do justly, and to love mercy, and to walk humbly with thy God?"), Dwight D. Eisenhower (Psalm 127:1: "Except the Lord build the house, they labour in vain that build it: except the Lord keep the city, the watchman waketh but in vain"), and George H. W. Bush (opened at random).

The Bible is still owned and cared for by New York City's Saint John's Lodge, which makes it available during each inauguration, should the newly elected president—the only person allowed to touch it with bare hands—choose to use it. ◆

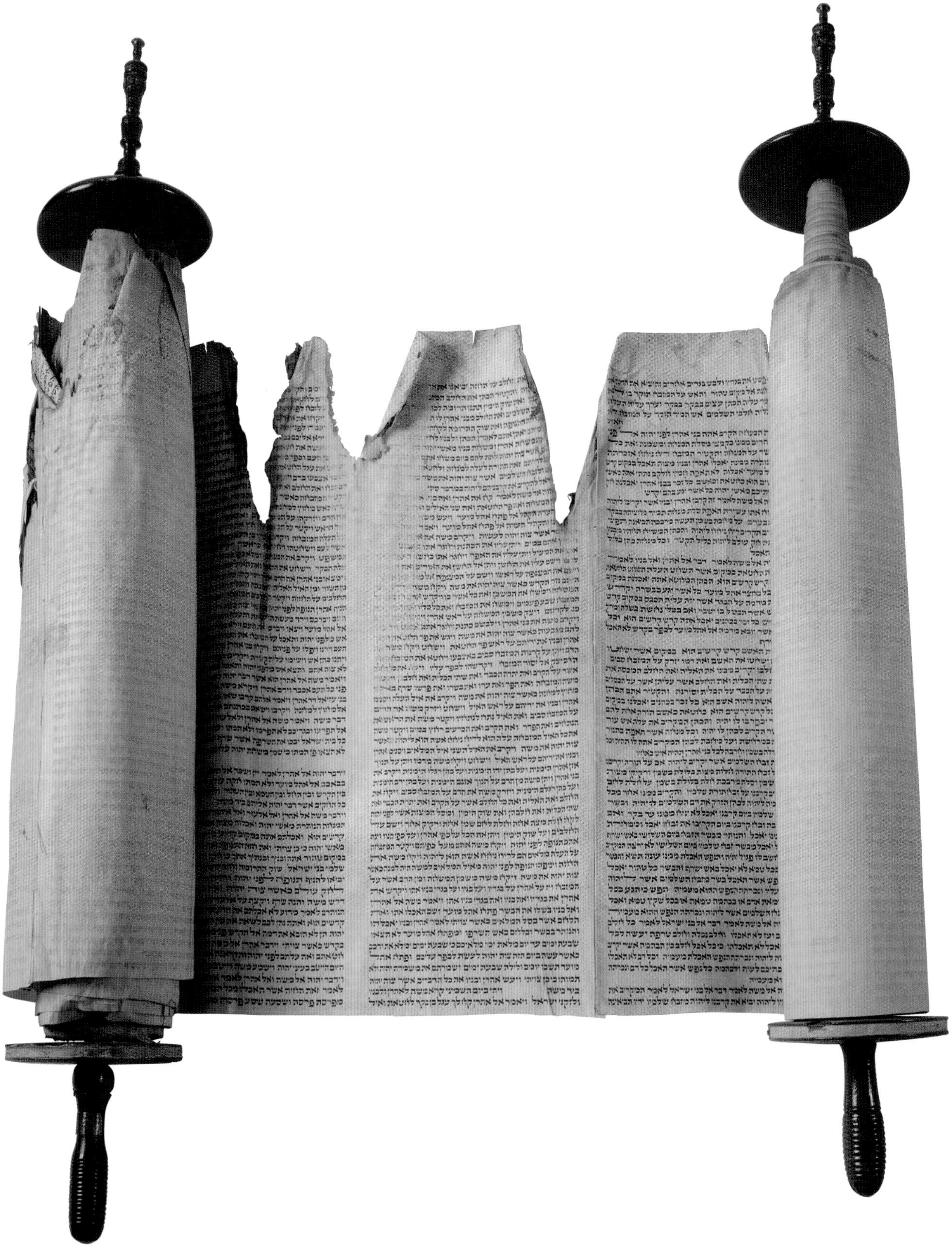

✳ *A Revolutionary Torah Scroll*

THE MEMBERS of the first Jewish community in North America arrived in 1654. Sephardic Jews who had sailed for the New World from Amsterdam, they had settled for a time in the Brazilian city of Recife but had been forced to leave when Portugal had wrested control of the South American colony from the Netherlands. Fearing the fires of the Portuguese Inquisition, which had begun in 1536 and targeted Jews as supposed threats to the Roman Catholic Church, twenty-seven Jewish refugees had pleaded with a Dutch ship captain to help them escape.

When they landed in the settlement of New Amsterdam, however, it seemed their troubles were only just beginning. The ship's captain claimed that his passengers had not paid sufficient fare and sued to recover his costs. The colony's governor, Peter Stuyvesant, had the Jews' belongings seized and sold to pay the damages, and he attempted to evict these new arrivals from the city.

Writing to his sponsors in the Dutch West India Company, Stuyvesant at first said that he "deemed it useful to require them in a friendly way to depart." But he did not maintain this amicable front for long. "Such hateful enemies and blasphemers of the name of Christ," he continued, should "be not allowed to further infect and trouble this new colony."

Yet the refugees too had written home. Leaders of the Recife Jews asked members of their community in Amsterdam to remind the colony's backers not only that Jews were allowed to live in Holland unmolested, but also that they were an important part of the very company from which Stuyvesant was seeking relief.

The Dutch West India Company's reply to Stuyvesant was not what he had hoped. Company representatives wrote,

> We would have liked to effectuate and fulfill your wishes and request that the new territories should no more be allowed to be infected by people of the Jewish nation, for we foresee therefrom the same difficulties which you fear. But after having further weighed and considered the matter, we observe that this would be somewhat unreasonable and unfair, especially because of the considerable loss sustained by this nation, with others, in the taking of Brazil, as also because of the large amount of capital which they still have invested in the shares of this company.

The "people of the Jewish nation," the company concluded, must be allowed to "travel and trade to and in New Netherland and live and remain there."

This would not be Stuyvesant's only rebuke for his reluctance to accommodate religious difference. In 1656, he made religious observances outside the Dutch Reformed Church illegal and was met with immediate resistance. Residents of the town of Flushing, concerned with the treatment that the colony's Quakers →

Torah scroll damaged in 1776 during the British occupation of Manhattan, Congregation Shearith Israel.

(page 85) might receive, issued the Flushing Remonstrance the following year. In an expansive list, it mentioned "Jews, Turks and Egyptians, . . . Presbyterian, Independent, Baptist or Quaker" and noted that "if any of these said persons come in love unto us, we cannot in conscience lay violent hands upon them."

From these eventful origins the vibrant multireligious population of New York City emerged, with the Jewish community building slowly over the decades that followed. It was nearly a century after the West India Company replied to Stuyvesant that the first native-born Jewish religious leader in America, Gershom Mendes Seixas, came of age and began to serve his community. As the cantor of New York's Congregation Shearith Israel (page 78), founded in 1729 but tracing its roots back to that first community from Brazil, he steered the synagogue's congregation through troubled waters before and after the Revolution, safeguarding many of its sacred objects during British occupation.

In August 1776, after the British pushed the Continental Army off Long Island, Washington and his troops set up an encampment on Manhattan. Within a few months, however, the British also took New York, which they occupied throughout the war. British and Hessian soldiers set fires, looted homes, and generally ransacked the city, causing most of those supporting independence to flee, including several hundred Jews.

When Hessian soldiers rode horses through the synagogue's sanctuary and set much of the building on fire, the Torah scroll seen on pages 90 and 92 was damaged. Burned edges are still visible on the parchment, which is no longer used during religious services but has been safeguarded by synagogue members for centuries as a reminder of their early history. Despite the desecration of their synagogue and the scattering of much of the congregation to Philadelphia, the members of Shearith Israel returned to prove themselves as resilient as the original twenty-seven Brazilian Jewish refugees had been.

In 1789, Seixas was one of fourteen religious leaders invited to attend Washington's inauguration on the steps of New York's Federal Hall (page 87)— a sign that the city accepted "people of the Jewish nation," as the Dutch West India Company had called them, at last. Though never formally ordained, and self-taught on many matters relating to Judaism, Seixas would ever after be called "the Patriot Rabbi of the Revolution."

While best remembered as the heroic leader of a congregation that endured despite having its most sacred objects burned during the Revolution, Seixas attended to the needs of his community in much more mundane ways as well. He was for a time the only available mohel—circumciser—in New York and so came to know many of the families in his spiritual care in an intimate way. Some fifty years ago, Thomas Kessner wrote in the *American Jewish Historical Quarterly*, "Gershom Seixas served in this capacity throughout his life, winning praise from a local doctor for his surgical expertise even at the age of seventy. . . . After the operation, Seixas would attend the child to check on his health and progress, often administering necessary medicinal remedies. These tasks sometimes ended in Pyrrhic finance when the hazzan [cantor] would in the end use most or all of his fee to pay for transportation and supplies."

Yet Seixas worked on behalf of not only his own people but all Americans. He became a pioneer of education, as one of the incorporators of Columbia University, and of charity, as a trustee of the New York Humane Society, seeing such work as an extension of his religious duty.

"I conceive we as Jews are more called upon to return thanks to benign Goodness in placing us in such a country," he once preached, "where we are free to act, according to the dictates of conscience, and where no exception is taken from following the principles of our religion." ◆

✳ *Thomas Paine*

James Watson, *Thomas Paine*, 1783. Mezzotint after Charles Willson Peale. After arriving in America in 1774, Paine became the Revolutionary era's foremost freethinker.

WHILE THE WAR FOR INDEPENDENCE is largely remembered as a secular affair sparked by concerns over taxation and representation, it also had religious roots— particularly among Christians who echoed the unofficial motto of the Revolution: "Rebellion to tyrants is obedience to God."

The power of framing liberty in such blatantly theological terms was not lost on patriots with no personal affection for religion. Even notorious freethinkers such as Thomas Paine—who once declared that "my mind is my own church"—recognized the potential impact of religious rhetoric and often drafted it into service. Though no fan of scripture (he wrote of the Old Testament, "With a few phrases excepted, it deserves either our abhorrence or our contempt," and of the New, "Is it not a species of blasphemy to call the New Testament revealed religion when we see in it such contradictions and absurdities?"), Paine could, when called upon to summon the devout to the cause of dissolving the union with England, thump the Bible as well as anyone.

Born in England in 1736, he did not arrive in the colonies until 1774. He had been in America less than two years when he published "Common Sense," his widely distributed work calling for independence from the British Crown. Paine's pamphlet made a moral case for revolution, intended to appeal to those who might not be persuaded merely by concerns about property or commerce. Written in a straightforward style ideal for oration in public settings, his publication was read aloud in taverns and at town meetings and quickly became the most popular essay printed in America at the time.

Though he did not base his arguments on religious beliefs or appeals to denominational allegiance or authority, throughout this short pamphlet, Paine built a scriptural case against monarchy, and he did so explicitly in the borrowed literary form of the sermon.

"A situation, similar to present, hath not happened since the days of Noah until now," he preached. "We have it in our power to begin the world over again. The birthday of the new world is at hand." Thanks to the ability of such passages to build bridges among various Christian denominations, many of his contemporaries credited Paine's pen with being as responsible for American victory as was George Washington's skill as a general. Though he is well known for his lack of belief, Paine nonetheless provides an example of how the fire of revolution might not have been lit if not for the spark thrown off by combining the rhetoric of political freedom with biblical imagery.

Following the American victory, Paine traveled to France to contribute to another revolution. He did not return to the United States until 1802, when he found he was no longer in step with the national mood. Because his later writings went too far in their mockery of faith, his star quickly faded in the country he had helped to free. ◆

COMMON SENSE;

ADDRESSED TO THE

INHABITANTS

OF

AMERICA,

On the following interesting

SUBJECTS.

I. Of the Origin and Design of Government in general, with concise Remarks on the English Constitution.

II. Of Monarchy and Hereditary Succession.

III. Thoughts on the present State of American Affairs.

IV. Of the present Ability of America, with some miscellaneous Reflections.

Man knows no Master save creating HEAVEN,
Or those whom choice and common good ordain.
                                    THOMSON.

PHILADELPHIA;
Printed, and Sold, by R. BELL, in Third-Street.
MDCCLXXVI.

Thomas Paine, "Common Sense," 1776. Paine's influential pamphlet occasionally used religious rhetoric to support the cause of independence.

✳ *Freeborn Garrettson's Saddlebags*

THE METHODIST MINISTER Freeborn Garrettson was a descendent of one of the first settlers of Maryland. For four generations, his plantation-owning family had relied on the labor of enslaved men and women. But in 1775, Garrettson heard a voice that would change his life. "One Sabbath morning, I continued reading the Bible till eight o'clock, and then, under a sense of duty, called the family together for prayer," he said. "While I was giving out a hymn this thought powerfully struck my mind: It is not right for you to keep your fellow-creatures in bondage. You must let the oppressed go free."

Despite his good fortune of having been born into wealth, he had struggled throughout his early life with a feeling of heaviness that he could not explain. Now he knew its cause and could not wait to rid himself of it. As he later remembered:

> I knew this was the voice of the Lord. *Till this moment, I never suspected that the practice of slave-keeping was wrong; having neither read anything on the subject, nor conversed with persons respecting its sinfulness.* After a minute's pause I replied, "Lord, the oppressed shall go free." I then addressed the slaves, and told them, "You do not belong to me: I will not desire your service without making you a sufficient compensation." I now found liberty to proceed in family worship. After singing I kneeled down to pray. But if I had the tongue of an angel I could never fully describe what I felt. All that dejection and melancholy gloom which I had groaned under, vanished away in a moment. A Divine sweetness ran through my whole frame. My soul was admitted into the depths of the Redeemer's love in an inexpressible manner! Praise and glory to his name forever!

Born in 1752, at the tail end of the First Great Awakening, Garrettson (shown opposite at the age of seventy-three) emerged from this religious experience as a major figure in early American Methodism, active mainly in New York, Maryland, and Delaware. He not only freed his own slaves, but also became an abolitionist, traveling with the saddlebags shown on page 98 to preach on plantations much like the one his family owned and to rebuke slaveholders for the sins he had only recently ceased to commit.

While the Bible was often used to justify slaveholding, among slavery's most stalwart opponents were Christians who argued for its abolition on religious grounds. Abolitionists often risked their lives for the unpopular idea that a nation built on forced labor must change its ways and repent. "It was God, and not man, that taught me the impropriety of holding slaves," Garrettson said, "and I shall never be able to praise him enough for it. My very heart bleeds for slaveholders, especially those who make a profession of religion." →

Portrait of the former slave owner Freeborn Garrettson, who became an abolitionist after hearing a voice during prayer. From Nathan Bangs, *The Life of the Rev. Freeborn Garrettson: Compiled from His Printed and Manuscript Journals, and Other Authentic Documents* (New York: T. Mason and G. Lane for the Methodist Episcopal Church, 1974).

Saddlebags of Freeborn Garrettson. The itinerant preacher used these bags while preaching abolitionism in Delaware beginning around 1775.

As a nineteenth-century account of his preaching career assesses, he was not a "reviler" of those who had not yet been enlightened as he had. On the contrary, "he was full of Divine tenderness and compassion for them." For this reason he attempted to avoid the creation of any unrest on the plantations he visited: "I endeavored frequently to inculcate the doctrine of freedom in a private way, which procured me the displeasure of some interested persons." He would not preach against slavery from the pulpit, but rather found it more effective to offer his personal testimony directly to those who might recognize their stories in his own.

His private approach, however, did not prevent him from making enemies. Throughout his daily travels, he endured threats of violence, which haunted his dreams. "I saw in the visions of the night many sharp and terrible weapons formed against me; but none could penetrate or hurt me," he wrote, "for as soon as they came near me they were turned into feathers, and brushed by me as soft as down. . . . I had a confidence in the morning that my beloved Lord would support me."

As Garrettson wrote to one of the founders of Methodism, John Wesley, in 1785, "Once I was imprisoned; twice beaten, left on the highway speechless and senseless; . . . once shot at; guns and pistols presented at my breast; once delivered from an armed mob, in the dead time of night, on the highway, by a surprising flash of lightning; surrounded frequently by mobs; stoned frequently: I have had to escape for my life at dead time of night."

Abolitionism was not the only unpopular opinion Garrettson held that frequently put him in harm's way. During the Revolution, he preached as vehemently against the war as he did against slavery. No loyalist, he opposed the tyranny of British rule, but he refused to enlist in the Continental Army or to take part in battle by any means. "These religious scruples excited violent opposition," one nineteenth-century account of his career noted. "In one instant he was assaulted by the way and beaten almost to death."

On another occasion, he recalled that his evangelizing activities had invited the attention of a lawman who had threatened to arrest the preacher and throw him in jail. Riding on his horse with saddlebags weighed down by Methodist tracts and abolitionist materials, Garrettson had given his antagonist a look of steely defiance. "I am going on the Lord's errand, and if you have power, here I am, take me," he had said, "but remember that the God against whom you are fighting, who made yonder sun, is just now looking down upon you; and I know not but that he will crush you to the earth, if you persist in fighting so furiously against him."

By the end of his life, in 1827, "going on the Lord's errand" had taken Garrettson through the United States and into Canada. His grave in Rhinebeck, New York, memorializes him by repeating a word that at times suggests dangerous rootlessness but that Methodism transformed into a badge of honor: *itinerant*. It reads, "Sacred to the memory of the Rev. Freeborn Garrettson, an itinerant minister of the Methodist Episcopal Church. He commenced his itinerant ministry in the year 1775."

Wherever he traveled, and whether in jail for his evangelism or preaching from a pulpit, he looked to his faith for comfort. "I had a dirty floor for my bed, my saddlebags for my pillow, and two large windows open with a cold east wind blowing upon me," he wrote of one period of imprisonment, "but I had great consolation in my dear Lord and could say, 'Thy will be done.'" ◆

✳ *Richard Allen's Hymnal*

Peter S. Duval, *Portrait of Richard Allen,* 1840. Lithograph.

WHILE FREEBORN GARRETTSON was not particularly successful in convincing slave owners to allow their enslaved laborers to go free (page 97), on at least one occasion his preaching did have the desired effect, and American religious history changed as a result.

On Stokely Sturgis's plantation in Kent County, Delaware, an enslaved young man named Richard Allen converted to Methodism in 1777. Just seventeen years old, Allen regarded the man he called Mr. Stokely with some affection and suggested that it might do the Sturgis family some good to invite a preacher to their home. Sturgis grudgingly agreed. When Garrettson arrived, he delivered a sermon on the Book of Daniel, with its warning about God's judgment: "Thou art weighed in the balance, and art found wanting" (5:27).

"In pointing out and weighing the different characters, and among the rest weighed the slaveholders," Allen said, "my master believed himself to be one of that number, and after that he could not be satisfied to hold slaves, believing it to be wrong." Sturgis did not simply let those he enslaved go free, however. Instead, he told Allen and his brother that they could buy their liberty for sixty pounds in gold or silver, or two thousand dollars. After finding extra work for five years to save sufficient funds, Allen bought his way out of bondage.

In the following years, he earned his living cutting cordwood, working in a brickyard, driving a wagon, and drawing salt. All the while, whether he was "sitting, standing or lying," he found himself in prayer. "While my hands were employed to earn my bread," he said, "my heart was devoted to my dear Redeemer. Sometimes I would awake from my sleep preaching and praying." He resolved to become a preacher, like the man who had helped convince his former owner that slavery was a sin. In February 1786, Allen arrived in Philadelphia and began his preaching career, uncertain though he was of his skills. "I strove to preach as well as I could," he said. "It was a great cross to me; but the Lord was with me." →

Bishop Richard Allen's hymnal, 1801. Founder of the African Methodist Episcopal Church, Allen was a prolific collector of hymns and published a number of hymnals in his lifetime, including this one, his first.

In Philadelphia, he met Rev. Absalom Jones, another former slave turned minister, and together they founded the Free Africa Society in 1787. For a time, both attended Saint George's Methodist Church, where some white members insisted that African Americans must use the balcony instead of being permitted to sit or kneel on the ground floor. When Allen, Jones, and other African Americans knelt to pray with the rest of the church on the ground floor, the trustees pulled Jones up off his knees.

"You must get up—you must not kneel here," a trustee said.

"Wait until prayer is over," Jones replied.

"No, you must get up now," the man said, "or I will call for aid and force you away."

"Wait until prayer is over, and I will get up and trouble you no more."

Other trustees arrived and a scuffle ensued, which, Allen later recalled, "raised a great excitement and inquiry among the citizens.... We all went out of the church in a body, and they were no more plagued with us in the church."

Following their poor treatment at Saint George's, Jones left the Methodists entirely to affiliate with the Anglican Church. Allen remained, however, professing loyalty to the denomination for what it had earlier done to change his life.

Ordained into the ministry by Bishop Francis Asbury, one of the leaders of Methodism in the United States, Allen began a congregation of his own in 1794, which he called the African Methodist Episcopal Church, commonly known as AME. His first worship services made use of a converted blacksmith shop, where an anvil held his Bible as he preached.

Within a decade, Allen's congregation had moved into a more permanent home and counted nearly five hundred members. Ten years further on, that number had more than doubled, to 1,272. By 1841, the church had outgrown two buildings and begun construction on a third, more permanent home. Mother Bethel AME Church, made of brick and stone and with more ornate interiors than the previous structures, was soon known as the Red Brick Church and became a recruiting center for African American soldiers during the Civil War. It was one of the most significant centers of African American culture in the country.

Richard Allen's hymnal, shown on page 101, was a source of both solace and challenge to many in the early republic. Considered within the story of Allen's slavery and the role that another preacher played in his freedom, it is a symbol of the capacity of the religious lives of Americans to influence one another in ways unexpected and often unseen.

Intriguingly, when Freeborn Garrettson made a record of the enslaved men and women whose freedom he had helped win, Allen's name was not among them. It is possible that he did not fully know what his ministry had wrought. ◆

✴ *Jarena Lee*

RICHARD ALLEN BROKE many social and cultural barriers (page 100), but he was perhaps the furthest ahead of his time when he granted approval to a woman who sought to preach in the African Methodist Episcopal Church.

Born to free African American parents in New Jersey in 1783, Jarena Lee grew up without being exposed to religion. Her family, she later wrote, was "wholly ignorant of the knowledge of God," and so it was not until her twenty-first year that she heard preaching that inspired her to worry over the state of her soul. In the period of searching that followed, she encountered several spiritual influences, from a Catholic woman who employed her to members of an Anglican church. Despite her attraction to a religious life, each experience, Lee said, "seemed to make this impression upon my mind, *this is not the people for you.*"

She began to feel differently when she heard Allen, then a bishop, preach in Philadelphia. "During the labors of this man that afternoon," Lee wrote, "I had come to the conclusion, that this is the people to which my heart unites." After joining the AME Church, she regularly had intense experiences in prayer, feeling the competing attentions of both benign spirits and the devil, until finally godliness won out. "During this," she said of such moments, "I stood perfectly still, the tears rolling in a flood from my eyes. So great was the joy that it is past description."

Peter S. Duval, *Portrait of Jarena Lee*, 1849. Lithograph. Lee was the first female preacher in the African Methodist Episcopal Church.

Five years after what she came to refer to as her "sanctification," Lee began to hear a call to preach. Though preaching was almost unheard of for women at the time, she proved to be persuasive. "Why should it be thought impossible, heterodox, or improper for a woman to preach, seeing the Savior died for the woman as well as the man?" she asked. "If the man may preach, because the Savior died for him, why not the woman, seeing he died for her also? Is he not a whole Savior, instead of a half one, as those who hold it wrong for a woman to preach, would seem to make it appear?"

While he was at first reluctant to do so, after hearing her persistent and persuasive arguments, Bishop Allen granted Jarena Lee permission to preach in 1823. In five years she traveled nearly two thousand miles, delivering sermons in Maryland, New Jersey, New York, and Pennsylvania.

When she wrote the story of her conversion and her preaching career in 1836, she began it with Joel 2:28, a scriptural passage that she considered irrefutable justification for her calling: "And it shall come to pass . . . that I will pour out my Spirit upon all flesh; and your sons and your daughters shall prophesy." ◆

✳ *American Samplers*

Sampler by B. Lazarus,
1843. This sampler includes
the letters of the Hebrew
alphabet, making it one of
a few known examples
of the art form displaying
familiarity with traditional
Jewish education.

WHILE RELIGIOUSLY INFORMED CLASSROOM educations of the kind that made use of books such as *The New England Primer* (page 40) were largely limited to boys in early America, girls received lessons that were at once spiritual and practical. Skills such as embroidery, often mastered by age ten, not only were domestic arts, but also served to display religious knowledge.

Many of the 137 samplers in the National Museum of American History's Textile Collection include elements demonstrating a familiarity with the Bible and moral instruction and thus might serve as windows onto the religious lives of girls whose spiritual development history often overlooks.

One sampler, stitched in New Jersey in 1788 by fourteen-year-old Rachel Kester, shows off its creator's talent with the needle by means of an inscription beginning with the words "Love the Lord and he will be a tender father." Other samplers of the era include short texts drawn from favored biblical passages and imagery full of scriptural allusions.

While the majority of the collection's samplers with religious content are explicitly Christian, samplers were also created by young Jewish girls, who occasionally added Hebrew letters as a decorative motif. Two examples from the Smithsonian collection were made by girls who recorded their names only as B. Lazarus (1843) and B. Hollander (1845). Given their shared time frame and the similarity of their designs—each includes only numerals, the Hebrew alphabet, and the Roman alphabet in multiple styles—it is possible that these were produced by students of the same teacher. Sadly, nothing more about them is currently known.

The earliest known sampler stitched in America was made by the daughter of the well-known *Mayflower* passenger Myles Standish, Loara, who was born in the 1630s in the Plymouth Colony settlement of Duxbury. Like Rachel Kester nearly a century and a half later, she chose a text for her sampler that would show her great ability with the needle and straightforward moral aspirations:

> Loara Standish is my name
> Lord guide my heart that I may do thy will
> Also fill my hands with such convenient skill
> As may conduce to virtue void of shame
> and I will give the glory to thy name.

Through the centuries of American sampler making that followed, designs became more ambitious, perhaps reflecting expanding understandings of the skills and knowledge that a young woman's education ought to include. Nine-year-old Elizabeth Orme's sampler from 1833, for example, has a large cornucopia of flowers and leaves above a verse of her own composition, all within a geometric carnation →

ABCDEFGHIJKLMNOPQRSTUVWX

ABCDEFGHIKLMNOPQRST UVWX

abcdefghiklmnopqrstuvwxyz.

ABCDEFGHIKLMNOPQ
RS UVW YZ 1234 5678 &c

ABCDEFGHIJKLM
NOPQRST UVW
XYZ 123456 7890.

abcdefghiklmnopqrstuvwxyz.

B   Lazarus. 1843

The star of Bethlehem

Brighter than the rising day
When the sun of glory shines,
Brighter than the diamond's ray
Sparkling in Golonda's mines
Beaming through the clouds of wo
Smiles in Mercy's diadem
On the guilty world below
The Star that rose in Bethlehem

Elizabeth Orme

Nov,th
1833
Age 9

border. Born in Washington, DC, Elizabeth had enough traditional religious knowledge to compose a poem about Bethlehem, but she was also worldly enough to include a reference (though misspelled) to Golkonda, the famed gem mine of southern India. Around the same time, and not too far from Elizabeth's home, a young girl named Mary Pets learned from Baltimore's Oblate Sisters of Providence (page 141) to stitch a sampler in one of the country's first schools for free African American children, the Oblate School for Colored Girls. Mary's sampler captures a view of the city in which she lived, as well as her views on the value of virtue ("the chiefest beauty of the mind, the noblest ornament of human-kind"), which are especially poignant given that she lived in a city in which only some were free.

While these later samplers do not have as great a variety of needle techniques as Loara Standish's, they do suggest that the view of the world from America had expanded over the nearly two centuries that separated one girl's lessons in Plymouth from two other girls' lessons in two of the young nation's major cities. All three samplers provide intriguing glimpses of the talents, the concerns, and the faith of young women in early America. ◆

✳ *Fraktur Baptismal Certificate*

FOR MANY PEOPLE in early America, religion was particularly significant at the beginning and the end of life, as seen in the elaborate remembrances of births and baptisms that the German immigrants of Pennsylvania created. Hand-illuminated Fraktur documents—such as the *Taufschein* (baptismal certificate) shown opposite, which celebrates the christening of Catharina Wachter in 1774—were a popular form of folk art that also served a practical purpose.

The word *Fraktur* originally referred to a style of German calligraphy whose letters appear fractured, bent, or broken. Over time, the name for this form of writing, which was used for official purposes, began also to refer to the embellishments that the calligraphers added. Like medieval monks illuminating a manuscript, Fraktur artists added vines, flowers, and small animals, especially birds. They became known for their mastery of elements such as the parrot motif, horn-blowing angels, and crowns of righteousness.

While birth and baptismal announcements were among the most common types, Fraktur drawings commemorated confirmations, weddings, and house blessings, too. Artists also made them for their own sake, as writing samples and floral scenes. Common graphic elements included birds, hearts, and flowers, blending sacramental purposes and traditional motifs. For the thousands of German-speaking immigrants who poured into the Mid-Atlantic region of the United States during the late 1700s and early 1800s, such certificates both affirmed that their individual futures would be lived in this young country and served as reminders that their collective past belonged to a land and a language that should not be forgotten.

Because much of their work is unsigned, many Fraktur artists are anonymous. In such cases, the inspirations for their images can only be guessed at. Of those who are known, however, a great many were schoolteachers. In this largely agrarian community of German-speaking immigrants, mainly members of Lutheran or Reformed churches, teachers were generally the only neighbors close at hand who were literate enough to perform the important task of recording marriages, births, and baptisms. The prevalence of teachers among Fraktur artists may rest on other practical concerns as well. Not only were they the ones with the paper and the pens, but they were also paid poorly enough that they were likely happy for the chance to make some extra money with a *Taufschein* or two.

Regarded as "primitive" or folk art by collectors, Fraktur drawings were at times remarkably intricate. Moreover, they reflect the intricacies of the religious lives of those for whom these works were created. Often depicted as a plain people who eschewed colorful expressions, the German immigrants who became known as the Pennsylvania Dutch had vibrant spiritual lives, complete with birds and angels that sang at their weddings and tulips that opened to announce their births. ◆

This *Taufschein* translates as follows: "To this married couple, Georg Wachter and his lawful wife, Catharina, born Weidmann, a daughter is born into this world, as: Catharina Wachter, born to this world in the year of our Lord Jesus 1774, the 14th day of January at about two o'clock in the morning in the sign of Aquarius (*according to Christian teaching, all people are conceived and born in sin, and all children shall be brought to Jesus. As is written by the Evangelist Mark, 10, v. 15, whoever is not received into the Kingdom of God as a child will not enter thus, unless united in God's merciful company through holy baptism*); and by Pastor Helmuth is baptized and named as notified above. Baptismal witnesses were Bernhard Gartner and his wife, Barbara. Catharina was born and baptized in America, in the Province of Pennsylvania, in Lancaster County, in Cocalico township.

Scarcely born into the world, it is only a short measured pace from the first step to the cool grave in the earth. O with every moment! Our strength diminishes, and with every year we grow more ripe for the bier. And who knows in what hour the final voice will awaken us, because God has not revealed this to anybody yet. Who tends to his house will depart from the world with joy. Because surety, in contrast, can provoke eternal death.

This model of the House that Noah had ... ...
... ...
... Charlotte Streatfield ... her godson ... the first of May 1829 ...

✷ *Sunday Toys*

ON THE CHRISTIAN SABBATH, many children were allowed to amuse themselves only with "Sunday toys," simple playthings that taught biblical or moral lessons. Sunday toys included play sets depicting the Garden of Eden or Noah's Ark, such as the one shown here, each of which might also have human figures and dozens of hand-carved animals.

Other playthings appropriate for the Sabbath included "church dolls," made of handkerchiefs, and a series of movable wooden squares tied together with ribbon and known as the Jacob's Ladder. Less immediately identifiable as religiously inspired than Noah's Ark, the Jacob's Ladder was permitted for its connection to a story told in Genesis about angels ascending and descending a ladder between heaven and earth.

Recalling his use of such toys, in 1870 Charles Dickens Jr. suggested that they were the amusements of a time when "children were easily satisfied":

> I clearly recollect that I had a great admiration for a plaything which was called sometimes Jacob's Ladder. . . . It consisted of six oblong pieces of wood, adorned with pictures on both sides, and so connected with tapes that when the top piece, which was held in the hand, was turned down, all the others would turn down likewise by an apparently spontaneous movement, causing a new series of pictures to be presented to the eye, which was highly gratified by the change, as were also the ears by the clattering of the wooden tablets and the tinkling of some little bells with which they were decorated.

Similar in content but not necessarily restricted to Sundays, some of the earliest board games in the United States sought to instill virtue in their young players while, of course, capturing their attention. The Mansion of Happiness, for example, the first board game commercially available in America, was sold as "an Instructive, Moral and Entertaining Amusement." Invented in 1800, the game was meant to be fun, but also warned against the dangers of a life spent ignorant of such virtues as keeping the Sabbath.

Yet Sunday toys were not only concerned with warning against vice through the denial or limiting of pleasure. As a popular nineteenth-century parenting manual entitled *Babyhood: The Mother's Nursery Guide* suggested, they were intended as a gentle way to occupy children at times when the adults in their lives might be engaged in quiet reflection. →

Noah's Ark play set, circa 1820. Play sets such as this one were among the most popular "Sunday toys," which allowed children to play while learning religious and moral lessons.

Those of us mothers to whom Sunday is the happiest and most sacred day of the week, long that our children should learn to love it too, but since we wish to teach them that it is a holy as well as a happy day, it is sometimes difficult to make it all we could wish to the little ones, and yet combine their pleasures with the quietness and reverence which we feel it desirable they should observe as becoming the sacredness of God's day of rest.

Children's Sundays should be happy days. . . . With this idea in mind, we instituted when they were very little the plan of Sunday toys and books, choosing those which were specially attractive and yet would conduce to quiet play; as, for example, boxes of animals, and such things as the children could play with while seated at the table, and all their prettiest books.

In this common approach, children were told not that they were limited only to Sunday toys on the Sabbath, but rather that *only* on the Sabbath were they permitted to use them.

These were kept separate from their every-day toys, and only allowed to be played with on Sunday. Even the very little ones very soon learned to look forward to this, and no sooner is breakfast over on Sunday morning than the demand for the best books and toys begins. This very largely obviates the necessity of having to ask them not to play roughly or noisily, for they are so absorbed in the enjoyment of their weekly treat that they do not think about or crave their everyday occupations.

While emphasis was placed on marking a special occasion, the more practical side of the Sabbath was not forgotten. When necessary, the *Nursery Guide* author notes, children should be reminded that "it is every body's resting day"; in order that others in the household might similarly enjoy a day of reflection, boys and girls "ought to be as quiet and give as little trouble as possible."

The Noah's Ark shown here, an early example of a Sunday toy, was gifted to a young girl in 1829, and it surely inspired many hours of quiet play. ♦

✻ Mourning Jewelry

FROM THE SEVENTEENTH to the nineteenth centuries, women wore mourning jewelry, such as the brooch shown opposite, to commemorate the deaths of loved ones. During the colonial era particularly, when the infant mortality rate was as high as 30 percent in some regions, religious imagery was employed to memorialize lost children. In this brooch, three child-angels identified with initials hover above two adult figures, most likely their parents.

While religious icons such as angels figured prominently in jewelry used to mourn children, darker images often appeared in similar pieces memorializing adults. Skulls and grave diggers' tools made such pieces not only reminders of family members who had died, but also memento mori accessories signaling the presence of death in an era that knew many hardships.

The rules of social propriety surrounding death were extensive. One nineteenth-century guide to appropriate behavior and personal presentation in every situation, *The Ladies' and Gentlemen's Etiquette: A Complete Manual of the Manners and Dress of American Society*, contains a long section on mourning, including the lengths of time required for the loss of various kith and kin—spouses, children, grandchildren, distant relations, and friends. According to the norms of the day, each form of grief imposed strictures not only on clothing, but also on jewelry. *The Ladies' and Gentlemen's Etiquette* states:

> Deep mourning requires the heaviest black of serge, bombazine, lustreless alpaca, de laine, merino or similar heavy clinging material, with collar and cuffs of crape. A widow wears a bonnet-cap of white tarletan, known as the "widow's cap." Mourning garments are made in the severest simplicity. They should have little or no trimming; no flounces, ruffles or bows are allowable. If the dress is not made en suite, then a long or square shawl of barege or cashmere with crape border is worn. The bonnet is of black crape; a hat is inadmissible. The veil is of crape or barege with heavy border. Black gloves and black-bordered handkerchief. In winter dark furs may be worn with the deepest mourning. Jewelry is strictly forbidden, and all pins, buckles, etc., must be of jet.

The one exception to such rules, mourning jewelry was part of a larger category of American folk art—including memorial painting, ceramics, calligraphy, and needlework—that flourished from the end of the eighteenth century until the middle of the nineteenth. That this coincided precisely with the Second Great Awakening, that period of increased religious devotion throughout the country, was no accident. The personal piety and individual affirmations of faith that itinerant preachers encouraged in open-air sermons drew largely on images of death and resurrection.

Mourning brooch, circa 1790–1810. Gold, glass, and ivory. Throughout colonial America and the young United States, distinctive jewelry and styles of dress signified that a family was grieving.

As these themes began to dominate the public imagination, they found aesthetic representation in depictions of death and loss that drew at once on Christian, romantic, and classical traditions.

As the nineteenth century progressed, memorial photographs replaced mourning paintings and needlework, but the mourning jewelry tradition endured. Particularly after the Civil War, the ability to express religious sentiment and personal suffering in a small but visible manner provided solace to a nation that had just encountered loss on a scale it had never seen before. ◆

✳ *Ephrata Cloister*

Ephrata Cloister, Lancaster County, Pennsylvania, founded in 1732. When Pietist immigrants arrived in Pennsylvania after fleeing religious persecution in Germany, some found refuge in the communal life of Ephrata Cloister. Like many American utopian experiments before and after it, it lasted only a short time before being all but abandoned.

AMONG THOSE WHO came to Pennsylvania to enjoy the religious freedoms established by William Penn (page 85) was a Pietist by the name of Johann Conrad Beissel. The movement known as Pietism had begun in Germany in the seventeenth century as an effort to reform state-sponsored Lutheran churches. Pietists often met in small groups to pray, read the Bible, and speak out against existing religious authority. Efforts to suppress such dissenting expressions of faith led to a series of emigrations, including those of the Mennonites, the Moravians, and the Dunkers, or German Baptists.

Fleeing his homeland because of such religious intolerance, Beissel arrived in Pennsylvania in 1720. As an early twentieth-century biography of him noted, he was at the time "about thirty years old, short in stature, high forehead, prominent nose, sharp piercing eyes, a skillful baker and an adept in music, and possessed of projects of a solitary life." It was in search of the last that he built, a year after his arrival in America, a log cabin in the Conestoga Valley in which to live and worship.

Despite his desire to live alone with his God, his personal charisma was such that others soon wished to share the solitary life with him. After his vocal opinions against Sunday worship (he believed Saturday was the true Sabbath) and in favor of celibacy caused a split within a nearby Pietist community, Beissel became the head of a new congregation. Though it was not his intention to be a religious leader, around him rose a complex of communal dwellings, chapels, barns, and workshops housing business enterprises for the common good.

Because Beissel's followers lived and worked communally, rose for prayers and singing in the middle of the night, and began to wear distinctive hooded, habitlike garments, many believed they were Catholic monks, and their home became known as the Ephrata Cloister.

"Beissel seemed to have strange power," his early biographer Samuel Grant Zerfass wrote. "When he established his hermitage at the Cloister it was then a desolate region, yet men and women came from distant parts and voluntarily assumed hardships, bearing burdens, drawing plows, sleeping on rude benches with a block of wood for a pillow." He also seemed to be strangely protected. "The

Ephrata pioneers were accused of being Jesuits sent there to seduce the populace," Zerfass noted. "Efforts were made by the surrounding people to burn down the entire community but the wind providentially changed the course of the fire and actually burned the barn and buildings of the chief instigator."

Ephrata soon found a place in American history not only as a peculiarly monastic Protestant community, but also as the site of the region's first successful publishing operations, which included a printing press, a book bindery, and even a mill for making paper. Among the significant publications for which the master printers of Ephrata were responsible was the first American edition of *Martyrs Mirror*, a 1,500-page book documenting the stories of those killed for their Christian faith. More formally known as *The Bloody Theater, or Martyrs Mirror of the Defenseless Christians, Who Baptized Only upon Confession of Faith, and Who Suffered and Died for the Testimony of Jesus, Their Savior, from the Time of Christ to the Year A.D. 1660*, it was second only to the Bible in religious importance in communities including the Amish and the Mennonites.

Thanks to a tireless work ethic and entrepreneurial spirit, the community built more than a dozen structures, many in a distinctive German style featuring multiple stories and high, steeply pitched roofs, in a little more than a decade. It also became known for the liturgical music and calligraphic arts that flourished in its contemplative atmosphere. Yet like many American religious experiments, Ephrata thrived for only a short time before declining. With the community so dependent on Beissel's personality and piety, his death in 1768 signaled the coming of the end.

Having been restored to their original condition in the middle of the twentieth century, the buildings and the property are open to the public, standing as a reminder of those who have come to America in search of places where they might explore new ways of living their faith. ◆

Music sheet, circa 1745. With singing central to its worship, Ephrata Cloister became known for producing ornate hand-drawn music sheets.

❋ *Cornplanter and Handsome Lake*

AT THE END OF the eighteenth century, the last bastion of autonomy of the Seneca people, one of the six Iroquois tribes, could be found in a village in the Allegheny Mountains called Jenuchshadego, also known as Cornplanter's Town.

Though he was a hereditary chief of the Seneca, Cornplanter was also the son of a Dutch fur trader and had moved through the colonies surrounding Native land with the name John Abeel. With his feet in both worlds, he was a skilled diplomat who had succeeded in safeguarding his people even as other Indian nations had disappeared.

It was this diplomatic spirit that led Cornplanter to invite Quakers to serve as teachers in his village. Providing lessons in such practical subjects as writing and agriculture, they also offered religious and moral instruction. These Quakers never succeeded in winning as many converts as they had hoped, but their influence could soon be seen in a new religious movement born of surprising circumstances in Jenuchshadego.

In 1799, Cornplanter's half-brother, Handsome Lake, was known as a troublemaker with a weakness for alcohol. For weeks during a hard winter, he was confined to a bunk of his half-brother's cabin. As he lay near death, he listened to Quaker lessons being taught in the next room, which may have contributed to a vision that changed not only his life but the lives of many of his people.

Following a miraculous recovery, the former ruffian announced that he had been given a revelation. From then onward, he would preach a new way of living to the Seneca. The Code of Handsome Lake, as his teachings became known, blended Quaker morality and abstinence from alcohol with traditional Iroquois beliefs and a new oral scripture about a people who had suffered at the hands of interlopers who had brought dubious gifts ("a flask of rum, a pack of playing cards, a handful of coins") from across the sea.

Handsome Lake's movement—known as Gai-wiio, or "Good message" in the Seneca language—grew slowly at first, but by the time of his death, in 1816, he had seen the small spark of his vision spread like wildfire. His teachings, transmitted orally first among his people and then to other Indian nations, inspired a spiritual revival among the Iroquois just when it seemed their way of life was destined to disappear. Their deepest beliefs revolved around an image of the home: the traditional Iroquois longhouse, in which many families lived together communally. Handsome Lake's teachings were soon also known as Longhouse Religion, as they used the structure as a symbol of the communal nature of all life.

Though undeniably influenced by Christian missionaries, Handsome Lake was for a time their greatest rival for the souls of Native Americans. He supplanted Cornplanter as the voice of their people and even earned the praise of President →

Frederick Bartoli, *Portrait of Cornplanter*, 1796. Oil on canvas. Also known as John Abeel, Cornplanter was a Dutch-Iroquois leader of the Seneca people.

Thomas Jefferson, who called him "brother" and urged all Indians to follow his example. "I am happy to learn you have been so far favored by the Divine spirit as to be made sensible of those things which are for your good and that of your people," Jefferson wrote in 1802, "and particularly that you and they see the ruinous effects which the abuse of spirituous liquors have produced upon them." Continuing in this vein, Jefferson made this new prophet seem not just the Seneca's leader but their Martin Luther:

> Go on then, brother, in the great reformation you have undertaken. Persuade our red brethren then to be sober, and to cultivate their lands; and their women to spin and weave for their families. You will soon see your women and children well fed and clothed, your men living happily in peace and plenty, and your numbers increasing from year to year. It will be a great glory to you to have been the instrument of so happy a change, and your children's children, from generation to generation, will repeat your name with love and gratitude forever.

Although it was Handsome Lake who would be remembered as a great religious leader, his half-brother also was known for his spiritual insight. As a man who moved between cultures and frequently found himself by virtue of his birth in diplomatic roles, Cornplanter faced practical challenges a man moved only by visions might not understand. Yet he, too, sought divine guidance he might share with his people.

"When the sun goes down he opens his heart before God, and earlier than the sun appears again upon the hills he gives thanks for his protection during the night," Cornplanter said. "He perceives that the Great Spirit will try his firmness in doing what is right." ◆

✳ *The Book of Mormon*

ACCORDING TO TRADITION, when Joseph Smith was a young man, he discovered golden plates inscribed with an ancient text buried in the ground of a hill called Cumorah in western New York. Though the text was written in a language unknown to anyone living, when Smith placed two "seer stones" that an angel had given him over his eyes, as if wearing a pair of spectacles, he was able to read it. He dictated a translation of the plates' contents to scribes and published the result as the Book of Mormon in 1830, when he was just twenty-five years old.

Even more remarkable than the story of their discovery, the story told on the golden plates did nothing less than rewrite religious history, putting ideas and figures from Christian lore on U.S. soil. The Book of Mormon was a new scripture explaining how Jesus Christ had visited earth far from the Holy Land of the Bible. After his resurrection, Smith said, the son of God had walked in the forests of America, appearing to the only people who had lived there at the time, the lost descendants of one of the tribes of Israel, known by Mormons as the Lamanites.

Smith had always been drawn to stories of Native America. His mother, who was also one of his earliest followers, recalled that this had been the case long before his discovery. "During our evening conversations, Joseph would occasionally give us some of the most amusing recitals that could be imagined," she once said. "He would describe the ancient inhabitants of this continent, their dress, mode of traveling, and the animals upon which they rode; their cities, their buildings, with every particular; their mode of warfare; and also their religious worship. This he would do with as much ease, seemingly, as if he had spent his whole life among them."

Though Smith launched perhaps the most successful new religious movement in American history, the questions that inspired it were far older, dating back to the earliest encounter between Europe and the Americas. One of the biggest theological problems that Europeans had faced after crossing the Atlantic was how to understand Native Americans, whose existence suggested that the God they believed had formed the universe had also created a population that did not fit into their biblical worldview. Spanish theologians had wondered if Native Americans had souls, while many Puritans had thought they were of the devil. Other colonial-era Christians, such as Roger Williams (page 26), had assumed, as Smith did, that the Bible must mention these people after all. Native Americans themselves, meanwhile, had their own range of responses to the Christian beliefs brought across the ocean, including conversion, adaptation, and resistance.

Presented as an entwined telling of hidden religious history and forgotten American prehistory, Smith's scripture spread quickly in a region that had by then seen more than its share of spiritual frenzies. At the time, western New York was known as the Burned-Over District, because it was said that there was no one left →

Manuscript pages, Book of Mormon, 1829. The faith's founder, Joseph Smith, dictated the Book of Mormon to a number of scribes. These pages include 1 Nephi 4:20–5:14 in the current edition of the Book of Mormon.

THE

BOOK OF MORMON:

AN ACCOUNT WRITTEN BY THE HAND OF MORMON, UPON PLATES TAKEN FROM THE PLATES OF NEPHI.

Wherefore it is an abridgment of the Record of the People of Nephi; and also of the Lamanites; written to the Lamanites, which are a remnant of the House of Israel; and also to Jew and Gentile; written by way of commandment, and also by the spirit of Prophesy and of Revelation. Written, and sealed up, and hid up unto the LORD, that they might not be destroyed; to come forth by the gift and power of GOD unto the interpretation thereof; sealed by the hand of Moroni, and hid up unto the LORD, to come forth in due time by the way of Gentile; the interpretation thereof by the gift of GOD; an abridgment taken from the Book of Ether.

Also, which is a Record of the People of Jared, which were scattered at the time the LORD confounded the language of the people when they were building a tower to get to Heaven: which is to shew unto the remnant of the House of Israel how great things the LORD hath done for their fathers; and that they may know the covenants of the LORD, that they are not cast off forever; and also to the convincing of the Jew and Gentile that JESUS is the CHRIST, the ETERNAL GOD, manifesting Himself unto all nations. And now if there be fault, it be the mistake of men; wherefore condemn not the things of GOD, that ye may be found spotless at the judgment seat of CHRIST.

BY JOSEPH SMITH, JUNIOR,
AUTHOR AND PROPRIETOR.

PALMYRA:
PRINTED BY E. B. GRANDIN, FOR THE AUTHOR.
1830.

Book of Mormon. First published in 1830, it has become one of the most-printed books in the world.

there whom the fire of the Holy Spirit had not baptized. Catching the end of the Second Great Awakening, the newly formed Church of Jesus Christ of Latter-day Saints spread west from its place of origin, establishing communities in Kirtland, Ohio; Independence, Missouri; Nauvoo, Illinois; and then on the frontier.

In frequent conflict with the federal government over issues including territory and polygamy, the people who came to be called Mormons issued their own currency and created their own state beyond existing U.S. borders. Named Deseret, it occupied an area that is now part of Nevada, New Mexico, and Utah, where figures such as Brigham Young took over the leadership of the church after an anti-Mormon mob murdered the church's founder in Carthage, Illinois, on June 27, 1844.

The Latter-day Saints' coins were minted with gold dust brought back by Mormon miners from California and were first produced to buy goods from the East. They came in denominations of $2.50, $5, $10, and $20 and were often crudely forged, with simple designs and hand-carved letters.

The $10 coin shown at upper left, produced in Salt Lake City, has the emblem of the Mormon priesthood below an all-seeing eye. It was made from unalloyed gold, and no more than ten of its kind are now known to exist. Mormon paper currency (below) is also rare and likewise provides a glimpse into the practical concerns of a new religious movement in search of a foothold on the frontier.

The first edition of the Book of Mormon, shown on page 123, was published within a decade of Joseph Smith's claimed discovery of the golden plates. Since then, more than 150 million copies have been published, making it among the most-printed books of all time. ◆

Mormon currency, 1847. As Mormons spread throughout the United States and then beyond its borders, they minted their own coins and printed their own promissory notes.

Mormon $5 note, 1837.

❋ The Peaceable Kingdom

THOUGH HE IS BEST KNOWN for tableaux so untouched by turmoil that predator and prey lie down together, the artist Edward Hicks was born into a world of conflict and sorrow. The Revolution was still raging at the time of his birth in Bucks County, Pennsylvania, and would soon deprive his loyalist family of their wealth. His mother died during his infancy, and his father, fearing what his political allegiance would mean when the war ended, sent Hicks to live in another family's home. The only saving grace of his childhood was that the family who took him in happened to be members of the Society of Friends, more commonly known as Quakers (page 85). To his turbulent young life, their faith brought a calm that he would later hope to share through his painting. →

Edward Hicks, *The Peaceable Kingdom*, 1826. Oil on canvas. This iconic bucolic scene, one of Hicks's sixty-two variations on the theme, also suggests some of the tensions present in early American life.

He had many more years of struggle, however, before he would be able to capture his iconic images of peace. As an adolescent, Hicks began an apprenticeship with a coach-making company, where he proved a competent carpenter but showed real skill in ornamentation. Yet as he had been sent away from his adopted home while learning a trade, he wandered from the straight and narrow. He abandoned himself to dice games, drinking binges, and, as he later said, "licentious lewdness."

It was only after entering into business with a member of the Society of Friends that Hicks reassessed his life, vowing to turn from the "ignorance, intemperance, impatient anger, and devilishness" that had ruled his youth to embrace faith and to use his talents for its benefit. He began regularly attending the Friends' meetings and soon sought to become a minister himself.

Perhaps because of the unsettled nature of his young life, as he grew older he spent long hours contemplating an image of stability and security described by the prophet Isaiah (11:6): "The wolf also shall dwell with the lamb, and the leopard shall lie down with the kid, and the calf and the young lion and fatling together; and a little child shall lead them." This passage would be an ongoing source of inspiration for Hicks, the theme of sixty-two surviving canvases of his in which animals at leisure create an American Eden. Often with a scene of human interaction tucked in the background, each *Peaceable Kingdom* painting suggests that we may ameliorate the unrest that seems an inevitable part of our existence by paying closer attention to divine creation.

Drawing inspiration from both the American landscape and the Bible, Hicks provided local settings for scriptural scenes, often depicting Quaker efforts to make peace with Native Americans through treaty negotiations and missionary work, as seen in the background of the version of *The Peaceable Kingdom* shown on page 125.

While the Quaker tradition gave Hicks a path toward personal peace, it also created further sources of conflict in his life. To begin with, the style of painting at which he excelled seemed vain and unnecessary to many Quakers. Still greater

disruption was caused by a bitter feud in the Society of Friends that Hicks's own cousin happened to spark. The writings of Elias Hicks (1748–1830), a Rhode Island farmer turned preacher, had an unexpectedly fractious effect on the community. His understanding of the importance of "immediate divine revelation" in religious life would have been uncontroversial to the earliest Quakers in America, who had risked the noose with their insistence that religion rested on an inner light available to all.

Yet by the end of the eighteenth century, many Quakers had become respectable citizens, and there was a divide between the largely affluent urban Quakers and the much less well-off rural Quakers, who took up Elias Hicks's call as a necessary reinvigoration of the faith. While the Hicksite revival would not formally split the Friends until 1826, in the early 1800s there were already rumblings about the true nature of divine revelation and who really had access to it. A writer complained in a Quaker journal called *The Friend*, "The facts are placed beyond all doubt, that there is an irreconcilable difference between the doctrines of our early Friends and those of Elias Hicks, in regard to the effects of the fall, the character of Jesus Christ, the benefits of his sufferings and death, with many other important principles of the Christian religion. Elias Hicks and his followers have departed from the original faith of the Society, and of the primitive believers."

The problem, this writer continued, was that the Hicksite branch of the faith had begun to argue that "we could not know the *least thing upon earth* without immediate revelation." In other words, every bit of knowledge was in its own way an experience of the divine. The implication of this, according to Elias Hicks's critics, was that even "the most wicked men upon earth" possess "immediate revelation." Disagreements over this particular issue ran hot enough that factions of the Society of Friends became far from amicable for a time.

Edward Hicks took his cousin's side in this schism, and his *Peaceable Kingdom* paintings, though still bucolic on the surface, began to reflect the volatility of the dispute. Nor were such divisions limited to the Quakers. His lifelong home of Pennsylvania, though founded as a "Holy Experiment" (page 86), was increasingly divided along religious lines, with individual communities growing more insular as their populations increased.

"The lamb, the kid, the cow, and the ox, are emblems of good men and women," Hicks said of his paintings, "while the wolf, the leopard, the bear, and the lion, are figures of the wicked. These last, we know, if they were confined in a small enclosure, would cruelly destroy each other, while the four innocent animals in the same enclosure would dwell harmoniously together." To look at his later images is to wonder if Hicks feared that animal nature might win out over faith, or if he had perhaps discovered that there was no escaping the conflicts from which he had hoped faith and art might deliver him. ◆

✴ Johnny Appleseed

Johnny Appleseed, 1871. The legendary figure, whose real name was John Chapman, traveled throughout the Mid-Atlantic states for both religious and agricultural reasons. From W. D. Haley, "Johnny Appleseed—A Pioneer Hero," *Harper's New Monthly Magazine* 43, no. 258 (November 1871).

AS VIBRANT AS both American religion and American folklore are, it is remarkable that they rarely overlap. The fantastic stories of larger-than-life characters on the frontier or in the early republic rarely have a spiritual dimension. Whether they are fictional figures such as Paul Bunyan and Rip Van Winkle or exaggerated heroes drawn from history such as Daniel Boone, our cultural champions are rarely depicted as having religious motivations.

A notable exception to this trend is John Chapman, better known as Johnny Appleseed. Born on September 26, 1774, in Leominster, Massachusetts, Chapman began his epic wandering in the young United States as a teenager. He traveled extensively throughout Ohio and Pennsylvania, establishing orchards and teaching others to tend them. These efforts made him a mainstay of American folk stories in the nineteenth and twentieth centuries. He is often depicted as an eccentric, wearing ragged clothing and a cooking pot on his head for a hat and always carrying a sack full of seeds that he cast about wherever he roamed, making apples—as well as apple cider and apple pie—emblems of the expanding nation.

In this, he did more than any other individual to change the reputation of a fruit that in the popular religious imagination had long stood for sin—as, for example, in the details on the ornate biblically themed spoon shown opposite. The serpent offered Eve just one apple; Johnny Appleseed gave them to Americans by the bushel.

While his legend is well known, the fact that he traveled to spread not only apple seeds but also seeds of the Gospel as a backwoods preacher has been largely forgotten. Chapman was a follower of Emanuel Swedenborg, an eighteenth-century inventor and scientist whose spiritual conversion late in life led him to advocate a radical reinterpretation of Christianity. Swedenborgianism proposed that a new era in humankind's religious development had begun, in which worship of God in the one person of Jesus Christ would replace the traditional notion of the Trinity, which understands divinity as the Father, the Son, and the Holy Spirit. Also called the New Church, this movement in fact saw itself as a return to Christianity's earliest days.

Usually portrayed clothed in tatters and barefoot, Chapman adopted his strange manner of dress more in allegiance to his understanding of the origins of his faith than because it served to advertise his horticultural labors. As one nineteenth-century account of his work notes, "Johnny's life was made serenely happy by the conviction that he was living like the primitive Christian." His faith, in fact, was once as central to his myth as his eponymous apple seeds. As one popular tale reported:

Toward the latter part of Johnny's career in Ohio an itinerant missionary found his way to the village of Mansfield, and preached to an open-air congregation. The discourse was tediously lengthy, and unnecessarily severe upon the sin of extravagance, which was beginning to manifest itself among the pioneers by an occasional indulgence in the carnal vanities of calico and "store tea." There was a good deal of the Pharisaic leaven in the preacher, who very frequently emphasized his discourse by the inquiry, "Where now is there a man who, like the primitive Christians, is traveling to heaven barefooted and clad in coarse raiment?" When this interrogation had been repeated beyond all reasonable endurance, Johnny rose from the log on which he was reclining, and advancing to the speaker, placed one of his bare feet upon the stump which served for a pulpit, and pointing to his coffee-sack garment, he quietly said, "Here's your primitive Christian!"

Effectively homeless for most of his life, by the time he died Chapman owned more than a thousand acres in Pennsylvania, Ohio, Indiana, and Illinois, which he had farmed profitably by using the experience he had gained through the years. He claimed to have covered four thousand miles across the young nation, which surely made him one of the most widely traveled Americans of his age. While he has earned his place in the mythology of the United States through his talent with fruit trees, it was his religious belief that inspired him to plant so many seeds in the ground. Decades after his death, newspapers around the country still remembered him as one of the most extraordinary and unlikely of American missionaries. ◆

Gold-washed silver serving spoon, nineteenth century.

✳ Carroll Family Tabernacle

WITH THE 1649 ACT CONCERNING RELIGION, the Province of Maryland sought to protect a variety of Christian sects from the negative attention of the colonial government. Yet though it is often referred to as the Toleration Act, its name is as misleading as its protection was fleeting.

In fact, the act called for toleration only for those "professing to believe in Jesus Christ." These believers, and only these believers, would henceforth be safeguarded from being "troubled, Molested or discountenanced for or in respect of his or her religion nor in the free exercise thereof within this Province, . . . nor any way compelled to the belief or exercise of any other Religion, against his or her consent."

Intended to protect Catholics at a time when their liberty was far from guaranteed, the Toleration Act also reflected the broad reality that no one religious group could count on maintaining a majority within the quickly shifting demographics of colonial populations. This was underscored just five years later when, in 1654, Catholics lost control of Maryland's governance and a law of opposite intentions was passed. The new Act Concerning Religion again preserved toleration for Christians, with the exception of adherents of "the Popish Religion commonly known by the name of the Roman Catholick Religion," who would not "be protected in this Province by the Lawes of England."

This act was in turn repealed when the Catholic Lord Baltimore reclaimed control just four years later, but that victory for the Roman faith also proved short-lived. In 1689, the Catholic government of the colony was again overthrown and public Catholic worship banned. In 1704, the Maryland Assembly passed the Act to Prevent the Growth of Popery within This Province, and it was the strictures included in this law that endured. Facing discrimination throughout the colonial period and the early republic, churches loyal to Rome were few and far between, leaving many of Maryland's Catholic faithful to worship in their homes.

The tabernacle shown opposite, which held the ritual elements of the Eucharist, was first used at St. Mary's Chapel in St. Mary's City and then was kept for generations by a prominent Maryland Catholic family, the Carrolls. Their most politically influential figure, Charles Carroll of Carrollton, was the only Catholic signer of the Declaration of Independence. Though far less devout than his cousin John (page 133), a Jesuit who would become the first bishop in the newly independent United States, Charles adhered to a particularly American version of the Roman faith. He once said,

> A good conscience and a virtuous life are certainly the greatest blessings
> we can enjoy on earth. I don't aim, nor never did, at canonization; I detest
> screwed up devotion, distorted faces, and grimace. I equally abhor those →

Tabernacle, seventeenth century. Originally built to store the Eucharist at an early Jesuit chapel in Maryland, this wooden liturgical furnishing was later used for the same purpose in the home of the Carroll family, which included several of the most prominent Catholics in the colony.

who laugh at all devotion, look upon our religion as a fiction, and its holy mysteries as the greatest absurdities. I observe my religious duties, I trust the mercy of God, not my own merits, which are none, and hope he will pardon my daily offences.

Despite their presence among the political elite, the Carrolls never forgot the precarious nature of being part of a religious minority. The feeling of always being at risk that this created endured throughout the family's long history in Maryland and even contributed to Charles Carroll's openness to rebellion.

"I can't conceive of how any Roman Catholic can consent to live in England or any of the British dominions," the young colonial said upon visiting the motherland in 1759. "Now where is the man of spirit that can behold the rod lifted up, tremble and kiss the hand of him that holds it?"

Carroll put these sentiments into action in the 1770s, when he began to publish letters in the Maryland press against increased fees for public officials. Signing his opinions pseudonymously, as "First Citizen," Carroll argued successfully against corruption in government and soon found himself in a political career that would lead him to become first an informal advisor to the Continental Congress, then a member of the state legislature, and finally a U.S. senator. Throughout the years, he remained, as John Adams once said of him, a man who "continues to hazard his all" for both his faith and his country. ◆

✳ *Archbishop Carroll's Chalice and Paten*

AFTER MARYLAND'S eighteenth-century anti-"Popery" law made it illegal for Catholics to practice their religion (page 131), priests were forced to use small acts of subterfuge to answer the spiritual needs of these faithful. Catholic clergymen at times rode through colonial America dressed in the garb of peddlers, with disguised liturgical items dangling like merchandise from their saddles. The "saddle chalice" was such an item. The cup, stem, and base of a specially designed ritual vessel for Communion wine could be joined in the shape of a bell, thus protecting the traveling priest from assault or arrest. →

Archbishop John Carroll's chalice and paten, eighteenth century, used during the sacrament of the Eucharist.

This was the situation into which John Carroll was born in 1735. The son of an Irish immigrant, he had advantages most Catholics lacked, not least of which were the large plantation that his family owned, through his mother's family, and wealth sufficient to send him to France for his education. While in France, Carroll joined the Society of Jesus and was ordained a priest at the age of twenty-six. At a time when it seemed that Jesuit influence in Europe might be waning (Pope Clement XIV had proposed placing limits on the society because of widespread concern over its political maneuverings), he decided to make the voyage back to America.

Within a year of his return to Maryland, Carroll had founded a parish, and the Continental Congress soon asked him to accompany his cousin Charles Carroll of Carrollton on a trip to Canada to enlist the Catholics of Quebec in the fight for independence. Though this journey was unsuccessful, the Carroll family's contribution to the cause significantly advanced their efforts to win the new nation's respect for their faith.

Five years after the end of the Revolution, John Carroll became the first Roman Catholic prelate in the United States. Around the same time, he founded Georgetown University in Washington, DC, so that young Catholics would no longer need to leave the country to receive a thorough religious education, and began to establish Baltimore as the foremost Catholic city in the country. He also called for the creation of several influential schools and religious communities, including the first U.S. seminary for the training of priests, and the Sisters of Charity, founded by Elizabeth Ann Seton (page 139), whom the bishop had personally mentored in the faith.

At the age of seventy, Archbishop Carroll led fundraising and construction efforts for the first cathedral in the United States, Baltimore's Cathedral of the Assumption (later named the Basilica of the National Shrine of the Assumption of the Blessed Virgin Mary; page 137). Overseen by Carroll, it quickly became a symbol of Catholics' climb toward religious equality in America, which he believed was good not only for the country but for Christianity itself.

"If we have the wisdom and temper to preserve," he once said, "America may come to exhibit a proof to the world that general and equal toleration, by giving a free circulation to fair argument, is the most effectual method to bring all denominations of Christians to a unity of faith."

By the time of his death in 1815, Carroll had set the Catholic Church in the young nation on a course that it would follow throughout its history. The founder of orders and institutions conceived to meet the spiritual needs of a quickly changing country, he encouraged the faithful to embrace the new and not be moved by "chimerical fears of innovation." ◆

"The Metropolis of American Catholicism"

DESPITE WIDESPREAD SENTIMENT against Roman influence in the English colonies and the early republic, the Catholic population of the young nation had grown sufficiently large by the end of the eighteenth century that it required a bishop to serve as both spiritual leader and advocate in the global church. After naming John Carroll as bishop (page 134), Pope Pius VI declared, "We commission the said Bishop elect to erect a church in the said city of Baltimore, in form of a Cathedral Church, inasmuch as the times and circumstances may allow."

Benjamin Latrobe, *Plan for the Baltimore Basilica*, 1797.

Time and circumstance conspired to make the undertaking of this commission slow indeed. It was seventeen years before the cornerstone for the church was laid and another fifteen before the cathedral opened its doors to the Roman Catholics of the nation.

Designed by Benjamin Latrobe, the architect appointed by Thomas Jefferson to design the U.S. Capitol, Baltimore's basilica employed novel building techniques that allowed it to soar above the city. Latrobe's innovative plan, particularly the use of inverted arches to support the enormous weight of the basilica's dome, signaled a new era in the architecture of American churches, which would soon include examples that rivaled the grandeur of European cathedrals.

Despite such lofty company and the contributions of wealthy Catholics, including the bishop's own family, the building was not completed without financial strain, reflecting the lives of most American Catholics of the time. Searching far and wide for funds, Bishop Carroll sent a letter in 1803 to Napoléon Bonaparte, who at the time headed the government of the French Republic as First Consul and was perhaps second only to the pope as a Catholic of global influence.

To General Bonaparte, First Consul.

General First Consul:—The Bishop of Baltimore in the name of the Catholics of the United States of America has the honor to implore your assistance for an enterprise which has need of your help. It is in accordance with this consideration, General First Consul, that the Catholics of the United States dare turn their eyes toward you in piety. After having suffered a long time under oppression, they enjoy, under a wise and moderate government, the free exercise of their worship, but they have no temple where they can assemble with becoming decency, and their past misfortunes have reduced them, so that they are unable to bear the expenses which such an edifice demands.

Are they presumptuous, General First Consul, in hoping that you will not disdain to favor their wish, and to prove to them your good-will for the construction of a cathedral in the city of Baltimore? Such a proof of your →

Lottery ticket no. 3391, dated September 18, 1805, and sold to raise funds for the Baltimore Basilica, the first Catholic cathedral in the United States.

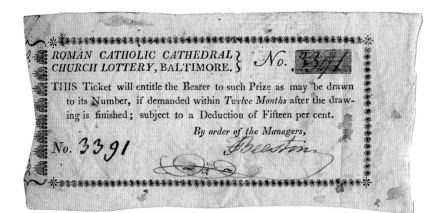

ROMAN CATHOLIC CATHEDRAL CHURCH LOTTERY, BALTIMORE. No. 3391

THIS Ticket will entitle the Bearer to such Prize as may be drawn to its Number, if demanded within *Twelve Months* after the drawing is finished; subject to a Deduction of Fifteen per cent.

By order of the Managers,

No. 3391

devotion to the welfare of the Church, in a country allied to your own, would cause the Catholics of the United States to share the sentiments which the people of France cease not to manifest for you.

Sincere though his respect for the French leader may have been, Carroll soon made the impolitic decision to perform the wedding of Napoléon's brother Jérôme-Napoléon Bonaparte to a local woman while the latter was visiting Baltimore. Irritated that a family member had married without his consent and with no clear political gain, Napoléon annulled the marriage by imperial decree after he became the emperor of France in 1804.

Lacking such high-placed backing, Baltimore's basilica was constructed between 1806 and 1821 with funds raised in part through the sale of lottery tickets to the city's growing immigrant Catholic population. In the first lottery, held in March 1805, a printer and a cabinetmaker shared a prize of ten thousand dollars. A forty-thousand-dollar jackpot was awarded in 1820 to two citizens of Baltimore who had purchased their tickets, according to press reports, "on the very morning the prize came out of the wheel." The size of these awards suggests that tens of thousands of tickets were sold to the residents of the city that Latrobe once called "the metropolis of American Catholicism."

Widespread support among the city's Catholics was not by itself enough to build the church envisioned in Rome and brought to fruition by Archbishop Carroll. The Maryland legislature passed twelve acts between 1795 and 1845 to make possible the construction and maintenance of the cathedral. ◆

✳ *Elizabeth Ann Seton*

Unknown artist,
*The Filicchi Portrait of
St. Elizabeth Ann Seton*,
circa 1804.

THE FIRST CATHOLIC SAINT born in the United States, Elizabeth Ann Seton did not embrace the Roman church until the age of thirty. By that time she was already a widow and a mother of five who had endured bankruptcy and quarantine for yellow fever, yet the most dramatic days of her life were still ahead of her.

Born into a wealthy New York City family in 1774, Elizabeth Ann Bayley married William Seton at nineteen and was a devout member of Trinity Episcopal Church →

in Manhattan. When her husband's health failed and his import-export business faltered, the Seton family traveled to Italy for what was intended as a short, recuperative stay. But then their lives took a tragic turn: William died in the port city of Livorno. Fortunately, his local associates took Elizabeth in.

This dark moment proved transformative, however. Through the influence of her hosts, Seton prepared for conversion to Catholicism, and she was formally accepted into the church in 1805 upon her return to New York. Three years later, after meeting resistance to opening a Catholic school in Manhattan, she was invited to do just that in Maryland, the seat of John Carroll's episcopal authority (page 131). Working with French priests of the Sulpician order, she established Saint Joseph's Academy and Free School in the rural town of Emmitsburg. Simultaneously, she began a religious community for women hoping to devote their lives to the poor through the church. The Sisters of Charity, as this order became known, was the first congregation of religious sisters in the United States.

Though she had known much loss in her life, she sought to transform her challenging experiences into service. "The accidents of life separate us from our dearest friends, but let us not despair," the widow once told the young women who had joined her order. "God is like a looking glass in which souls see each other. The more we are united to Him by love, the nearer we are to those who belong to Him."

When the Roman Catholic Church canonized her in 1975, it was in recognition that her work in setting the foundation for the parochial school movement had transformed education for generations of U.S. Catholics. "Elizabeth Ann Seton is a saint. St. Elizabeth Ann Seton is an American," Pope Paul VI declared in 1975. "All of us say this with special joy, and with the intention of honoring the land and the nation from which she sprang forth as the first flower in the calendar of the saints. Elizabeth Ann Seton was wholly American! Rejoice for your glorious daughter. Be proud of her. And know how to preserve her fruitful heritage." ◆

※ Mother Lange of Baltimore

ELIZABETH CLARISSE LANGE was born in the late eighteenth century in Santiago de Cuba's French-speaking enclave, likely the daughter of refugees who had left Haiti during or shortly before its revolution began in 1791. By the midpoint of the War of 1812, she had arrived in Baltimore, where a community of free black Francophone Catholics from Haiti had settled after fleeing from the same unrest that had sent her family to Cuba.

At the time, there was no public education available for African Americans, either free or enslaved (nor would there be until after the Civil War). Lange opened her home to children desiring an education and then, with the support of the archbishop of Baltimore and the Sulpician priest Rev. James Nicholas Joubert, founded the Oblate Sisters of Providence, a religious institute dedicated to educating African American girls. While its purpose was the education of the young, its mission had the added benefit of establishing one of the first consecrated communities for women of color in the Roman Catholic Church.

The woman now known as Mother Mary Lange made solemn vows and joined the Oblate Sisters of Providence on July 2, 1829, along with three other women. Together they expanded their school, which began to offer to the African American girls of Baltimore educations similar to those received by white children, as seen in the needlework sampler stitched by a student of the Oblate Sisters shown on page 107.

Portrait of Mother Mary Elizabeth Lange, Oblate of the Sisters of Providence, circa 1850. Tintype.

Throughout the 1830s, Mother Lange served as the superior of the newly formed religious order and, another nun later remembered, "always delighted to tell the young Sisters of the customs and processions carried on in Santiago." Alongside her sisters, Mother Lange not only offered education to the young but frequently took in orphans, nursed the sick, and assisted former slaves with their transition to freedom. Her seriousness of purpose was a surprise to some, particularly her family. When her own mother relocated to the United States, Mother Lange made room →

Two crucifixes and a religious medal worn by Mother Mary Elizabeth Lange. These items, worn by Mother Lange throughout her life, were recently rediscovered in Baltimore when her remains were exhumed as part of the Roman Catholic Church's canonization process. They are kept sealed in a glass case in the motherhouse of the Oblate Sisters of Providence, the religious institute she founded.

for her with the Oblate Sisters. Her mother, however, was not nearly so pious as Mother Lange had become. She passed her time among the sisters, teaching them Haitian and Cuban dances she remembered from her youth, and drew her devout daughter's wrath when the dancing kept the sisters from hearing the bell calling for meditative silence.

Living nearly one hundred years, Mother Lange died in 1882. She wore the crucifixes and religious medal shown below throughout her life; they were recently rediscovered when the Oblate Sisters exhumed her body as part of the petition for her sainthood. If she is canonized, the objects found with her remains will become religious relics and so must remain sealed by ceremonial red ribbon throughout the process, which is known as the cause for sainthood.

A contemporary of Elizabeth Ann Seton (page 139) and Archbishop John Carroll (page 135), Mother Lange was a lesser-known figure instrumental in establishing Baltimore as America's first vibrant Catholic city, as well as a pioneer of African American religion and education. ◆

✳ *Mikveh Israel*

Mikveh Israel. Etching. Founded in the 1740s, Mikveh Israel was the first synagogue in Philadelphia.

THE REVOLUTION BROUGHT unexpected changes to the lives of many American Jews. With fighting along the Atlantic coast and the British occupying Manhattan, large centers of Jewish population in cities including New York, Richmond, and Charleston emptied as families left behind their homes and synagogues to relocate to Philadelphia. By then, Jewish presence in the city founded by William Penn (page 85) had been noted for more than a century, and it promised to be a refuge during a dangerous time. →

The first organized Jewish community in Philadelphia, Mikveh Israel, was founded in the 1740s and became a spiritual home away from home for Jews displaced by the war. Gershom Seixas arrived from New York's Shearith Israel (page 79) to lead a congregation gathered from across the former colonies. With a swelling membership, the community built its first permanent home in 1782. It continued to grow throughout the nineteenth century and occupied a succession of larger buildings, opening its fifth home in the bicentennial year of 1976.

From the beginning, Mikveh Israel played a significant role in American history. A decade after its founding, when the Constitutional Convention was meeting in Philadelphia, the synagogue's president became an impassioned public voice in defense of religious freedom. An immigrant from Germany, Jonas Phillips keenly felt the promise of what America might mean to religious minorities like himself. In September 1787, he composed a letter concerned with religious requirements for those who hoped to serve in the government. Identifying himself as "one of the people called Jews of the City of Philadelphia, a people scattered & dispersed among all nations," he noted that among the provisions of the Constitution of Pennsylvania was a clause requiring all officeholders to "acknowledge the Scriptures of the old and New testament to be given by divine inspiration."

"To swear and believe that the New Testement was given by devine inspiration is absolutely against the religious principle of a Jew," he wrote, "and is against his Conscience to take any such oath." As a veteran of the Revolution, Phillips was particularly concerned that the sacrifices those of his faith had made during the war might go forgotten. He wrote:

> It is well known among all the Citizens of the 13 united States that the Jews
> have been true and faithful, and during the late Contest with England
> they have been foremost in aiding and assisting the States with their lifes
> and fortunes. They have supported the Cause, have bravely faught and
> bleed for liberty which they Can not Enjoy.
>
> Therefore if the honourable Convention shall in ther Wisdom think fit
> and alter the said oath and leave out the words "and I do acknowledge the
> scripture of the new testament to be given by devine inspiration" then the
> Israeletes will think them self happy to live under a government where all
> Religious societys are on an Eaquel footing.

While it cannot be known what effect this single letter had on the Constitutional Convention, ultimately Phillips's wish was granted. Article VI of the U.S. Constitution explicitly states that "no religious test shall ever be required as a qualification to any office or public trust under the United States." ◆

✳ *Rebecca Gratz*

Thomas Sully, *Portrait of Rebecca Gratz*, 1831. Oil on canvas. The educator Rebecca Gratz was a member of one of Philadelphia's most prominent Jewish families.

A DAUGHTER OF ONE of the most prominent families who belonged to Mikveh Israel (page 143), Rebecca Gratz was a philanthropist, an educator, and a pioneer of what Judaism might mean to women in America.

Born in Philadelphia in 1781, Gratz grew up with twelve siblings at the center of the city's upper-class society. From its earliest days under the leadership of William Penn (page 85), Pennsylvania had been a place where Jews could prosper despite standing apart from the religious majority. Gratz's father had →

arrived in America from Silesia as an orphan but soon made his fortune. His children, Rebecca included, played and learned alongside well-to-do Christians, with their social status a tie that bound them together despite different creeds.

It was through her many friendships with Philadelphians outside the city's Jewish community that Gratz developed an outlook involving both calm acceptance of religious difference and fervent defense of the faith in which she had been raised. Though she did not widely share her thoughts on such matters during her life, her posthumously published letters provide a view of what it meant to be a woman and a Jew in the early republic.

It is only through Gratz's words, for example, that we can experience the dedication ceremony for the opening of Mikveh Israel's new home in 1825: "I have never witnessed a more impressive or solemn ceremony or one more calculated to elevate the mind to religious exercises," she wrote. "The shul [synagogue] is one of the most beautiful specimens of ancient architecture in the city . . . the decorations are neat yet rich and tasteful—and the service commencing just before the Sabbath was performed by lamplight."

Gratz also wrote extensively about what attending religious services meant to a family in the unique position of achieving high social standing while remaining religious outsiders. "We all go Friday evening as well as on Saturday morning," she wrote to her brother Benjamin, who had married a Christian woman. "My dear Brother when I enter that temple and I pray that I may again see you worshipping within its walls—I know your faith is unchangeable and will endure even tho' you are alone in a land of strangers."

Beginning as a teenager, Gratz was an indefatigable organizer on behalf of charitable causes. She cofounded the Female Association for the Relief of Women and Children in Reduced Circumstances at the age of nineteen in 1801, went on to launch the Philadelphia Orphan Society (1815) and the Female Hebrew Benevolent Society (1819), and inspired Jewish religious schools through her educational efforts in response to the Christian Sunday School movement.

Often ecumenical in her approach (as in the nonsectarian Female Association), she nonetheless did not shy away from seeking to serve her own community. Looking over her attitude toward faith throughout her life, Rebecca Gratz once remarked, "I claimed the privilege of not being inimical to any man's religion, yet being firmly attached to my own." ◆

James Madison's Notes for a Speech on Constitutional Amendments

FROM THE MOMENT when Thomas Jefferson penned the words "We hold these truths to be self evident," Americans have excelled at making lists. And no list has been as important as the Bill of Rights, amendments to the U.S. Constitution proposed by James Madison in a speech delivered to Congress on June 8, 1789, with the aid of a sheet of sparse notes. Jotted on a single leaf of paper measuring just five by eight inches, his handwritten outline nonetheless provides a view into one of the most significant developments in the nation's history.

Though there is no one more closely associated with the first ten amendments, Madison was an unlikely champion of the cause of listing protections guaranteed to citizens of the United States. To be sure, he had long been an outspoken advocate of religious liberty in his home state of Virginia. His 1785 Memorial and Remonstrance against Religious Assessments stated his position plainly: "The Religion then of every man must be left to the conviction and conscience of every man; and it is the right of every man to exercise it as these may dictate." Yet when it came to the federal Constitution, he did not believe that naming freedom of religion, or other individual rights, was necessary.

Early in the process of ratification, adding a Bill of Rights to the Constitution was primarily a concern of Madison's anti-Federalist opponents. While Madison would later claim that he had "always been in favor of a Bill of Rights," he opposed such an addition on the grounds that naming some protections but not others could have the undesired effect of limiting rather than safeguarding the rights of Americans.

As the states considered ratification, however, it became apparent that many would not approve of the document without such an enumeration. To avoid starting from scratch with a new Constitutional Convention, Madison spoke directly to the anti-Federalist critique. "If we can make the Constitution better in the opinion of those who are opposed to it, without weakening its frame, or abridging its usefulness in the judgment of those who are attached to it," he said, "we act the part of wise and liberal men to make such alterations as shall produce that effect."

After reviewing hundreds of amendments suggested at the state ratifying conventions, Madison proposed nineteen points that might be used to edit or amend the original text. A congressional committee abridged his list to twelve, ten of which were ultimately affirmed.

There were forces for and against explicit protections for religious liberty in the years following the Revolution. In Madison's Virginia, the long-standing colonial establishment of the Anglican Church came to an end after independence, but few believed religious institutions should have no role in public life. Arguing that religion was essential for the morality of the young nation, Patrick Henry proposed a system of state support for multiple Christian denominations →

in 1784 to diffuse the focus on Anglicanism. His proposal was considered religiously tolerant in its day, but Madison and Jefferson thought it did not go far enough (page 192). They pushed for the state to remove itself entirely from the business of promoting religion of any kind.

It was this victory against eighteenth-century supporters of religion in Virginia that inspired the federal protections to which twenty-first-century supporters of religion often appeal. When we also consider that the Constitution and the Bill of Rights intended to leave such matters to the states, many of which had officially established churches until well into the nineteenth century, the question of when exactly the national freedom of religion was secured becomes still more muddled.

Madison, for his part, did not include the word *religion* in the notes for his speech but instead mentioned "Freedom of Conscience." Nor did the subject rate a specific mention in his "Reasons for urging amend[men]ts," which had only four points:

1. to prove fedts. [Federalists] friends to liberty
2. remove remaining inquietudes.
3. bring in N.C. & R. Island.
4. to improve the Constitution

In the speech itself, he was more expansive on the subject, stating, "The civil rights of none shall be abridged on account of religious belief or worship, nor shall any national religion be established, nor shall the full and equal rights of conscience be in any manner, or on any pretext infringed."

More than two and a quarter centuries later, religious liberty is one of the most emblematic of American freedoms. Though we now consider it a timeless quality of the nation's character, it was born of a moment of political compromise. ◆

The South

In the early days of the southern colonies, Anglicanism played a role similar to Puritan Congregationalism in the North. It was at once the officially established church and a social force so dominant that the influences of other religious traditions are often difficult to see.

Required by law to attend public worship in their local Anglican church, colonial Virginians could be fined if they failed to turn up in the pews. Such affronts made spiritual alternatives attractive, but also ensured that belonging to other churches was dangerous. By the middle of the eighteenth century, the number of Baptists in the South began to rise. Dissenters, as they were called, often faced violence, arrest, and prison for their beliefs. After the Revolution, the persecution that Baptists had suffered in Virginia was perhaps the single most important factor in the fight for religious liberty in the new United States.

Yet like New England and the Mid-Atlantic, the South was home to great religious diversity beyond Christian disagreements. Charleston had a thriving Jewish community, while on slaveholding plantations in Georgia, the Carolinas, and Louisiana, traditions brought from Africa, including Islam, Yoruba, and Akan, at first were practiced in secret and then blended with the Christianity that many of the enslaved eventually embraced. Through the combination of elements derived from many faiths, distinctive forms of American worship were born.

A View of Saint James Church, Goose Creek, from the Parsonage, circa 1800. Watercolor on paper. This Episcopal church in South Carolina was built in the 1710s.

✳ George Whitefield's Pulpit

DURING COLONIAL AMERICA'S first period of dramatic religious upheaval, the eighteenth century's Great Awakening, a quickly growing portion of the population left old ways behind in search of a new kind of faith. Called the New Lights—as opposed to the Old Lights, traditional believers—they replaced droning sermons and dour prayer services with hugely popular open-air revivals, building on long-simmering dissatisfaction with existing worship styles to give rise to newly dominant denominations such as Methodism.

The man often credited with jump-starting this phase of American religious life, the itinerant evangelist George Whitefield, was known for stirring orations calling into question the divisions among Christians. Standing on a balcony in Philadelphia, he once called out to the sky to ask "Father Abraham" who could be found in heaven.

"'Any episcopalians?' 'No!'" Whitefield preached. "'Any presbyterians?' 'No!' 'Any baptists?' 'No!' 'Have you any Methodists there?' 'No!' 'Have you any independents or seceders?' 'No! No!'" He shouted with dramatic exasperation, "'Why, who have you then?'"

The answer he provided, as if in the voice of Abraham himself, was a rebuke to the sectarianism that had defined the differences among the many communities that made up the people now beginning to consider themselves simply Americans: "'We don't know those names here.'"

For Whitefield, questioning these divisions grew out of personal experience. Born in England in 1714, he had begun his ministerial career as an Anglican. He had been educated first in his hometown of Gloucester and then at Oxford, where he met the Wesley brothers, Charles and John, cofounders of Methodism (page 155).

Young Whitefield joined the Wesleys in what they called the Holy Club of Oxford, whose members undertook such practices as regular Communion and fasting in order to live more spiritual lives. Derided by other students for their strict adherence to such "methods," the Holy Club took "Methodists" as a name of pride.

When the Wesleys left England to bring their approach to faith to the colony of Georgia, Whitefield remained behind. He was ordained as a priest in the Anglican Church and soon became known for his dynamic preaching style, which in fact was too dynamic for some congregations. With pulpits often closed to him, he began to preach in the streets, where it was said he could draw crowds as large as thirty thousand.

In the 1730s, Whitefield followed the Wesleys to Georgia and helped Methodism become the fastest-growing denomination in American history. Traveling throughout the colonies, he covered more than five thousand miles in a single year, preaching open-air sermons from makeshift stages and portable pulpits—including the one pictured on page 154, which he used perhaps two thousand times. →

Though undeniably dramatic, Whitefield's sermons were not simply performances of one man's emotional presentation of his faith, but rather opportunities for all those who heard him to get in on the act. Crying, singing, testifying, those in thrall to Whitefield's words newly believed their own experiences to be as significant as those of any religious authority.

When Whitefield preached in Philadelphia, his contemporary Benjamin Franklin was often in the audience. Franklin became a great admirer of Whitefield's oratory skill and, it seems, of the power it had to unnerve those set in their ways. "In 1739 arriv'd among us from England the Rev. Mr. Whitefield, who had made himself remarkable there as an itinerant Preacher," Franklin wrote in his autobiography. "He was at first permitted to preach in some of our Churches; but the Clergy taking a Dislike to him, soon refus'd him their Pulpits and he was oblig'd to preach in the Fields."

Franklin was taken by the positive effects that the preacher seemed to have on the city. "It was wonderful to see the Change soon made in the Manners of our Inhabitants," he said. "From being thoughtless or indifferent about Religion, it seem'd as if all the World were growing Religious; so that one could not walk thro' the Town in an Evening without Hearing Psalms sung in different Families of every Street."

Supporting Franklin's impressions of Whitefield, paintings and drawings from the period show audiences enthralled by his dynamic new preaching style. He was not without his critics, however, as can be seen in political cartoons of the day, which depict Whitefield receiving demonic messages while delivering his sermons. Yet the

Pulpit, mid-eighteenth century. The itinerant preacher George Whitefield used this portable pulpit as he preached in open fields throughout the English colonies during several trips to America from 1738 to 1770.

trends in worship that he helped to establish—dramatic preaching, outdoor revivals, emotional outpourings of personal testimony—outlived not only his detractors but the man himself. Thanks to Whitefield, the New Lights had won, opening Americans to ever more innovative religious expression.

Many have proposed that the work of Whitefield and others like him opened Americans to far more than that. As the historian Mark Noll noted, "The awakeners preached a higher, more spiritual vision of the church, yet the result was decline in the very notion of church and a transfer of religious commitment from the church to the nation." Throughout the lands of the republic about to be born, identification with particular denominations became less intense as many awakened to the idea of considering themselves Americans first of all. ◆

✳ The Wesley Brothers

Far left J. Tookey, *Portrait of John Wesley*, 1791. Engraving.

Left Thomas Addis Emmet, *Portrait of Charles Wesley*, 1880. Engraving.

THE RAPIDLY CHANGING CHARACTER of religion in the early United States was due largely to the astonishing growth of a single denomination: Methodism. Surprising though this may be, it becomes all the more so when one considers that this new approach to Christianity arrived in America with a pair of English brothers who between them did not stay even five years on this side of the Atlantic.

The Wesley brothers—the elder, John, was born in 1703, and the younger, Charles, in 1707—grew up in the Anglican Church and attended Oxford University, where they created an informal prayer group that struck their fellow students as off-puttingly strident. Though mocked as the "Holy Club," the Wesleys and their like-minded friends made no secret of their desire to live deeply religious lives. Thought to be overly methodical in their style of devotion to the Bible and the Book of Common Prayer, they were derided as "Methodists," but, far from insulted, they took the name as their own.

At the request of the Georgia governor James Oglethorpe, the Wesleys sailed for America as missionaries to the colony in 1735. Charles remained only a year, and John not much longer. While the younger brother returned to England and began writing hymns (page 156), the older preached without much success to Native Americans and opened an orphanage, which he struggled to maintain. Despite the failures of their missionary endeavors, however, their time in the colonies transformed them. Though ordained already, the brothers soon experienced religious conversions, opening each minister to more dynamic expressions of faith. →

Title page, Charles Wesley hymnal, 1742. Methodist circuit riders made hymns a central part of their evangelizing mission, distributing hymnals such as this one wherever they traveled.

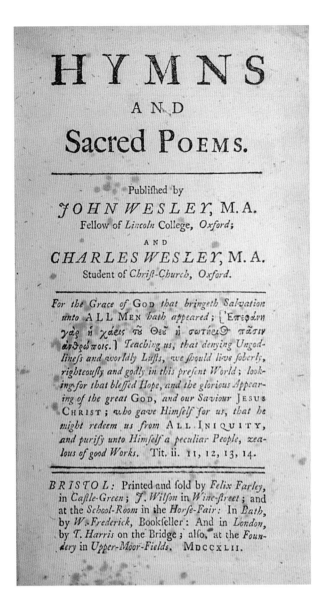

HYMNS
AND
Sacred POEMS.

Publiſhed by

JOHN WESLEY, M.A.
Fellow of *Lincoln* College, *Oxford;*

AND

CHARLES WESLEY, M.A.
Student of *Chriſt-Church, Oxford.*

For the Grace of GOD *that bringeth Salvation unto* ALL MEN *hath appeared;* [Ἐπεφάνη γὰρ ἡ χάρις τῷ Θεῷ ἡ σωτήριος πᾶσιν ἀνθρώποις.] *Teaching us, that denying Ungodlineſs and worldly Luſts, we ſhould live ſoberly, righteouſly and godly in this preſent World; looking for that bleſſed Hope, and the glorious Appearing of the great* GOD, *and our Saviour* JESUS CHRIST; *who gave Himſelf for us, that he might redeem us from* ALL INIQUITY, *and purify unto Himſelf a peculiar People, zealous of good Works.* Tit. ii. 11, 12, 13, 14.

BRISTOL: Printed and ſold by *Felix Farley,* in *Caſtle-Green;* *J. Wilſon* in *Wine-ſtreet;* and at the *School-Room* in the *Horſe-Fair:* In *Bath,* by *W. Frederick,* Bookſeller: And in *London,* by *T. Harris* on the Bridge; alſo, at the *Foundery* in *Upper-Moor-Fields.* MDCCXLII.

The Wesleys planted the seeds of Methodism in America, but it fell to their former Oxford classmate and Holy Club member George Whitefield (page 152) to cultivate and harvest them. Whitefield's first trip to America, to oversee the Georgia orphanage, overlapped with John Wesley's departure for England. Nonetheless, the three men continued to influence one another and would powerfully affect the nation soon to be born.

In 1740, there were no Methodist churches in the thirteen colonies. In 1770, there were twenty. Less than a hundred years later, the United States had nearly a thousand times that number. By comparison, the number of Anglican and Congregational churches, formally established throughout the southern and northern colonies respectively, grew only by single-digit multiples. To Christians in early America, Methodism clearly offered something that other churches did not. ◆

✳ *Francis Asbury's Powder Horn and Trunk*

B. Tanner, *Portrait of Francis Asbury*, 1814. Engraving, after a painting by J. Paradise.

WHILE TOWERING CHURCH STEEPLES looming over iconic town greens dominate many visions of religion in early America, in fact the vast majority of the population of the young nation did not live anywhere near a house of worship. Most people lived in thinly settled rural areas, and often their nearest neighbors would not have been members of the same church, even if there had been one to attend.

"All sects are mixed, as well as all nations," J. Hector St. John de Crèvecoeur, a French chronicler of the young nation, wrote in 1782. Describing the modern-seeming experience of passing by a number of houses and knowing that in one →

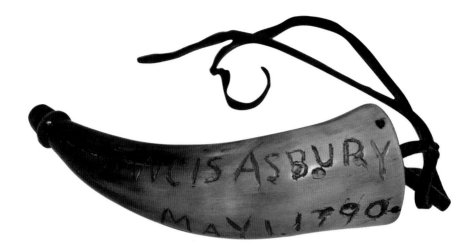

Francis Asbury's powder horn, 1790. Though not known to have owned a gun, Asbury carved his name on this horn, which he evidently carried on his journeys.

lived a Lutheran, in another a Calvinist, and in a third a Catholic, he noted that each "works in his fields, embellishes the earth, clears swamps." In time it might come to pass that the daughter of the Catholic would marry the son of one of the Protestants, and the young couple might move far from their parents. In such a case, "what religious education will they give their children?" This question, created by distance and the seeming ease with which Americans altered their religious affiliations, was soon answered by a church more willing than most to go wherever potential members might be found.

Though George Whitefield (page 152) and the Wesley brothers (page 155) brought Methodism to America and established the tradition of the itinerant preacher, it was the later arrival Francis Asbury who most successfully built upon this foundation. One of the first two Methodist bishops in the United States, he was perhaps singularly responsible for the growth of the denomination there.

"Whither am I going? To the New World. What to do? To gain honor?" he wrote during his journey across the Atlantic from England in 1771. "No, if I know my own heart. To get money? No: I am going to live to God, and to bring others so to do."

Unlike gifted orators such as Whitefield, Asbury did not delight in being the focal point of a crowd's attention. His great skill was instead in organization. He created districts of neighboring churches and organized a system whereby preachers would travel from town to town to provide religious instruction, rather than serving as pastor to a single flock. By necessity, these circuit riders traveled vast distances in the largely rural nation, and their willingness to endure such hardship for the sake of spreading their message virtually guaranteed that Methodism would draw new members in places where no other churches could be found.

Not content to simply plan such a network, Asbury rode through it more than anyone else. It is estimated that he traveled some three hundred thousand miles over the course of a career that lasted nearly half a century. Even more important for the growth of his church, he ordained four thousand others to follow in his footsteps.

Though there had been few Methodists in America before the Revolution, by the middle of the following century there were more than a million.

The changes that the circuit riders wrought were not just spiritual. They regularly distributed Bible tracts and hymnals, such as the one shown on page 156, and stressed the importance of learning to read as they stretched the nation's borders westward. "When I came near the American shore," Asbury once wrote, "my very heart melted within me to think from whence I came, whither I was going, and what I was going about. But I felt my mind opened to the people, and my tongue loosed to speak. I feel that God is here, and find plenty of all we need."

During Asbury's four decades as a traveling preacher, he ventured deep into the frontier with the small trunk shown below, carried on horseback. Of course, he was a primarily a minister rather than a frontiersman. Though he carved his name on the powder horn shown opposite in the spring of 1790, scholars note that the bishop is nowhere recorded as having owned a gun. ◆

Francis Asbury's trunk, circa 1784. One of the first two Methodist bishops in America, Asbury traveled thousands of miles on horseback from 1771 to 1816, often carrying this trunk filled with evangelizing material.

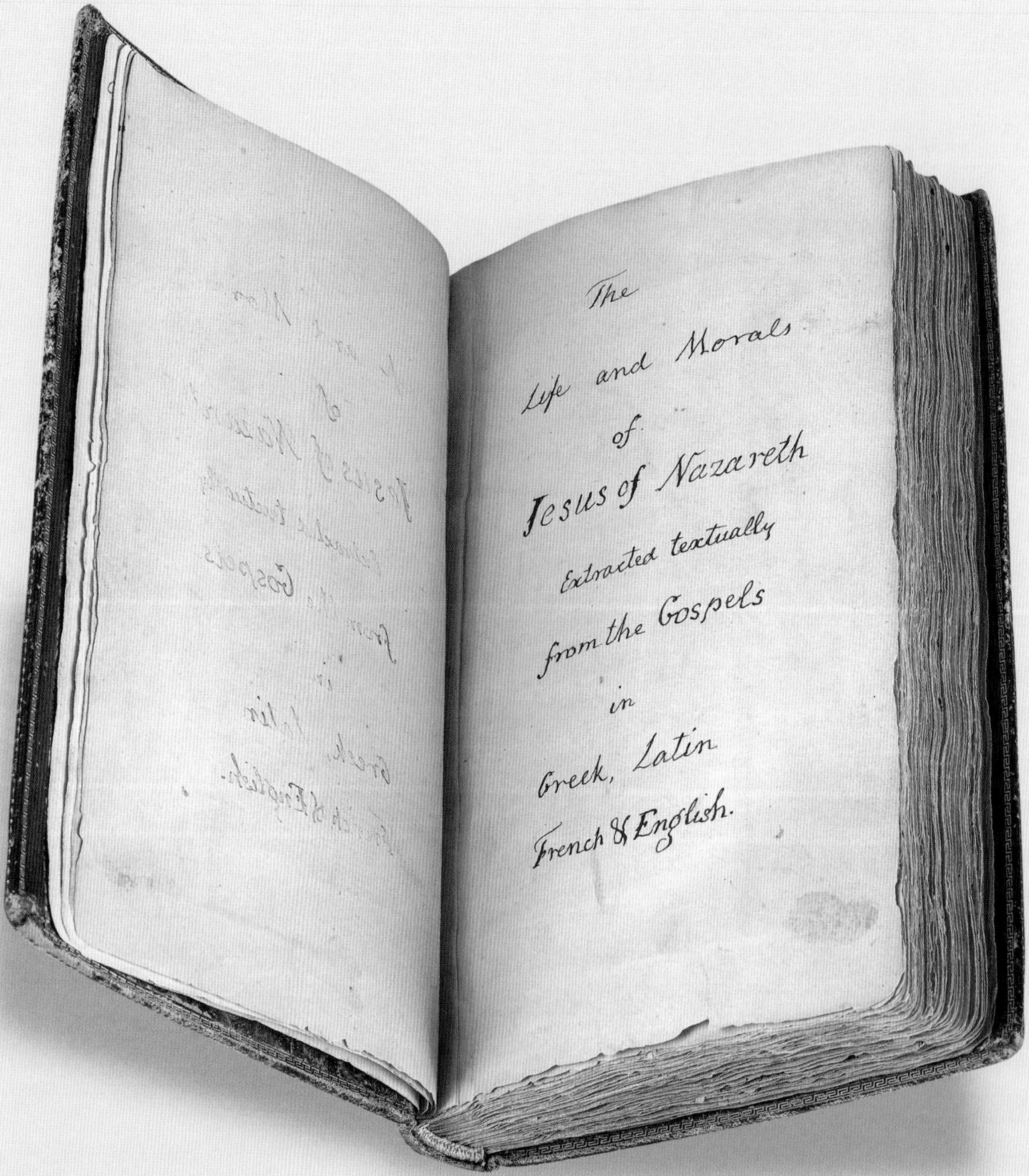

The

Life and Morals

of

Jesus of Nazareth

Extracted textually

from the Gospels

in

Greek, Latin

French & English.

The Life and Morals of Jesus of Nazareth

OF THE 6,487 of his books that Thomas Jefferson planned to sell to the federal government as the core of a new Library of Congress in the winter of 1815, about three hundred dealt with religious subjects. Among the volumes selected for shipment from Monticello to Washington, DC, Jefferson included a score of Bibles, a Qur'an, a history of "heathen gods," and works by deist philosophers. Such heterodox titles reflected his opinion that religion should be a personal affair, guided by curiosity and reason (page 67).

As wide-ranging as Jefferson's religious collection was, it did not contain the book that provides the purest expression of his religious ideas. In fact, he had not yet created it. A labor of love during his long retirement, the eighty-four-page redacted edition of the New Testament that he called *The Life and Morals of Jesus of Nazareth* was the product of decades of thinking about scripture, religion, and the latter's role in society. Beginning in 1819, the seventy-seven-year-old Jefferson worked with a penknife and glue to excise sections from the Gospels in English, French, Latin, and Greek and paste them into his own version of the sacred text (pages 162–63).

The Jefferson Bible, as the resulting text is also known, makes no mention of turning water into wine or walking on water but reorganizes the words and biography of Jesus to avoid repetition while recounting his life chronologically. To the sage of Monticello, the man from Nazareth was a great teacher and moral exemplar, and that was enough. "Jesus did not mean to impose himself on mankind as the son of God," he wrote. The miracles and supernatural elements that make up so much of the traditional story of Jesus's life Jefferson regarded as fictions grafted on to the biography of a historically significant figure. The dogmas that had grown out of these fictions, he believed, were little more than the "Abracadabra" of priests.

Frequently accused of heresy and even atheism, Jefferson knew that his approach to scriptural interpretation would be too much to accept for those with more traditional perspectives. He discussed *The Life and Morals of Jesus of Nazareth* only with a few friends and never imagined it would be widely distributed.

Among his trusted confidants on matters of faith was the patriot and physician Benjamin Rush. Long before he put penknife to paper to craft his alternate scripture, Jefferson wrote the doctor a letter outlining his thoughts on Christianity, as well as his frustration that they were so often misperceived.

> Dear Sir,
>
> In some of the delightful conversations with you, in the evenings of 1798–99, and which served as an anodyne to the afflictions of the crisis through which our country was then laboring, the Christian religion was sometimes our →

Thomas Jefferson, *The Life and Morals of Jesus of Nazareth*, 1820. Jefferson created this work at Monticello after retiring from public life.

topic; and I then promised you, that one day or other, I would give you my views of it. They are the result of a life of inquiry & reflection, and very different from that anti-Christian system imputed to me by those who know nothing of my opinions. To the corruptions of Christianity I am indeed opposed; but not to the genuine precepts of Jesus himself. I am a Christian, in the only sense he wished any one to be; sincerely attached to his doctrines, in preference to all others; ascribing to himself every *human* excellence; & believing he never claimed any other. . . . In confiding it to you, I know it will not be exposed to the malignant perversions of those who make every word from me a text for new misrepresentations & calumnies. I am moreover averse to the communication of my religious tenets to the public.

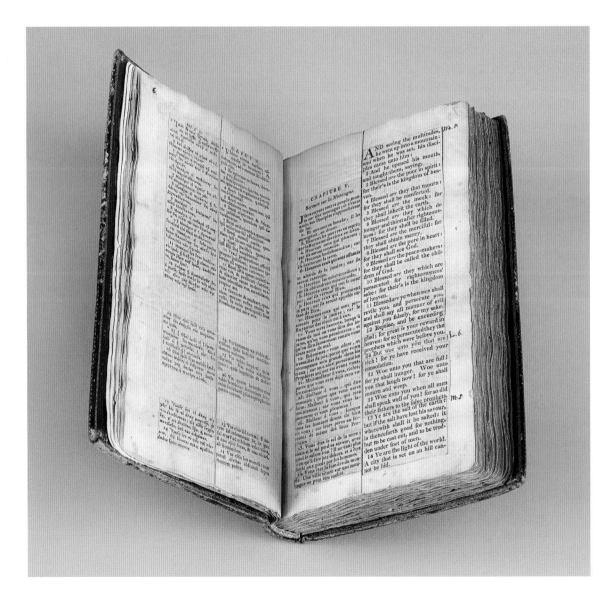

Jefferson was known to say he was "of a sect by myself." Yet the reception of *The Life and Morals of Jesus of Nazareth* suggests that many Americans shared his views. Having produced a single copy of the manuscript in his lifetime, he bequeathed the leather-bound volume to his daughter Martha in his will. It passed down through generations of his descendants until his great-granddaughter Carolina Randolph sold it to the Smithsonian's librarian Cyrus Adler in 1895. Nine years later, an act of Congress decreed that the text be published for the first time. For fifty years, every newly elected senator received a copy of the Jefferson Bible upon taking the oath of office.

It was fitting that the manuscript was passed down through family, as Jefferson had always made his most personal statements regarding religion to those closest to him. In a letter written in 1787, he urged a nephew to consider all sides when it came to questions of religion. As he said of this process:

> If it ends in a belief that there is no God, you will find incitements to virtue in the comfort & pleasantness you feel in its exercise, and the love of others which it will procure you. If you find reason to believe there is a God, a consciousness that you are acting under His eye, & that He approves you, will be a vast additional incitement; . . . if that Jesus was also a god, you will be comforted by a belief of his aid and love. In fine, I repeat that you must lay aside all prejudice on both sides, & neither believe nor reject anything because any other persons, or description of persons, have rejected or believed it. Your own reason is the only oracle given you by heaven.

Jefferson's attempt to craft a scripture he could believe in is clear evidence that he not only gave this advice, but also lived by it himself. ◆

✵ *Thomas Jefferson's Qur'an*

George Sale, *The Koran, Commonly Called the Alcoran of Mohammed,* 1764. Thomas Jefferson bought this edition of the Qur'an while studying law in Williamsburg, Virginia.

THOMAS JEFFERSON'S COPY of the Qur'an provides a further example of how he thought about religion. The edition he owned, *The Koran, Commonly Called the Alcoran of Mohammed*, was translated by the Englishman George Sale, who, despite being the translator of the primary text of Islam, was hardly sympathetic to the faith. In fact, he believed it was only a matter of time before God would bring about its end. "Providence has reserved the glory of its overthrow," he wrote.

Yet Sale presented the book to readers not in the spirit of triumphalism but as a matter of education. "To be acquainted with the various laws and constitutions of civilized nations, especially of those who flourish in our own time, is, perhaps, the most useful part of knowledge," he wrote. "If the religious and civil institutions of foreign nations are worth our knowledge, those of Mohammed, the lawgiver of the Arabians, and founder of an empire which, in less than a century, spread itself over a greater part of the world than the Romans were ever masters of, must needs be so."

To put the spread of the Muslim faith into context, the edition of the Qur'an that Jefferson read paints a picture of the peoples of the lands Islam would conquer as not unlike the Greeks and Romans, who eventually shed classical mythologies in favor of monotheism: "The idolatry of the Arabs . . . chiefly consisted in worshipping the fixed stars and planets, and the angels and their images, which they honoured as inferior deities, and whose intercession they begged," Sale wrote. "It was from this gross idolatry . . . that Mohammed reclaimed his countrymen, establishing the sole worship of the true God among them."

Encountering the text for the first time as a law student living in Williamsburg, Virginia, in 1765, Jefferson purchased it for the wholly practical reason of gaining a better understanding of a text relevant to some of the world's legal systems. He might have been surprised to learn that one day 242 years later, the first Muslim member of the House of Representatives, Minnesota's Keith Ellison, would use the very book that Jefferson bought as a young man to take his oath of office. Acquired out of intellectual curiosity and preserved as part of a collection of texts transported from Monticello to the Library of Congress, it came to serve this higher purpose in a nation more religiously diverse than Jefferson could have imagined. ◆

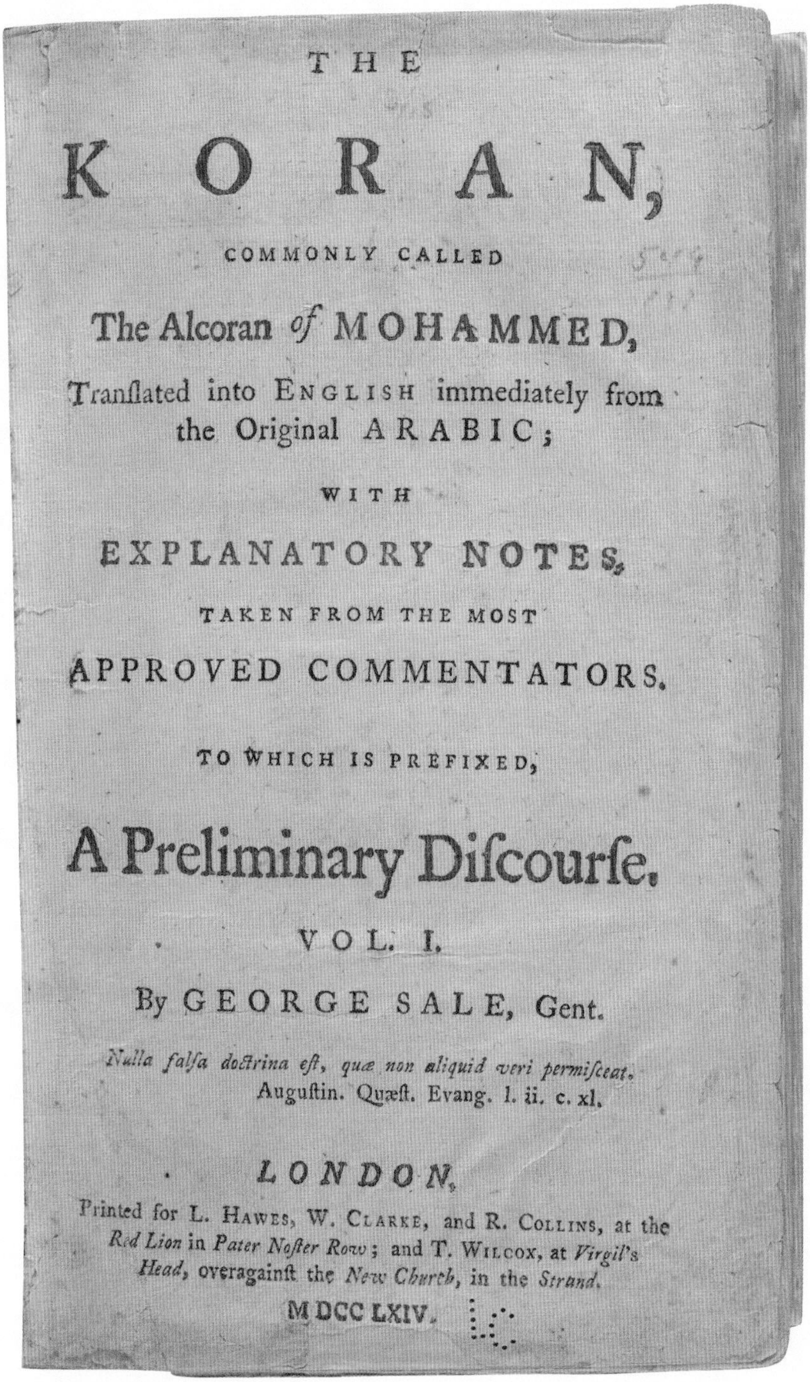

THE
KORAN,

COMMONLY CALLED

The Alcoran *of* MOHAMMED,

Translated into ENGLISH immediately from
the Original ARABIC;

WITH

EXPLANATORY NOTES,

TAKEN FROM THE MOST

APPROVED COMMENTATORS.

TO WHICH IS PREFIXED,

A Preliminary Difcourfe.

VOL. I.

By GEORGE SALE, Gent.

Nulla falfa doctrina eft, quæ non aliquid veri permifceat.
Auguftin. Quæft. Evang. l. ii. c. xl.

• LONDON,

Printed for L. HAWES, W. CLARKE, and R. COLLINS, at the
Red Lion in Pater Nofter Row; and T. WILCOX, at Virgil's
Head, overagainft the New Church, in the Strand.
MDCCLXIV.

✳ The Bilali Document

Pages of the Bilali
Document, early
nineteenth century.
Written by Bilali
Muhammad, this is the
only known Islamic text
written by an enslaved
Muslim in America.

DESPITE EFFORTS TO SUPPRESS THEM, the religions of the enslaved—including Islam, Yoruba, Akan, and other African traditions—managed to survive in America through adaptation, secrecy, and occasionally isolation. Early in the nineteenth century on remote Sapelo Island, Georgia, a man named Bilali Muhammad composed this thirteen-page Arabic text, the only known work of Islamic instruction written by an enslaved Muslim in the United States.

Sapelo Island is best known as a home of Geechee/Gullah culture, a complex of linguistic, handicraft, and spiritual traditions tracing their lineage directly to the first enslaved populations in the region. One example is religious meetings known as ring shouts, which often include rhythmic hand clapping accompanied by songs sung by men and women moving in a circle. While "shout" in this instance refers to a style of singing, it may also derive from *saut*, a word of Arabic origin describing "a religious ring dance in which the participants continue to perform until exhausted." The call-and-response worship style of many American churches today can be traced in part to spiritual traditions like this, which are older than the nation itself.

While Bilali Muhammad's document is singular, the broad strokes of his life were not. He was but one of the perhaps 20 percent of African-born men and women who followed Islam before losing their faith and their communities when transported as captives first to the English colonies and later to the young United States. Their presence is affirmed in documents such as a Virginia law of 1682 that explicitly refers to men and women of "Mohammedan parentage" taken from regions of Africa where Islam was the dominant religion.

Largely forgotten today, enslaved Muslims were a well-known presence in America throughout the eighteenth and nineteenth centuries. Plantation owners across the South made it a point to add Muslims to their labor forces, relying on their experience with the cultivation of indigo and rice. A small number of enslaved Muslims were recognized for their skills and learning, including a man named Abdul-Rahman Ibrahim ibn Sori, a prince in his homeland whose plight drew wide attention. A newspaper account noted that he had read the Bible and admired its precepts, but added, "His principal objections are that Christians do not follow them."

What little we know of the life of the Bilali Document's author can be gleaned from the work of a nineteenth-century Christian writer, William Brown Hodgson. A self-taught linguist who had married into a family wealthy enough to allow him to pursue his obscure interests, Hodgson had heard from a Sapelo Island plantation owner of the peculiar manners of a dozen or so of his enslaved laborers. Led by Muhammad, also known as Old Tom, this small community of Muslims managed to keep certain aspects of their preenslavement religious lives intact. →

"This Mohammedan, the trust-worthy servant of Mr. Spalding, of Sapelo Island, Georgia, died recently, at an advanced age," Hodgson wrote in 1860. "He adhered to the creed, and to the precepts of the Koran. He wrote Arabic, and read his sacred book with constancy and reverence. It is understood that his numerous descendants, who are Christians, buried him with the Koran resting on his breast." Referring specifically to the Bilali Document, Hodgson added, "He left various written papers, supposed to be ritual, which, I hope, may be preserved."

Many Christian writers saw the faiths that enslaved men and women brought from Africa as inferior to their own, and often as a threat to the spiritual welfare of the nation. Yet there was still some grudging respect. Another Christian observer of Muslim slaves, Theodore Dwight, wrote:

> Mohammedan learning . . . forms an essential part of the Moslem system. . . . [Islam] favors, nay, requires, as a fundamental principle, the free and universal reading and study of their sacred book; and, instead of withholding it from the people under penalties of death and perdition, it establishes schools for all classes, primarily to teach its languages and doctrines. Extracts from the Koran form the earliest reading lessons of children, and the commentaries and other works founded upon it furnish the principal subjects of the advanced studies. . . .
>
> Readers who have neglected Africa may not be prepared to believe that schools of different grades have existed for centuries in various interior negro countries, and under the provisions of law, in which even the poor are educated at the public expense, and in which the deserving are carried on many years through long courses of regular instruction.

Though nothing of this kind was possible among the Muslims of the early United States, the efforts of people such as Bilali Muhammad to keep their beliefs alive in a hostile land are a testament to the resilience of faith. ◆

✳ Omar ibn Said

WHILE NOT MUCH IS KNOWN about the man who wrote the Bilali Document (page 166), other Muslims enslaved in America left behind detailed accounts of their lives.

In 1807, when Omar ibn Said was taken from his homeland in what is now Senegal, he was thirty-seven years old. A pious man, he had been a teacher of religion to the youth of his village. "Then there came a large army who killed many people," he later recalled. "They took me, and brought me to the great sea, and sold me into the hands of the Christians, who bound me and sent me on board a great ship and we sailed upon the great sea a month and a half, when we came to a place called Charleston. And in a Christian language, they sold me."

After three years of slavery in South Carolina, he made his escape. He traveled north for days before being recaptured in Fayetteville, North Carolina, where his life took another turn. Locked in a jail cell, he prayed facing east in the manner he had learned as a child, then took up a piece of coal from a fire and began to write Arabic words on the walls, most likely verses from the Qur'an.

Soon word of these activities spread and a crowd gathered at the jail. Fearing for the runaway slave's safety, Fayetteville's sheriff arranged for Ibn Said's sale to a family prominent in state politics and active in the Presbyterian church. Under their influence, he soon converted to Christianity, became a fixture at Sunday services, and wrote an account of his experiences.

Composed in Arabic in 1831 but not translated into English until 1848, "The Life of Omar ibn Said, Written by Himself" is framed as a conversion narrative, yet it suggests that he never fully left his former faith behind. "In the name of God, the merciful, the compassionate," he wrote, starting his life story with the *Basmala*, the phrase that begins the Qur'an. When he had lived as a follower of Mohammed in a Muslim land, he explained, "to pray, I said: 'Praise be to Allah, Lord of the Worlds; the Compassionate, the Merciful.'" Finding himself in a land filled with Christians, however, he discovered that other prayers were required:

> Now, I pray in the words of our Lord Jesus the Messiah: "Our Father, who art in heaven, hallowed be thy name, thy Kingdom come, thy Will be done, on earth as it is in Heaven. Give us this day our daily bread and forgive us our trespasses as we forgive those who trespass against us, and lead us not into temptation but deliver us from the evil one for thine is the Kingdom, the power, and the glory for ever and ever. Amen."

Joining his biography to verses from the Qur'an and an acknowledgment of the Christian faith that he had adopted, Ibn Said created not just a tale of conversion but a more complicated story of how religious traditions have combined and influenced one another in the lives of Americans. →

Later in life, he briefly found an unlikely celebrity as a supposed example of the good that could come from bringing the enslaved to the Christian faith. A magazine writer gave him the nickname Uncle Moro and painted his enslavement in a positive light.

> Being of a feeble constitution, Moro's duties have been of the lightest kind, and he has been treated rather as a friend than a servant. The garden has been to him a place of recreation rather than a toil, and the concern is not that he should labor more but less. The anxious efforts made to instruct him in the doctrines and precepts of our Divine Religion, have not been in vain. . . . Mohammedanism has been supplanted in his heart by the better faith in Christ Jesus.

Omar ibn Said's own understanding of his faith was likely far more nuanced. His autobiography suggests that the spiritual nature of religious conversion is never without its practical dimension. Even after he began to attend church services, he took stock of the country where he had found himself sold into bondage, and he posed a question to the Christians who held him captive: "O people of America, O people of North Carolina. . . . Do you have such a good generation that fears Allah?" he wrote. "Are you confident that He who is in heaven will not cause the earth to cave in beneath you, so that it will shake to pieces and overwhelm you?" ◆

Omar ibn Said, in a photograph taken circa 1860.

✳ *Trade Beads*

Glass beads, date unknown, Louisiana. Such "trade beads" were often carried by enslaved women and men for spiritual protection.

THE MOST WIDELY READ first-person account of American slavery, *Narrative of the Life of Frederick Douglass* (1845), describes the improvised religious items that enslaved men and women often turned to for solace and protection. Once, when Douglass was on his way to confront an overseer named Covey, who had mistreated him, a friend urged him to find a particular plant and keep it in his pocket, in accordance with traditional African beliefs:

> He told me, with great solemnity, I must go back to Covey, but that before I went, I must go with him into another part of the woods, where there was a certain root, which, if I would take some of it with me, carrying it always on my right side, would render it impossible for Mr. Covey, or any other white man, to whip me. He said he had carried it for years; and since he had done so, he had never received a blow, and never expected to while he carried it.

Many of the enslaved men and women brought by force across the Middle Passage were followers of West African belief systems, perhaps mostly Yoruba, Obeah, and Akan. All of these experienced some amount of hybridization in America, where formerly vital distinctions between tribal identities became far less important than fostering a shared community of the enslaved that might contribute to their survival. The advice to Douglass to carry a root at times of danger was part of a larger cultural system often called hoodoo or conjure, comprising folk magic practices that drew on ceremonies and stories both passed down through the generations and invented anew.

Along with roots and other natural items, enslaved men and women often kept polished beads for spiritual protection. Prevented from maintaining the cultural traditions with which they had been raised, they improvised religious practices with the materials available to them. "Trade beads," as they were often known, were made of polished stone, glass, scraps of metal, or shells. Their true value came in how they were used. Worn as adornments or amulets, they were also bartered, awarded, or given as gifts.

While some of these beads were crafted after their owners were enslaved, many had been kept and traded as tools of commerce in home countries before being carried across the Atlantic. A mid-nineteenth-century account of the variety of trade beads provides a view of a complex system of use and significance. Some beads, known as *popo*, were believed to have been dug out of the ground in Africa, "relics of ancient traffic" that were highly prized. Others were carved and distributed differently from region to region. The account notes:

> Some of the opaque beads, called "agras," . . . are exchanged for oil, ivory, and gold, at Accra, Lagos, and Cape Coast Castle. . . .
>
> The flat "agras" are perforated discs, measuring about five-eighths of an inch in diameter, and about a quarter of an inch in thickness. They are used in the slave trade on the west coast of Africa. The slave beads used by the Portuguese and Spaniards on the same coast are globular, opaque glass beads, some measuring as much as an inch in diameter. Others are six-sided tubes of opaque white glass, rather more than two inches in length.

An earlier account by a traveler to West Africa notes how such beads might be used. Parents would "tie strings of beads around the children's hands, feet and neck, and fill their hair with little shells, which they greatly esteem." At times so many beads and shells might be present that they seemed to form a net of protection. "For they say that as long as the young child is draped with this Net, the Devil cannot catch the child or carry it away; but without it would be carried away by the Devil. They highly esteem . . . the Beads which they hang around the neck of the little child and they consider it protection against vomiting, falling, bleeding, harmful animals, unhealthiness, and for sleeping well."

Beads were often seen as attributes of the gods. The Yoruba orisha (or minor deity) Osanyin is said to be the spirit of herbal healing. "Osanyin, so it is believed," the Yale art historian Robert Farris Thompson has noted, "was born with beads shining about his body. Moreover, beads are important to Osanyin because he associates their colors with the hues and qualities of the forest herbs. Thus some of the sylvan fronds are said to be bright green, while other herbs are yellow, black, red, or even white, and each hue denotes a different kind of curing power." Likewise, beads were thought to have varied attributes according to their color, though all were believed to have definite "powers of restoration."

Connected as they were with memories of homelands, landscapes, and traditions lost, as well as notions of childhood protection, these beads took on deeper significance as rare, treasured objects once those who kept them were sold into bondage. While beads came in all colors and shapes, the most valued tended to be blue. As the color of the sky, blue may have suggested heaven, or freedom. ◆

❊ *Nat Turner*

Newspaper cartoon following Nat Turner's rebellion, 1831. The uprising led by the preacher Turner on August 21, 1831, struck fear into the hearts of plantation owners in part because it drew on religious themes to inspire the enslaved.

ON AUGUST 21, 1831, an enslaved thirty-year-old man named Nat Turner lifted a hatchet against the family that had claimed to own him since his birth, sparking a revolt against slavery in remote Southampton County, Virginia, that would eventually leave more than a hundred dead. His story is well known; its religious roots are often forgotten.

Following the uprising, the Virginia press frequently referred to Turner as a "fanatic preacher." While his fanaticism is open to debate, he had shown himself to be precocious in spiritual matters from an early age. As a boy, he drew admiring attention for his piety, even from those who would one day rue having encouraged him to learn to read and write.

"My master, who belonged to the church," he later remembered, "and other religious persons who visited the house, and whom I often saw at prayers, noticing the singularity of my manners, I suppose, and my uncommon intelligence for a child, remarked I had too much sense to be raised, and if I was, I would never be of any service to any one as a slave."

Convinced that he was set apart for some special purpose, Turner sought to cultivate his natural gifts. "All my time, not devoted to my master's service," he said, "was spent either in prayer, or in making experiments in casting different things in moulds made of earth, in attempting to make paper, gunpowder, and many other experiments, that although I could not perfect, yet convinced me of its practicability if I had the means."

The young man became a self-taught minister and as such was permitted to visit nearby plantations, where he delivered sermons to other enslaved men and women. He often noticed "the confidence of the negroes in the neighborhood, even at this early period of my life, in my superior judgment" and soon began to see himself as not only a leader but a prophet.

One day, while working at his plough, he heard spirit voices urging him to bring about the "Kingdom of Heaven" on earth. Moved by what he took to be an experience akin to those of biblical prophets, he was baptized in a river, like Jesus himself when he had begun his mission, and then, Turner said, "I heard a loud noise in the heavens, and the Spirit was loosened, and Christ had laid down the yoke he had borne for the sins of men." In the model of Christ, he decided, he would "fight against the Serpent, for the time was fast approaching when the first should be last and the last should be first."

Turner was shaped not only by the lessons he learned from his study of Christian scripture, but also by the traditional beliefs his mother and grandmother had brought with them across the Middle Passage. Those participating in such traditions understood the "Spirit" that Turner had heard speak not as the Holy Spirit →

HORRID MASSACRE IN VIRGINIA.

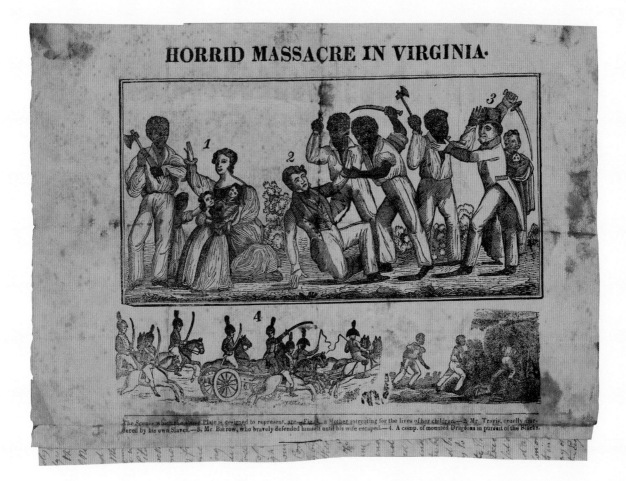

The Scenes which the above Plate is designed to represent, are,—Fig. 1—a Mother intreating for the lives of her children.—2. Mr. Travis, cruelly murdered by his own Slaves.—3. Mr. Barrow, who bravely defended himself until his wife escaped.—4. A comp. of mounted Dragoons in pursuit of the Blacks.

of the Gospels but as a Yoruba figure called Eshu or Legbo, the god of messages, able to communicate with elements of the natural world.

"Laboring in the field, I discovered drops of blood on the corn as though it were dew from heaven," Turner recalled, "and I then found on the leaves in the woods hieroglyphic characters, and numbers, with the forms of men in different attitudes, portrayed in blood, and representing the figures I had seen before in the heavens." These messages, together with the prophetic model of the Bible, formed the revelation that led to his rebellion.

"He stimulated his comrades to join with him by declaring to them that he had been commissioned by Jesus Christ," the *Richmond Telegraph* reported after his capture, "and that he was acting under inspired direction in what he was going to do."

The ambition and scope of the attacks sometimes referred to as the Southampton Insurrection shocked the nation, but many who had witnessed the powerful orations of enslaved and formerly enslaved preachers were not surprised. Uprising seemed to be the subtext of many of their interpretations of scripture. A proslavery sermon published in Virginia in 1825 noted:

> I venture to predict if ever that horrid event should take place, which
> is anticipated and greatly dreaded by many among us, some crisp-haired
> prophet, some pretender to inspiration, will be the ring leader as well
> as the instigator of the plot. By feigning communication with heaven, he
> will rouse the fanaticism of his brethren, and they will be prepared for
> any work, however desolating and murderous. The opinion has already
> been started among them, that men may make such progress in religion,
> that nothing they can do will be sinful, even should it be the murder
> of those whom they are now required to obey!

Turner was hanged along with many of those who followed him, but though his uprising failed, he succeeded in highlighting the radically different purposes to which religion could be put in the matters of slavery and the future of the country. ◆

❈ Emanuel African Methodist Episcopal Church

CHARLESTON'S OLDEST African American church, Mother Emanuel, as it is commonly known, was founded as the Hampstead Church in 1816, and it won early renown as a site of resistance to slavery and mistreatment. Targeted with harassment by city officials, members of the church were regularly arrested for violating restrictions on worship and education among the enslaved. Church leaders took part in the planning of a slave revolt in 1822, resulting in the execution of the head of the uprising, Denmark Vesey, and other organizers.

Had it been successful, the Vesey revolt might have been the most bloody in American history. The plan, hatched at the church, was to storm the state armory in Charleston, overtake the city, and then escape by boat to Haiti. Twenty-three years before the planned uprising, Vesey had won a lottery and purchased his freedom from slavery. He then worked as an independent carpenter and quickly rose through the ranks of African American society in Charleston. A committed Christian, he first belonged to a Presbyterian church that put restrictions on black membership, and then was involved in founding the state's first African Methodist Episcopal church.

Emanuel AME Church, Charleston, South Carolina, founded in 1816. Its current home, pictured here in 1910, was completed in 1891.

In addition to making Mother Emanuel a symbol of the struggle for freedom, the church's role in the 1822 revolt revealed the multiple religious perspectives operative in the broader African American community even after the majority of its members had become Christians. Sharing the leadership of the planned uprising with Vesey, and also his fate on the gallows, a man known to history only as Gullah Jack persuaded African-born slaves to join the fight. Though Vesey had recruited him at the church, Jack had a reputation as a "conjureman," a practitioner of traditional African healing and magic arts. He claimed invincibility and offered charms and spells to make all those who followed him invincible as well. An 1822 newspaper account of the planned revolt reported:

> It appears that this was in agitation for a considerable length of time. [The conspirators] formed themselves into a society, and held meetings at a farm that they could approach by water, to avoid being stopped by any patrols. . . . →

Religion and superstition were used by the more cunning to delude the incredulous African into the plot. Gullah Jack was considered invincible; he could not be hurt nor killed by any means whatever; but a blow from him would mean instant execution. At one of these meetings, they had a fowl dressed and put on a table—Gullah Jack performed some ceremony of witchcraft over it; when he was done an instant scramble was made for the fowl, everyone trying to get a piece, then says Jack, "so do we pull the Buckra [white men] to pieces."

When information about the plot was revealed, Vesey, Jack, and more than a hundred others were arrested. Three dozen were hanged.

The court record of Gullah Jack's condemnation provides a window onto the fear that traditional African beliefs inspired in slaveholders. As it delivered its death sentence, the court declared:

In the prosecution of your wicked designs, you were not satisfied with resorting to natural and ordinary means, but endeavored to enlist on your behalf, all the powers of darkness, and employed for that purpose, the most disgusting mummery and superstition. You represented yourself as invulnerable; that you could neither be taken nor destroyed and that all who fought under your banners would be invincible. While such wretched expedients are calculated to inspire the confidence, or to alarm the fears of the ignorant and credulous, they excite no other emotion in the mind of the intelligent and enlightened, but contempt and disgust. Your boasted Charms have not preserved yourself, and of course could not protect others.

In the aftermath of the revolt, the church was burned to the ground and all-black congregations were outlawed in Charleston. Members of the community met and worshipped in secret until after the Civil War. When finally they were able to rebuild, the lead architect was Robert Vesey, a son of the executed leader. ◆

❊ *Embroidered Exodus*

THE STORY OF THE EXODUS—when the God of the Bible led Moses and his people out of bondage—has long had a special resonance in America. The Puritans who crossed the Atlantic to escape religious persecution reimagined England as Egypt, the ocean as a desert, and New England as the promised land. A century and a half later, when a new nation emerged from the colonies, John Adams, Benjamin Franklin, and Thomas Jefferson proposed using a related image on a seal for the republic. Beneath the words "Rebellion to Tyrants Is Obedience to God," it showed the Israelites passing through the Red Sea with Pharaoh's army chasing them.

For many in the generations that followed, Exodus remained a touchstone. With the young nation cast as ancient Israel, George Washington inevitably became its Moses. As the New Jersey Presbyterian pastor John Carle preached in a sermon shortly after Washington's death, "In several instances during the war between Great →

Elizabeth J. Crosswell, *Moses and the Bulrushes,* 1825–35. This silk embroidery depicts a scene from the biblical Book of Exodus.

Britain and America, there were seasons as dark and gloomy as that of the Israelites, and the people were so sorely afraid; but the American Moses hushed the murmurs of the people—dispelled the gloom, and opened a passage through the waters."

Another eulogist, Peter Folsom of New Hampshire, made the connection even more dramatically: "Moses led the Israelites through the red sea; has not Washington conducted the Americans thro' seas of blood?"

During the War of 1812, the Massachusetts pastor John H. Stevens saw the return of war to American soil as divine retribution. He wrote:

> After God had done such great things for Israel, and had settled them in the good land of Canaan in peace, where they enjoyed his word and ordinances, and every blessing, we should have supposed they would have forsaken all other gods, and feared, worshipped, and served the Lord Jehovah with all the heart. But instead of this they sinned against him. . . .
>
> And has not our nation in this particular, done as Israel did, forsaken God, and done great evil in his sight?

Even as some Americans were casting themselves as Israelites in a retelling of the biblical saga, however, others saw the new nation as another Egypt keeping a people in bondage. Though almost none of the men and women brought to these shores in chains were Christians when they arrived, in time most adopted the faith and began to search its stories for solace. Like many Americans before them, the enslaved looked for themselves in the Bible's pages.

Of course, so too did plantation owners, as in the embroidered silk depiction of the Exodus story shown on page 179. In the biblical story, the infant Moses is taken from among the bulrushes by the attendants of Pharaoh's daughter, who raises the baby as her own. The three women are here depicted wearing dresses popular in the South throughout the 1830s.

Their lightly tinted complexions also highlight the dramatically divergent resonances of scripture for different American populations in the era of slavery. When hearing the Exodus story, Christian plantation owners and their families identified with the enslaved Israelites rather than the slave-owning Egyptians. For enslaved Christians, meanwhile, the story of Moses leading his people out of bondage was a symbol of hope that they too might one day be free.

Ultimately, this struggle would lead another president, Abraham Lincoln, to be perhaps even more closely associated with Moses and the Exodus story than Washington had been. The Philadelphia synagogue Mikveh Israel (page 143) adopted resolutions declaring Lincoln "one of the best and purest presidents, who like the law-giver Moses brought a nation to the verge of the haven of peace, and like him was not allowed to participate in its consummation."

Crafted a generation before the Emancipation Proclamation, this silk depiction of a scene from Exodus captures a moment when the religious vocabulary that the nation used to define itself was in flux. While biblical stories have long helped Americans to understand themselves, they have rarely had only one meaning. ◆

❋ Stickball

AMONG THE CHEROKEE and other southeastern Native American peoples, stickball (also known as *a-ne-jo-di*, "little brother of war") was no mere athletic pastime but rather a ritual battle enacting the struggle between good and evil, played to settle disputes between tribes and to give pleasure to the Creator. Developed as a means for competing tribal communities to come to terms, the game soon became a sacred performance that was frequently violent but nonetheless avoided the full costs of combat.

Preparations for each match began weeks before the action itself. The players not only exercised to reach top physical shape, but also engaged in ritual activities to train their spirits as well as their bodies. Those readying themselves adhered to a strict diet designed to discourage characteristics that would not serve them well on the field of play. They avoided eating the meat of rabbits because they felt it would make them as timid as the animal itself, as well as that of birds or frogs, which they →

Caddos and Choctaws playing baggataway, now known as lacrosse, image 1900.

believed would make their bones brittle. For seven days before and seven days after each game, players were also instructed to remain celibate.

These weeks of training would culminate in an elaborate ball-play dance the night before the game, during which the entire community would perform conjuring ceremonies, spiritual songs, and other rites believed to insure a favorable outcome. Dressed in ceremonial attire and gathered in groups of men and women chanting sacred lines, they hoped the gods who helped them would also hinder their opponents.

As the nineteenth-century anthropologist James Mooney wrote, "To further incite them to strain every nerve for victory, two settlements, or sometimes two rival tribes, were always pitted against each other, and guns, blankets, horses—everything the Indian had or valued—were staked upon the result. The prayers and ceremonies of the shamans, the speeches of the old men, and the songs of the dancers were all alike calculated to stimulate to the highest pitch the courage and endurance of the contestants."

While stickball matches involved the entire community, at the center of the ritual were those wielding religious authority. "Even so simple a matter as the ball game is not left to the free enjoyment of the people," Mooney added, "but is so interwoven with priestly rites and influence that the shaman becomes the most important actor in the play."

For all of stickball's religious import, however, the anthropologist highlighted its physical intensity. "It is a very exciting game as well as a very rough one," he observed. "Almost everything short of murder is allowable in the game, and both parties sometimes go into the contest with the deliberate purpose of crippling or otherwise disabling the best players on the opposing side. Serious accidents are common."

George Catlin, *Ball-Play of the Choctaw—Ball Up*, 1846–50. Oil on canvas.

An alternate assessment of stickball gatherings can be found in the work of the frontier painter George Catlin, who traveled with fifty Native Americans and chronicled their lives throughout the 1830s. The spectacle of the game so impressed him that he once called it "a school for the painter or sculptor, equal to any of those which ever inspired the hand of the artist in the Olympian games or the Roman forum." In his views of the game, Catlin sought to capture both the massive scale of tournaments that could involve a thousand players and the individual dignity of those involved in a centuries-old ceremony that was vital to their culture.

The games were played with sticks of hardwood, such as hickory, fitted with nets of loosely woven hide. Like modern-day lacrosse, which derives from a similar game played by northern tribes, stickball involved throwing and catching a ball that scored when shot into a goal. Unlike in lacrosse, however, a single match could last for days.

Along with other traditions of the southeastern tribes, the ritual battles of stickball moved west with the Indian Removal Act, signed into law by President Andrew Jackson on May 28, 1830. Affecting the Chickasaw, Choctaw, Seminole, Muscogee/Creek, and Cherokee peoples, the act authorized the federal government to offer tribes unsettled territories west of the Mississippi River in exchange for Indian lands that were now considered the property of the states.

When the Cherokee resisted this forced relocation, they were marched out of the lands they had called home for generations. The Trail of Tears killed thousands and marked a significant turning point in the religious lives of many Native Americans. Among other things, Indian removal increased the rates of adoption of Christianity. Missionaries accompanied the fifteen thousand men, women, and children on their journey. In conditions that claimed a least a quarter of the lives of those traveling—including outbreaks of cholera, supply shortages, extreme weather, starvation, and exhaustion—Christian ministers found fertile ground for their evangelizing efforts (see, for example, the hymnal on page 184). One missionary personally led groups of Cherokee into Indian Territory: of the Wales-born Baptist Evan Jones, it has been said that he and his family "converted more American Indians to Christianity than any other Protestant missionaries in America." →

Stickball sticks, nineteenth century. This Cherokee game was not merely a diversion, but also a religious ritual.

Pages in a Cherokee hymnal, 1830. While many Native Americans eventually embraced Christianity, the majority of the Cherokee were not converted until they were uprooted from their homes and forced to march the Trail of Tears in 1830. Many missionaries saw this as an opportunity, producing materials such as this hymnal in the Cherokee language.

The missionaries' role in the relocation was not accidental. President Jackson himself had stated that the ultimate goal of removal was for the southeastern tribes to "cast off their savage habits and become an interesting, civilized, and Christian community."

Yet while the turmoil of relocation challenged and in many cases changed their traditional beliefs, stickball, along with certain other religiously influenced rites, continued in the Southwest, where it is still played today. ◆

✺ *The Ten Thousand Name Petition*

THREE MONTHS AFTER fifty-six delegates to the Second Continental Congress signed the Declaration of Independence, nearly two hundred times that many Americans affixed their names to a document they viewed as equally important. The spiritual equivalent to declaring independence from England was formal separation from the religious institution inextricably connected to the Crown; thus, immediately after the Revolution, dissenting members of minority Christian denominations in Virginia used petitions to force the issue of religious freedom for those outside the Anglican Church.

The most notable was the document shown on page 186, the so-called Ten Thousand Name Petition, which was delivered to the state's legislative session in October 1776. It includes more than a hundred pages of signatures opposing the support of religious instruction through assessments levied for the benefit of particular churches irrespective of the affiliations of those being taxed. Despite gathering the thousands of names for which it became known, this petition was only one of hundreds submitted over the decade that followed. Within a single legislative session nine years later, for example, nine petitions catalogued Virginians' disapproval of religious assessments.

Virginia's dissenters undoubtedly helped secure full religious rights for members of denominations other than the Church of England in their state. But more than that, these appeals were part of a larger freedom-of-conscience movement that later served as a model for religious liberty in the nation as a whole. The text of the Ten Thousand Name Petition reads:

To the Honourable the President and House of Delegates

The Petition of the Dissenters from the Ecclesiastical establishment in the Commonwealth of Virginia—Humbly sheweth

That your Petitioners, being (in Common with the other Inhabitants of the Commonwealth) delivered from British oppression Rejoice in the prospect of having their freedom maintained and secured to them and posterity inviolate; the hopes of your Petitioners have been raised and confirmed by the Declaration of your Honourable House with Regard to equal Liberty. Equal Liberty! that invaluable Blessing; which though it be the Birth right of every good member of the State has been what your Petitioners have been Deprived of in that by Taxation their property hath been wrested from them and Given to those from whom they have received no equivalent.

Your Petitioners therefore haveing long groaned under the Burden of an Ecclesiastical establishment beg leave to move your Honourable House that →

Ten Thousand Name Petition, 1776. Thousands signed this petition for religious liberty in Virginia shortly after independence was declared.

this as well as every other yoke may be Broken and that the oppressed may go free that so every Religious Denomination being on a Level, Animosities may cease and that Christian Forbearance, Love and Charity may be practised toward each other while the Legality Interferes only to support [. . .] their Just Right and Equal Liberty.

And your Petitioners shall ever pray.

While singular statements on behalf of religious liberty such as the Virginia Statute for Religious Freedom, which Thomas Jefferson drafted in 1777, rightly received credit for prefiguring the course the nation would take, the Ten Thousand Name Petition serves as a reminder that there were many other voices in the chorus. ◆

✴ *John Leland*

THOUGH BORN in Massachusetts, the minister John Leland made his most significant contributions to American religion in Virginia. Throughout the 1770s and 1780s, his Baptist denomination chafed against the privileged position of the Anglican Church. Since Virginia's founding in 1624, taxes had supported Anglican clergymen, while ministers of all other churches had faced imprisonment and fines if they failed to obtain the license required of all those known as dissenters. The Revolution did not put an end to this tension but rather brought it to a head, as the framers of the new state constitution sought to address religion's proper role in society.

One side of this debate maintained that though England had been defeated, the Anglican Church, which had roots there, remained of vital importance in America and should continue to receive support. Opposing this group were those who believed that religion should be a private matter left out of the public square. Yet the most persuasive voices in the debate in Virginia belonged to those who had experienced firsthand the dangers of religious establishment: Christians who had chosen to go to jail rather than support a church to which they did not belong.

Portrait of John Leland, 1854 (detail). Leland was a Baptist minister and advocate for religious liberty. From Writings of the Late Elder John Leland (New York: G. W. Wood, 1845).

Leland arrived in Virginia in 1775 and immediately became an influential advocate for his fellow Baptists. Writing impassioned letters to James Madison, he reminded the future author of the Bill of Rights (page 147) of the persecution of dissenters and urged that religious freedom should be the law of the land for both his home state and the new nation.

After Virginia passed its Statute for Religious Freedom in 1779 (page 186), disestablishing the Church of England, Leland returned to his native New England to continue the struggle in Connecticut and Massachusetts, which both continued to provide state support to the Congregational Church.

A gifted preacher, Leland was also well versed in politics. He understood early on that religious communities would become powerful constituencies in the United States. In Virginia, he had rallied Baptist support for Madison's congressional campaigns, and he had perhaps his most lasting influence as a behind-the-scenes advocate for the addition of the Bill of Rights to the Constitution. Having seen →

the abuse that religious dissenters faced under the system of established churches, Leland argued for the inclusion of individual rights and protections, particularly guarantees of religious liberty. Among the most persecuted religious minorities in the early republic, Baptists such as Leland put pressure on the government to guarantee religious liberty for all. In a February 1789 letter, he asked Madison to inform him if the freedom of religion might be threatened in any way.

Sir,

I congratulate you in your Appointment, as a Representative to Congress; and if my Undertaking in the Cause conduced Nothing else towards it, it certainly gave Mr. Madison one Vote. I expect that Congress will be very busy for some years, in filling a continental Blank with a Code of general Laws; and I think it will be very Judicious to send those Laws very liberally into the States, that their Eyes may always be open. No Danger of the Destruction of Liberty where the Community is well informed. Ignorance always brings on either Mutiny or Lethargy, which equally pave the Way for Tyranny. If Mr. Madison can get Leisure enough in Congress it would please my Fancy to have a List of all the Names of the Members of Congress; in which State they reside, and which House they fill: and it would inform my Mind to have an Account of all our National Debts; to what Powers they are due, and at what p[e]r Cent; and likewise of our internal debt. . . . No doubt, there will be printed Statements, at proper Times; but I am so little acquainted with the literary and political World, that without the Aid of a particular Friend, I shall never see them. If I could see all the Laws I should be glad, altho' in Person, I have little Use for them. One Thing I shall expect; that if religious Liberty is anywise threatened, that I shall receive the earliest Intelligence.

Leland's support of Madison proved beneficial to each man's interests. During the presidential election of 1800, the minister hoped to have the same sort of relationship with Thomas Jefferson. He caused a stir in 1802 when he enlisted Baptist dairy farmers in Cheshire, Massachusetts, to make a 1,235-pound wheel of cheese inscribed with the motto "Rebellion to tyrants is obedience to God," which he then had delivered to the White House.

President Jefferson warmly received the Cheshire "mammoth cheese" in recognition of the minister's decades of support of their common cause. The outspoken Baptist and the man who once took a blade to the Bible (page 163) shared an unwavering concern for religious liberty, despite the differences in their beliefs. ◆

✳ Baptist Collection Basket

RELIGIOUS LIBERTY in the United States was built on the principle that there would be no established religion. In the English colonies, Congregational churches in the North and Anglican churches in the South had received public support as promoters of education, social welfare, and moral virtue. Taxes not only provided for the upkeep of houses of worship, which often served both civic and spiritual purposes, but also paid ministers' salaries.

This changed in the early United States. The First Amendment to the U.S. Constitution did away with the establishment of religion on the federal level in 1789. Over the next few decades, individual states followed suit, some more quickly than others. Massachusetts, whose system of church support functioned largely on the local level, had religious taxes until 1833. But even in the states that lagged behind, the coming transformation was clear: regardless of their previous formal connections to government, every congregation would now be required to raise its own funds.

The need to collect money directly from churchgoers, rather than indirectly through the taxes they paid, was a practical matter that had surprising religious implications. Some communities continued the long-held tradition of renting prime pews to wealthier members (in many colonial-era churches, one can still see plaques inscribed with the names of those who paid for the privilege of sitting close to the pulpit), while others began to seek donations from worshippers as they gathered for Sunday services.

In time, passing the plate became a ceremony all its own—a moment when mundane needs and otherworldly aspirations were entwined. While not ubiquitous in American churches until later in the nineteenth century, the practice was sufficiently accepted by the 1820s that gently mocking portrayals of the ritual began to appear in the press.

Public donations to the church, it was feared, might turn sanctuaries into places of bald commerce. In 1824, the *New York Evening Post* recounted the tale of a shoemaker who asked a pastor to preach on a particular passage of scripture. "When the collection plate was handed around," the reporter wrote, the shoemaker "drew from his pocket a pair of new shoes suited to the parson's measure, and deposited them in the plate."

Similarly, some raised concerns that these donations created status separation at a moment when Christians should feel most united. A poem in a Boston paper addressed this point soon after the New York cobbler made his unexpected offering. →

Collection basket, nineteenth century. This handwoven basket was used for decades to hold monetary offerings made to a Baptist church in Virginia.

'Tis thus the rich man walks away
With a swagger in his gait.
He knows the price that he can pay
As he passes the "offering" plate.
For Sunday is the rich man's day,
To him exclusive given.
Sin is no sin with those who pay,
And buy their right to Heaven!

Yet from the earliest days of passing the plate, simple gifts were also accepted—as can be seen in the delicate, handmade offering basket shown on the previous page, which helped to maintain a Baptist church in Virginia throughout the nineteenth century. Far from being a sign of the rich receiving special attention or of churches becoming overrun with commercial transactions, this basket might instead be seen as a symbol of Virginia's role in shaping a new conception of how American religious institutions would be supported.

When the Virginian Patrick Henry debated the Virginian Thomas Jefferson on religion's relationship to the state, Henry took for granted that a certain amount of state support would be necessary if churches were to continue to offer services for the good of society. Jefferson, meanwhile, insisted that religions functioned best when no one was forced through taxation to support denominations with which they did not agree. A dozen years before the Bill of Rights, Jefferson's Virginia Statute for Religious Freedom stated that "to compel a man to furnish contributions of money for the propagation of opinions which he disbelieves and abhors, is sinful and tyrannical."

A third Virginian, James Madison, took an even more extreme position. Writing against "A Bill establishing a provision for Teachers of the Christian Religion" in 1785, he suggested that state support for religious endeavors was "a contradiction to the Christian Religion itself." He had come to this conclusion in part because of the experiences of Virginia Baptists, whose desire to see all denominations support themselves and the state favor none had led to the collection of funds from congregants through a ritual that became a vital part of worship. ◆

✳ *George Mason's Baptismal Bowl*

Monteith, mid-eighteenth century. Silver. In the family of the patriot George Mason, this bowl, generally used for chilling wine glasses, doubled as a christening font.

THIS SILVER MONTEITH—a large bowl used to chill wine glasses—doubled as the patriot George Mason's christening basin. While not designed for religious purposes, it served generations of the Mason family as a ritual item. In his will, Mason noted that all of his children had been christened in the bowl, which he hoped would "remain in the family unaltered for that purpose."

According to the scholar Lauren Winner, objects such as this one highlight the willingness of Anglicans in America to mix the domestic and the ecclesiastic, the profane and the sacred. It is also a surprising symbol of controversy: the question of whether baptism could be performed at home was a source of conflict among Anglicans in colonial Virginia. Winner writes:

> In a society in which the sacred is set apart from the secular, a bowl like the Masons' does not make much sense. In a society that draws a sharp boundary between the things of God and the things of man, punch bowls do not sit on altars, and baptismal bowls are not used at parties. If we look without such presuppositions at the Masons' bowl, however, we can begin to see a form of religion and a form of society in which baptizing and tippling were close kin. . . . The bowl's doubleness suggests the ways that religion and ordinary life were intertwined in the households of Virginia's Anglican gentry. →

This bowl's dual purpose likely also indicates a simple preference for seeing family religious rituals held at the Mason estate Gunston Hall rather than in a house of worship, reflecting Mason's opinion that religion was more a private matter than one that should be open to the pressures of communal life. "Religion, or the duty which we owe to our Creator, and the manner of discharging it, can be directed only by reason and conviction, not by force or violence," he wrote. "All men should enjoy the fullest toleration in the exercise of religion, according to the dictates of conscience, unpunished and unrestrained by the magistrate, unless, under the color of religion, any man disturb the peace, the happiness, or the safety of society."

While Mason has never received as much attention as his fellow Virginians Thomas Jefferson (page 67) and James Madison (page 147) for his part in shaping the principle of religious liberty in the United States, he was responsible for the 1776 Virginia Declaration of Rights, which guarantees the freedom of the state's citizens to live according to their conscience.

For Mason, the practice of religion began in the home, among family, and extended from there into society. "It is the mutual duty of all," he wrote, "to practice Christian forbearance, love, and charity towards each other." While Mason referred only to Christians in such statements, thanks to his work in Virginia, religious freedom was also available to those of other faiths, and of no faith. Though he was an Anglican, he opposed the preferential treatment that his church had long received as the established church of the state.

"Anglicans, Roman Catholics, Evangelicals, Jews, and unbelievers were placed on the same civil footing" in Virginia, the early twentieth-century archivist H. J. Eckenrode wrote. "It may be said, then, that Virginia was ahead of the world at the time when the Bill of Rights was adopted, making the first legal statement of the principle of religious liberty." If this was so, it may have been at least in part because of how men such as Mason considered religion and its associated rituals. As Winner notes:

> For some Christian communities in early America, baptism dramatically interrupted daily life. . . . But at Gunston Hall, baptism was neither dramatic nor an interruption. There, religious meanings and religious practices were integrated elegantly into daily life. The Christian life into which George and Ann Mason's children were inaugurated was wholly compatible with life in the world—with worldly success and worldly pleasure. . . . The bowl that had once held water that cleansed children from sin returned to the dinner table, where it was transformed, quite unmiraculously, back into a monteith holding water used to chill upside-down wine glasses. ◆

✵ George Washington's Christening Robe

THE RELIGIOUS OPINIONS held by the nation's first president have long been the subject of debate. He was at once a church vestryman and a Freemason, and he appears to have entertained deist notions. He was known to pray, but also to avoid certain religious rituals such as Communion, which he apparently left church services early to miss from time to time. Some of the more pious depictions of his career—such as a popular painting showing General Washington kneeling in prayer at Valley Forge—do not have a basis in fact.

Yet for the all the questions that his adult commitments inspire, there is no disagreement about when his religious life began. George Washington became a member of the Anglican Church with his christening on April 5, 1732, during which he was wrapped in this silk brocade gown.

While many infants at the time were baptized in churches, Washington was christened at home. In this, his family was far from unique. Religious rituals in early America were practiced not only in houses of worship and in the open air, but also at home, often with clergymen visiting to preside over improvised liturgical objects (page 191). This blending of the domestic and the sacred was typical of a time when many expected religion to play a role in every aspect of life. Washington's christening was likely attended not only by his parents, but also by his two godfathers and one godmother. The event was recorded in the family Bible.

George Washington's christening robe, 1732. Silk. Baptized at home, as were most wealthy Anglicans in colonial America, Washington was wrapped in this robe for the occasion.

Nearly a century ago, Washington's christening robe was already drawing visitors to the Smithsonian. "In the National Museum," Robert Shackleton wrote in 1922, "there is a child's christening robe, of white silk brocade, a robe so delicate and attractive that it would draw attention even if it were not associated with any known individual. Its interest is therefore immensely added to when it is learned that it was the christening robe of George Washington."

Now as then, standing in its presence provides a direct connection to a moment before the nation's infancy, when the man who would be the first American president was only an infant himself. ◆

Martha Washington's Bible

"WHEN THE MIND is deeply afflicted by those irreparable losses which are incident to humanity," Martha Washington once wrote, "the good Christian will submit without repining to the dispensations of divine Providence, and look for consolation to that Being who alone can pour balm into the bleeding heart, and who has promised to be the widow's God."

When she wrote these words, America's first First Lady had just become a widow for the second time. She had lost her first husband, Daniel Parke Custis, when she was just twenty-five. The irreparable loss she endured forty-three years later also belonged to the nation. At such trying moments, she turned to her Bible.

Scripture provided the Washingtons with images of rest and peace. In their letters, a verse from the Book of Micah (4:4) is shorthand for their longing for a period of life free from war and the concerns of state: "But they shall sit every man under his own vine and under his own fig tree, and none shall make them afraid."

Bound in plain calfskin, Martha Washington's Bible was once covered with homespun linen likely made at Mount Vernon. Its most distinctive features are six large folded maps, depicting such locales as Jerusalem and King Solomon's Temple. Its three hundred illustrations are copperplate engravings first published in London in 1715. The artist, John Sturt, was best known at the time for his popular illustrations for John Bunyan's *The Pilgrim's Progress*. His work suggests that reading this Bible was not just a religious but also a sensory and aesthetic experience, and his illustrations provide a window onto the hour or more that Martha Washington is said to have spent in prayer and reflection each day.

While the importance of faith in her husband's life has been a matter of debate among historians (page 193), Martha Washington's own devotion has never been questioned. As she wrote to a friend who tried to console her after George's death, "The precepts of our holy religion have long since taught me that, in the severe and trying scenes of life, our only sure rock of comfort and consolation is that of Divine Being, who orders and directs all things for our good." →

Martha Washington, circa 1800–25. Oil on canvas.

Title page of Martha Washington's Bible, 1783. Washington was known to read her Bible daily, and she took solace in scripture after her husband's death.

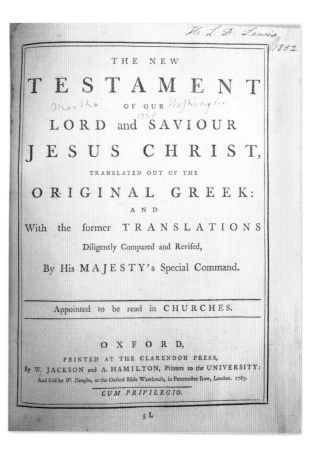

Like many family Bibles of the era, this volume of scripture served not only for worship and reflection, but also for record keeping. Five blank pages allowed ample room for the family tree of Lawrence Lewis, who married Martha's granddaughter Eleanor Parke Custis. The first entry reads: "Lawrence Lewis, born 4th April, 1767. Nellie Parke Custis Lewis, born 31st March, 1779; married at Mount Vernon, on Friday, 22d February, 1799, in the presence of General and Mrs. Martha Washington."

The view that this record provides of the private lives of the most famous family in the young nation is all the more poignant because the general would not live to see the end of 1799. As Martha soon wrote to her consoling friend:

> Bowing with humble submission to the dispensations of providence, and relying upon that support which he has promised to those who put their trust in him, I hope I have borne my late irreparable loss with Christian fortitude. To my feeling heart, the sympathy of friends, and the evidences of universal respect paid to the memory of the deceased, are truly grateful. But, while these alleviate our grief, we find that the only source of comfort is from above.

As a physical object, this Bible served the first First Lady as a place to note joyous moments of birth and celebration, while the lessons within offered solace even during her darkest hours. ◆

✳ *The Jews of the South*

Solomon Nunes Carvalho, *Interior of Beth Elohim Synagogue, Charleston, South Carolina*, 1838. Carvalho's painting was created from memory: the temple, dedicated in 1794, burned down in 1838 and was replaced two years later with the present-day structure.

FOLLOWING THE INAUGURATION of George Washington in 1789, the six major Jewish congregations in the United States—in New York, Philadelphia, Savannah, Richmond, Charleston, and Newport—announced their intention to send a letter of congratulations to the new president on behalf of all American Jews. That three of these congregations called the South home was no accident; at the time, many considered the southern states to be Jewish America's center of gravity. In the view of the leadership of the synagogues in Virginia, Georgia, and South Carolina, it was only right that a communiqué to the president from the Jewish people should originate in the South. →

Disagreements over who should write this letter delayed the process for months, however. In the meantime, Washington visited Newport and received the letter to which he wrote his famous response declaring that the "Government of the United States . . . gives to bigotry no sanction" (page 35). Likewise, the congregation in Savannah decided to send a letter of its own.

When the collaborative letter was finally sent, it represented just four of the original six congregations and somewhat awkwardly apologized for the delay. Its writer, Manuel Josephson, was a German-born merchant who was not from one of the southern congregations but from Mikveh Israel in Philadelphia (page 143). He delivered it when he had the opportunity to meet Washington a year after the inauguration.

The Address of the Hebrew Congregations in the cities of Philadelphia, New York, Charleston and Richmond.

Sir,—It is reserved for you to unite in affection for your character and person, every political and religious denomination of men; and in this will the Hebrew congregations aforesaid yield to no class of their fellow-citizens. We have been hitherto prevented, by various circumstances peculiar to our situation, from adding our congratulations to those which the rest of America have offered on your elevation to the chair of the federal government. Deign then, illustrious sir, to accept this our homage.

The wonders which the Lord of Hosts hath worked in the days of our forefathers, have taught us to observe the greatness of his wisdom and his might throughout the events of the late glorious revolution; and while we humble ourselves at his footstool in thanksgiving and praise in the blessing of his deliverance, we acknowledge you, the leader of the American armies, as his chosen and most devoted servant. But not to your sword alone is our present happiness to be ascribed; that indeed opened the way to the reign of freedom; but never was it perfectly secure till your hand gave birth to the federal constitution—and you renounced the joys of retirement to seal by your administration in peace, what you had achieved in war.

To the eternal God, who is thy refuge, we commit in our prayers, the care of thy precious life: and when, full of years, thou shalt be gathered unto the people, thy righteousness shall go before thee, and we shall remember amidst our regret, "that the Lord hath set apart the godly for himself," whilst thy name and thy virtues will remain an indelible memorial on our minds.

Manuel Josephson.
For and in behalf and under the authority of the several Congregations aforesaid.
Philadelphia, 13th Dec. 1790.

Washington replied the same day. His response, while offering less of a forceful evocation of the meaning of American religious liberty than his letter to the Newport synagogue does, is notable for its suggestion that "the power and goodness of the Almighty" were at work during the Revolution.

To the Hebrew Congregations in the cities of Philadelphia, New York, Charleston and Richmond:

Gentlemen,—The liberality of sentiment towards each other which marks every political and religious denomination of men in this country, stands unparalleled in the history of nations.

The affection of such a people is a treasure beyond the reach of calculation: and the repeated proofs which my fellow-citizens have given of their attachment to me, and approbation of my doings, form the purest source of my temporal felicity. The affectionate expressions of your address again excite my gratitude and receive my warmest acknowledgments.

The power and goodness of the Almighty were strongly manifested in the events of the late glorious revolution: and his kind interposition in our behalf, has been no less visible in the establishment of our present equal government. In war he directed the sword, and in peace he has ruled in our councils. My agency in both has been guided by the best intentions and a sense of the duty which I owe my country.

And as my exertions have hitherto been amply rewarded by the approbation of my fellow-citizens, I shall endeavour to deserve a continuance of it by my future conduct.

May the same temporal and eternal blessings which you implore for me, rest upon your congregations.

George Washington

❋　❋　❋

Among the founders of the southern Jewish communities who received Washington's blessings, there was one who might have been particularly pleased to hear the president's assurances. Unfortunately, he did not live long enough to see the independence of the country he had made his own.

One of the earliest Jewish success stories in America, Moses Lindo arrived in the Carolinas twenty years before the Revolution with a fortune he had built through his prominent indigo-trading firm in London. While he crossed the ocean to be closer to a supply he thought equal to any in the world, his emigration also came at a time when there were abundant reasons for an English Jew to abandon his mother country for the colonies.

Throughout the eighteenth century, the status of Jews in England was uncertain, sometimes seeming to improve with tolerant acts of Parliament, only to be set back by anti-Jewish sentiments that flared up at the slightest provocation. The year that Lindo set sail, 1756, was, ironically, the centenary of Oliver Cromwell's readmittance of Jews into the kingdom, the end of a three-hundred-year ban on their ability to openly live, do business, and practice their faith. Since that time, Jews born in England had secured some rights, but those born abroad still were not permitted to hold elected office unless they were willing to convert to Anglicanism. Intended as →

a defense against Catholic elements in the kingdom, the so-called Sacrament Test caught Jews in its net as well.

As a native-born Briton, Lindo would not have faced such a test of his faith, but he nonetheless sought a place where he might live more freely. Primarily intended as a means to naturalize Protestants born outside England, the Plantation Act of 1740 also allowed religious minorities, including Jews and Quakers, who were willing to live in the American colonies for at least seven years the opportunity to become British subjects with full rights. For someone such as Lindo, who seems never to have considered conversion, relocating family and business interests made sense.

From the moment of his arrival in Charleston, Lindo made new contacts throughout the colonies while continuing to exploit his relationships with the Jewish merchant classes of England and Holland, building a business successful enough that the governor of South Carolina soon named him the inspector general of all indigo in the province, which Lindo declared "equal to the BEST French."

The quality of the material in which he traded was likely not the only factor that Lindo considered when determining where to settle in the colonies. Charleston by then was on its way toward becoming the unofficial capital of the North American Jewish community—a designation further solidified by Lindo's success.

The first Jews had arrived in the city as early as 1695. Within a decade, Sephardic Jews of Spanish and Portuguese ancestry had come from England and Holland in sufficient numbers that they were noted as voters in general elections. Midway through the eighteenth century came a new wave of Jewish immigration, from the colonies farther south, where fighting with Spain caused many to flee north.

By the time of the Revolution, the Carolinas were home to the largest part of the perhaps three thousand Jews in America. Lindo himself died in 1774, but immigrants who followed in his footsteps maintained the region's reputation as the most open to Jewish religion and culture in America. This lasted until later in the century, when waves of German and Eastern European Jews settling in New York, Philadelphia, and Chicago shifted the center of Jewish American life.

Yet even after that transformation, Lindo's Charleston still influenced the religious lives of many U.S. Jews. The American branch of the modernizing movement Reform Judaism was born here in 1824, when Congregation Beth Elohim began to consider using English rather than Hebrew in its worship, among other liturgical innovations. According to the synagogue's late-nineteenth-century rabbi Barnett Elzas, it may have been inevitable that South Carolina would be the starting point for such a revolution.

Describing how the situation that Moses Lindo had faced in England could lead so quickly to new approaches to Jewish life in America, Elzas wrote, "It took the Jews of England over one hundred and fifty years to win by steady fighting, step by step, the civil and religious equality that were guaranteed to the first Jew who set foot on South Carolina soil. Is it to be wondered at that the Jew in an atmosphere of perfect civil and religious freedom should develop far more rapidly and in a different way from that in which he developed in the stifling atmosphere at home?" ◆

Thomas Jefferson's Letter to the Ursuline Sisters of New Orleans

To the Soeur Therese de St. Xavier farjon Superior, and the Nuns of the order of St. Ursula at New Orleans.

I have recieved, holy sisters, the letter you have written me wherein you express anxiety for the property vested in your institution by the former governments of Louisiana. the principles of the constitution and government of the United states are a sure guarantee to you that it will be preserved to you sacred and inviolate, and that your institution will be permitted to govern itself according to it's own voluntary rules, without interference from the civil authority. whatever diversity of shade may appear in the religious opinions of our fellow citizens, the charitable objects of your institution cannot be indifferent to any; and it's furtherance of the wholesome purposes of society, by training up it's younger members in the way they should go, cannot fail to ensure it the patronage of the government it is under. be assured it will meet all the protection which my office can give it.

I salute you, holy sisters, with friendship & respect.

Thomas Jefferson, letter to Soeur Therese de St. Xavier Farjon and the nuns of the Ursuline Sisters of New Orleans, May 15, 1804.

EXPANSIONS OF AMERICA'S BORDERS have often raised questions of religious freedom. With the Louisiana Purchase of 1803, heavily Catholic French territories became part of the United States. While it is often noted that this single land deal increased the size of the United States by more than eight hundred thousand square miles, nearly doubling it, as well as radically changing the nation's economy and its access to natural resources, it also had religious implications. New populations with new beliefs and concerns suddenly joined the majority-Protestant country →

Ursuline Convent, French Quarter, New Orleans, completed in 1752.

and naturally wondered what America's promise of religious liberty would mean for them. Concerned for their rights and their property, the Roman Catholic nuns of the Ursuline Convent of New Orleans wrote to Thomas Jefferson to inquire if they had anything to fear. In his reply of May 15, 1804, Jefferson assured the Sisters that their convent would not only be protected, but also would remain "sacred and inviolate."

The response was a relief to the Sisters, who by then had fought for decades with both civil and religious authorities for their right to own property and to control the income they earned there. Since the convent's founding in 1727, they had endured scrutiny as women who sought financial autonomy and feared their challenges would increase when they joined a nation not known for being hospitable to their faith.

Jefferson's tone was nothing if not conciliatory, but he surely knew the Sisters' worries were not unwarranted. The history of anti-Catholic sentiment in America was by then much older than the nation itself. Hatred of the Roman Catholic Church, as personified in the figure of the pope, provided a common cause for an increasingly diverse population of Protestants. With emigration becoming a distant memory for the descendants of the original colonists, Rome had come to represent for some the jettisoned constraints of Europe, a reminder of a bloody past now replaced by the limitless possibility of independence.

Jefferson himself, in fact, was prone to see Catholics as somehow unfit for democracy. For this, he faulted both their clergy—"In every country and in every age," he wrote, "the priest has been hostile to liberty"—and the laity, whom he suspected of being too much in authority's thrall to govern themselves. "History, I believe, furnishes no example of a priest-ridden people maintaining a free civil government."

Of course, Jefferson made no such comments to the Ursuline Sisters, but rather insisted that their good works would earn their new fellow-citizens' acceptance, no matter the prevalence of existing prejudices. "Whatever diversity of shade may appear in the religious opinions of our fellow citizens," he wrote, "the charitable objects of your institution cannot be indifferent to any."

After the Louisiana Purchase, the members of Ursuline order joined the United States without incident, but the decades that followed would prove they were right to be wary. Nuns especially soon became the targets of renewed anti-Catholic sentiment. In incidents such as the 1834 burning of a convent in Charlestown, Massachusetts, the "charitable objects" of such institutions were often overshadowed by the kind of bigotry that had caused the New Orleans Sisters to write their new president for reassurance. ◆

✳ *Marie Laveau*

Frank Schneider
after George Catlin,
Portrait of Marie Laveau,
1920s. Oil on canvas.
Laveau was called the
"Queen of the Voudous"
in early New Orleans.

WHEN THOMAS JEFFERSON wrote to the Ursuline Sisters of New Orleans (page 201), he could have had no idea that another young Catholic woman in that city would soon play a prominent religious role of a very different kind. For nearly a century, Marie Laveau would be known as the Queen of the Voudous. She embodied the flexibility of religious identity in this hotbed of cultural hybridity.

Formally known as vodoun, the syncretic religion more often called voodoo was made most famous in the United States by this free African American →

churchgoing Catholic. It offered a potent mixture of African, Caribbean, and European beliefs and practices, all of which Laveau had mastered at an early age.

Born in 1794 in Spanish Louisiana to an enslaved mother and a French father, she was said to have been a "beautiful, bright-eyed intelligent little Creole" in her youth, whom "the men who made New Orleans famous in those days were almost in daily attendance upon." As a young woman, Laveau became known as a healer, host, and chef. She was a sought-after entertainer of high and low alike. "Lawyers, legislators, planters, merchants all came to pay their respects to her and seek her offices," the *New York Times* reported. "She would allow no other house to be called more hospitable than her own."

She offered not mere distractions, however, but a powerful blend of the healing traditions that had by then intermingled in the region for centuries. It was said that

> her skill in medicine . . . and her ability as a nurse made her desirable at the sick-bed. Marie had a large, warm heart and tender nature and never refused a summons from the suffering, no matter how dangerous the disease. Wherever she went, she labored faithfully and earned life-long friends. During yellow fever and cholera epidemics she proved herself a noble, disinterested woman going from patient to patient administering to the wants of each and saving many from death.
>
> People were not all as enlightened and unprejudiced as they are now, and failing to understand how she arrived at her conclusions, they could imagine no better source than Voudouism. At first she encouraged this idea and delighted to cover her actions with an air of mystery.

In addition to healing, she offered services in divination and prophecy. Her satisfied customers so secured her reputation that her daughter, also known as Marie Laveau, carried on the family business, creating an American Voudoun dynasty.

While the elder Marie Laveau's legend has been recounted for generations in New Orleans and beyond, all who knew her had to admit that they had not known much of her that could be verified. Her secrets, her obituary concluded, "could only be obtained from the old lady herself, but she would never tell the smallest part of what she knew, and now her lips are closed forever and, as she could neither read nor write, not a scrap is left to chronicle the events of her exciting life." Perhaps by design, her mystery, and the spiritual practices it inspired, endured long after her death. ◆

✵ Cane Ridge Meeting House

LATE IN THE SUMMER of 1801, the Presbyterian minister Barton Stone hosted a sacramental meeting at his small stone church in Paris, Kentucky. Along with other Presbyterians, he invited area Methodists and Baptists to attend. The multiday gathering that resulted was an unexpected milestone in American religious history. Quickly outgrowing the tiny building, the Cane Ridge Revival became known as the first "camp meeting," with worship dispersing far into the surrounding countryside. It drew as many as ten thousand worshippers and is often credited as being one spark leading to the Second Great Awakening, which was just beginning to reignite the religious devotion of the nation.

Cane Ridge Meeting House, Paris, Kentucky, built in 1791.

Tales of the intensity of faith on display at Cane Ridge spread quickly and then were repeated for decades. As one letter from 1802 reported, "The people met on Friday morning, and continued till Wednesday evening, night and day, without intermission, either in the public or private exercises of devotion; and with such a degree of earnestness, that heavy showers of rain were not sufficient to disperse them."

Later in the century, the meeting's legend had only increased, with stories of its excesses suggesting a time when religion had allowed a brief release from usual behaviors and social expectations. "It began as an ordinary religious awakening, grew in fervor as it progressed, and finally reached a stage which would probably puzzle a psychologist," the *Indianapolis News* reported in 1875. "Many, if not most, of those affected by the appeals from the pulpit, were seized with strange convulsions, palsied shakings of the limbs and head, wild and uncontrollable contortions, often falling senseless or into trances, or running aimlessly about."

While such descriptions made revivals seem otherworldly to those who had never experienced one themselves, the men and women in attendance at Cane Ridge found in such extremes of worship precisely the outlet for their devotion that they had been missing. The Methodist revivalist Peter Cartwright, for example, recalled arriving as "a guilty, wretched sinner." Within a day, he found himself a changed man. "On the Saturday evening of said meeting, I went, with weeping multitudes . . . and earnestly prayed for mercy."

That such radical transformations could occur is hardly surprising, given how intense the experience seems to have been. "It was not unusual for one, two, three, and four to seven preachers to be addressing the listening thousands at the same time from the different stands erected for the purpose," Cartwright recalled. "It was said, by truthful witnesses, that at times more than one thousand persons broke out into loud shouting all at once, and that the shouts could be heard for miles around. . . . The heavenly fire spread in almost every direction." ◆

Beyond the Borders

The early United States did not contain all the spiritual influences that would eventually shape the religious character of the nation. The lands to the west and the south of the country's earliest borders were home to an even greater diversity of beliefs and practices, which today are as much a part of our past as the iconic churches of New England.

For centuries in the Caribbean, the Gulf Coast, and the Southwest, Spanish Catholicism, Native American, and African traditions interacted to create vibrant expressions of cultures at crossroads. The religious statuary of Puerto Rico and the animal-skin paintings of New Mexico both display elements of syncretism, a blending of religions so entwined that it is difficult to see where one ends and another begins.

In the middle of the nineteenth century, the already complex multireligious environment of the Southwest became even more so with the introduction of new traditions from across the Pacific. As they had from the east, new peoples arrived on American shores from the west to remake a land with beliefs and practices of their own.

Postcard depiction of Mission San Miguel, San Luis Obispo County, California, founded in 1797.

✴ *San Rafael Santo*

LONG BEFORE ANY EUROPEANS arrived in the Americas, the peoples of many Caribbean islands carved sacred figures out of wood. Originally called *zemies*, these statues functioned as mediators between the human and the divine realms. They were at once works of art and objects of devotion.

In Puerto Rico during the first decades of the sixteenth century, this tradition evolved to include depictions of Catholic saints. Santos, as the statues had come to be called, soon played a role in communal worship, private prayers, and public events. Though the names of the figures had changed along with the beliefs that they both influenced and embodied, the act of crafting celestial characters from humble materials endured.

More formally known as *santos de palo*, or "saints of wood," Puerto Rican religious statues were made entirely from a single length of rough-hewn timber in the early days of the art form. Later, as artisans wanted to present saints in ever more elaborate gestures and poses, separately rendered limbs, hands, and heads were attached to the bodies of santos. To allow for more expressive facial features, wax was introduced, often mixed with chalk to add color and detail. These statues range in size from just a few inches (often crafted for home use) to several feet tall—large enough to be displayed for veneration inside a church.

This eighteenth-century depiction of San Rafael the archangel is a classic example of the Puerto Rican santo form. Its vibrant colors show its maker's mastery of homemade paints to supply shades that have lasted for centuries, while its golden wings, two separate pieces attached to the statue's back, demonstrate that the art had moved beyond its original blocky designs.

Along with San Miguel and San Gabriel, San Rafael is one of the three archangels (here referred to by their Spanish names) who appear in scripture and whom Catholics revere. Rafael is mentioned in the Book of Tobit, which tells a story about a righteous Israelite who is stricken blind. During a time of hardship for Tobit's family, Rafael appears in the form of a man to protect Tobit's son while he travels and then to heal Tobit himself, saving him from a despair that had caused him to wish for death. As he watches the angel depart, Tobit prays, "Praise the eternal God, praise the one who rules. He punishes us; then he shows us mercy. He sends us down to the world of the dead, then he brings us up from the grave" (13:1–2).

This San Rafael, as well as the santos on the following pages, came to the National Museum of American History as part of a gift of more than three thousand objects gathered by the Puerto Rican folklorist and historian Teodoro Vidal. The 622 santos that he collected on the island provide a view of an art form that began at the intersection of indigenous and Spanish cultures and continues today. ◆

✷ San Juan Nepomuceno Santo

KNOWN IN ENGLISH as Saint John of Nepomuk, the Catholic patron saint of the sacrament of confession never left Europe during his life but began a symbolic journey to America a century before Columbus set sail.

In the spring of 1393, a priest by the name of Jan Velflín was tortured and then drowned in a Prague river on the orders of King Wenceslas IV of Bohemia. Accounts of the reason for this royal punishment vary but often rest on the priest's siding against the king in a political dispute over the management of an influential abbey. According to the saint's popular legend, however, his only crime was hearing the confession of the queen and then refusing to tell her husband what she had said under the promise of silence known as the seal of the confessional.

Because of his heroic forbearance, Velflín became the patron saint of confessors and a hero of priests—particularly members of the Society of Jesus, also known as the Jesuits, who often found themselves in similar disputes with ecclesial and temporal powers. As the Jesuits and their influence spread throughout the world during the age of Spanish and Portuguese exploration, images of the saint who had become known in Iberia as San Juan Nepomuceno were carried wherever they went.

The santo opposite was likely carved in the mid-eighteenth century in the town of San Germán in Puerto Rico's southwestern corner. It is believed to be the work of Felipe de la Espada, a prominent creator of santos from a family of wood carvers of African ancestry. Together with his son Tiburcio, he built many of the island's most significant altarpieces, which he peopled with statues similar to the one shown here.

While many such figures were small enough to be used at home, the large size of this example suggests that it was used in places where a significant group of people would have seen it. Its display, and the cult of San Juan Nepomuceno generally, likely encouraged new converts to participate in the ritual known as penance, which involves the confession of sins in the presence of a priest. Puerto Rican artists working in other media also reinforced the suggestion that clergy could be trusted with such information. One of the island's earliest recognized fine artists, the eighteenth-century painter José Campeche, depicted the saint with a halo of letters around his head spelling out the Latin word *tacui*, "I did keep silent."

Velflín's international popularity is an indication that such guarantees of confidentiality transcended borders. Images of the murdered cleric can be seen not only in countries that the Jesuits visited during the colonial period, but also throughout the region in which he lived. While European depictions often show the saint with a finger to his lips, as if refusing to divulge the sins he has heard, in this American santo he stands with his arms wide and his head slightly tilted, a posture suggesting that he is ready to listen. ◆

San Juan Nepomuceno santo, circa 1754. Wood. San Juan is the patron saint of the sacrament of confession.

❋ *Virgen de Monserrat Santo*

FROM THE MOMENT when Christopher Columbus raised a banner bearing a cross on the shore of the island of San Salvador, stories drawn from the Christian faith have been planted in the soil of the Americas. Across the centuries, perhaps no religious phenomenon has proved as popular, flexible, and enduring in this regard as apparitions of Mary, the mother of Jesus.

At the end of the sixteenth century, a farmer in the village of Hormigueros in southwestern Puerto Rico cried out to the Virgin Mary when a bull attacked him. According to legend, the farmer, Gerardo González, was miraculously saved by the saint's intercession. The bull's legs broke under its own weight, and its head fell toward the earth as if it were bowing in prayer. In gratitude, González built a church on the spot of his brush with death and dedicated it to the figure of the Mother of God known as Our Lady of Montserrat.

This depiction of the Virgin traces its origins to a mountain in the Catalonia region of Spain where, tradition maintains, Catholic shepherds once hid to escape invading Moorish armies. The shepherds heard singing and saw lights emanating from a small cave. Upon investigating, they discovered a statue of a woman seated with a child, which all presumed to be Mary and Jesus.

Yet just as Christianity in America has often blended symbols of European and indigenous beliefs, it is possible that the identification of the discovered statue as a figure of the Virgin Mary did much the same. As Stephen Benko, a scholar of the intersections of pagan Rome and early Christianity, notes, "The iconography of Isis and [her son] Horus was basically adopted by Christians when they started to portray Mary and Jesus as Mother and Child." In the Americas, this iconography would make a further journey. Derived from pagan roots, the image of the Mother and Child mingled with different non-Christian influences to create a novel expression of faith.

This santo of the Virgen de Monserrat was completed in the late eighteenth century. The four figures it shows are the Virgin and the infant Jesus looking down from above, and the farmer González and the stricken bull below. One of the Virgin's hands holds an orb that stands for Christ's dominion over the world. Her other hand is open, reaching down as if to separate her devoted follower from the beast. It is at once a scene from a famous miraculous tale and a reflection of how the faithful regard the presence of the Mother of God in their lives. Two hundred years after the miracle of the bull, González's story had become an important part of the island's national and religious identity. ◆

✺ Cathedral Basilica of Saint Augustine

Postcard depicting the Cathedral Basilica of Saint Augustine, Florida, dedicated in 1797. Home to the oldest Roman Catholic parish in what is today the United States, the cathedral stands on land that was used for churches under Spanish and English rule before Florida became the twenty-seventh state in 1845.

BUILT ON ONE of the oldest church sites in the continental United States, Florida's Cathedral Basilica of Saint Augustine was dedicated in 1797 on land that had supported houses of worship since the sixteenth century. The first church there, constructed when Spanish territory extended to present-day Georgia, lasted only a short time before it burned to the ground during an English attack led by the sea captain Sir Francis Drake in 1586. The hastily erected replacement was also lost to a fire. A century later, in 1702, a third church was destroyed, but the colonists of Saint Augustine vowed to build again.

For a time it appeared that they would not have the chance. Midway through the eighteenth century, the Spanish abandoned the region to England and with it, it seemed, the prospect of Catholicism surviving as a significant cultural force in this part of the Americas. Yet when the English began to plan settlements of their own here, they discovered the climate might be better suited to southern Europeans than to colonists from the British Isles. Thanks to the recruiting efforts of the Scottish-born physician Andrew Turnbull, who had a Greek wife and knew the Mediterranean region well, more than a thousand farmers and other laborers came over from Italy, Minorca, and Greece. Though the colony they built, called New Smyrna after the city of Mrs. Turnbull's birth, suffered devastating losses from disease, the newly arrived settlers succeeded in bringing the Catholic faith back to the area, then known as British East Florida. They did not, however, manage to build a church of their own.

After the Spanish regained control of the area in 1784, they discovered that nothing remained of Saint Augustine's ecclesiastic structures but a "pile of useless masonry." One of the first initiatives called for was the building of a cathedral to replace the churches that had been lost. The settlement's diverse population, including prominent planters, skilled artisans, and workers of both European and African descent, contributed money and labor to its construction. An Irish priest in the service of the Spanish Crown, Father Miguel O'Reilly, dedicated the cathedral in 1797. Originally sent to America to minister to the Minorcans, O'Reilly managed to remain in the region through its changes in temporal power and served generations of Florida's Catholics as both priest and teacher. A nearby property that he purchased to serve as the new cathedral's rectory is the oldest dwelling still standing in the city.

The present church structure combines Spanish mission and neoclassical styles, which give it the appearance of having always watched over the city. Already in the nineteenth century it was often referred to as "the old cathedral," perhaps in part because it could boast "the oldest bells in America," as one account from the time put it. Remnants of the prior destroyed churches, the bells are stamped with dates as early as 1689. The tones used to call the faithful to worship here remained unchanged as Florida fell under Spanish and British rule and finally joined the United States in 1845. ◆

✳ Popé

Cliff Fragua, *Popé*, 2005. Marble. The leader of the Pueblo Revolt of 1680, Popé became a model of religious resistance among the peoples of the Southwest. This statue, in the U.S. Capitol's National Statuary Hall, is an indication that his story still resonates.

BY THE MIDDLE of the sixteenth century, Spanish explorers were bringing a potent blend of Christianity and military might into the American Southwest. The conquistador Francisco Vázquez de Coronado marched from the land then known as New Spain, present-day Mexico, as far north as territory that later became the state of Kansas. Along the way, he began wars against the indigenous peoples who crossed his path, sparking resentments that would continue for more than a century.

Traveling with Coronado's soldiers, Spanish missionaries attempted to quell hostilities by converting the Pueblo Indians, Tewa-speaking people who had previously lived undisturbed in dozens of large settlements, also known as pueblos. Despite massive efforts by Franciscans that included baptizing thousands, local religious practices not only endured but became formidable sources of resistance. Dances invoking kachinas, the spirit beings of Pueblo cosmology, were used to maintain traditional knowledge and allegiances in the face of Christian teachings, which were often offered with force.

After the suppression of native religions intensified in 1675, a spiritual leader known as Popé emerged to marshal the most effective uprising against the spread of Christianity in the western United States. A healer and a shaman, he had been arrested on charges of sorcery during the heightened effort to quash indigenous beliefs. Many of the dozens of holy men taken captive then were executed. Popé was not killed but was beaten, which left scars across his back. On his release, he was adamant about fighting Spanish influence.

Born in the pueblo of San Juan in what is now New Mexico, Popé lived in the neighboring pueblo of Taos at the time of his insurgency. Such connections allowed him to create alliances not only among a number of pueblos, but also with the Apache people to the east. In the summer of 1680, Popé and other disaffected leaders gathered a force of eight thousand, which vastly outnumbered the European settlers in the area. In a series of attacks that came to be known as the Pueblo Revolt, hundreds of Spaniards were killed, including more than twenty Franciscan friars. After the survivors fled, Popé hoped to erase every sign of the faith that had been imposed on the Pueblo villages. He destroyed Catholic churches, images, and ritual objects and punished those among his people who used the Spanish language or the Spanish names they had been given.

Popé's rebellion succeeded in keeping the Spanish out for more than a decade following his first attacks, until after his death. The Spanish retook much of the region in 1692, but Popé's memory endured even as many of his former followers converted to Christianity. Though his efforts ultimately failed, his beliefs survived through adaptation, as can be seen in the blended Christian–Native American practices still found at some Catholic churches in the area. ◆

✳ Retablo *of Santo Niño de Atocha*

Retablo of Santo Niño de
Atocha, 1840–50.

EVEN BEFORE POPÉ and the Pueblo Revolt (page 216), New Mexico was a site of interreligious blending and conflict. While for the most part this involved Spanish Catholicism and indigenous traditions, other influences can be seen as well.

As in the English colonies and the early republic, many of the enslaved laborers brought into New Spain carried spiritual traditions of their own with them. The enslaved North African known as Esteban de Dorantes adds surprising diversity to the well-known story of American exploration and conquest. Born into a Muslim family in Morocco circa 1500 and sold into slavery as a teenager, he converted to Christianity in Spain before being taken by his owner on an expedition to the

Americas. Through an unlikely series of events, he became one of the first men to cross the North American continent. His travels through what are now Texas and New Mexico, as well as the subsequent journeys of hundreds of North African slaves attached to the 1540 expedition of Francisco Vázquez de Coronado, provide intriguing hints of the presence of Muslims at the heart of the land that would become the United States.

Esteban is just one example of how Islamic history entwined with religion in early America. Another is one of the most popular depictions of Jesus Christ throughout Mexico and the Southwest, El Santo Niño de Atocha, or the Holy Infant of Atocha. When Spain was under Islamic rule in the thirteenth century, the town of Atocha remained home to many Christians. According to medieval accounts, the Christian men there were taken prisoner by Moorish soldiers and allowed to eat only what the children of the town brought them. A boy dressed as a pilgrim visited nightly, offering food from a gourd that never seemed to empty. When some suggested that this boy must be the Christ child, the veneration of El Santo Niño de Atocha was born.

Perhaps because of his appeal to others who had endured the invasion of a new religion, the Holy Infant of Atocha became particularly popular in the Americas. Early in the nineteenth century, a prominent planter in the New Mexican village of El Potrero, Severiano Medina, fell gravely ill and prayed for relief. After his recovery, he constructed a shrine to El Santo Niño in the foothills of the Sangre de Cristo Mountains. Soon it became a pilgrimage site, attracting the attention of the religious brotherhood called the Penitentes. Known for their service to the community and for their often extreme religious discipline, they traced their history to medieval Europe's flagellant orders of monks, who would whip themselves in repentance for the world's sins. During their arduous devotional practices, such as carrying crosses great distances across desert terrain, the Penitentes recited lengthy litanies, including a poignant invocation of the legendary child:

> Holy Infant of Atocha,
> Little pastor of your sheep,
> Accept this soul into your flock
> And pardon its lament.

The image shown opposite depicts the child in a form of devotional art known as a *retablo*. It was made in Santa Fe six centuries after the legend of the prisoners and their miraculous preservation began to spread throughout northern Spain. Like the travels of Esteban de Dorantes, the journey of El Santo Niño de Atocha to America provides a view into how the religious conflicts of the Old World came to influence the New. ◆

✸ *Mission Elk-Hide Painting*

Possibly Francisco Xavier Romero, elk-hide painting, eighteenth century. Combining indigenous techniques with Christian subject matter, hide paintings such as this one, showing Saint Anthony of Padua holding the infant Jesus, provided decoration in many churches throughout the Southwest.

THE TRADITION OF MAKING images on animal hides dates back centuries in America. As early as 1540, the Spanish explorer Francisco Vázquez de Coronado recorded seeing "skins . . . very well dressed"; within a century, settlers were so taken by the elaborate paintings adorning Native American ceremonial robes that they shipped them back in great numbers for display in Europe. In 1805, the Lewis and Clark Expedition sent Thomas Jefferson a painted hide, which he featured prominently in the "Indian Hall" that greeted guests to Monticello.

Long before European Americans and their descendants took an interest, various tribes developed this distinctive art form, which now provides an unparalleled view of Native American life. The earliest hide paintings feature complex geometric patterns as well as scenes of battle and other significant events, all of them drawn from histories and symbol systems largely unchanged for generations. The hides also offer a glimpse of a culture in the midst of a transition that would reshape every element of its civilization. With the arrival of Catholicism in the Indian lands of the Southwest, the paintings began to assimilate Christian themes and images into indigenous forms.

The elk-hide painting shown opposite depicts Anthony of Padua holding the infant Jesus. The medieval Italian saint wears a brown robe tied with a rope and his hair in a tonsure—both indicators that he was a follower of Saint Francis of Assisi—and he stands above a book that is likely the Rule of the Franciscan Order. Saint Anthony was said to be such a gifted preacher that he could communicate with people of all stations and even to nonhuman audiences. In a famous story dramatizing this gift, a school of fish came to the surface of the water as he delivered a seaside sermon.

The Spanish missionaries attempting to spread the Gospel among the Pueblo people badly needed such communicative ability. Their desire to translate the essentials of Christianity across a divide of language and culture led these Franciscan friars to learn from local artists how to render Christian images in forms to which they hoped the Pueblo would more readily respond. Churches built throughout the region that would become New Mexico incorporated depictions of Catholic saints alongside symbols more immediately recognizable by prospective converts.

Painted with tints made from local plants, this elk-hide Saint Anthony was completed in the eighteenth century, possibly by the Mexico City–born cobbler and self-taught artist Francisco Xavier Romero. Discovered in a mission church in New Mexico late in the nineteenth century, it has been part of the Smithsonian's collection almost since the founding of the institution. ◆

❋ Retablo *of Our Lady of Guadalupe*

WITHIN HALF A CENTURY of the arrival of European beliefs in the Americas, Christian efforts to convert the indigenous peoples were well underway. Among the early converts was a middle-aged Aztec man who had one of the most influential religious experiences in history.

According to legend, fifty-seven-year-old Juan Diego was visited four times in 1531 by the Virgin Mary, the mother of Jesus Christ. On Tepeyac Hill in central Mexico, he met a woman whose skin seemed to emit light. Making her identity known to him, she declared, "My dear little son, I love you. I desire you to know who I am. I am the ever-virgin Mary, Mother of the true God who gives life and maintains its existence. He created all things. He is in all places. He is Lord of Heaven and Earth."

She instructed him to have a church built on the place of their meeting and to tell the local bishop what he had seen. When the bishop did not believe him, the Virgin visited Juan Diego again, this time promising to give him signs with which to convince those in doubt. Miraculous events followed, including seemingly impossible healings and flowers that bloomed in the wintertime. The Aztec carried several of the latter inside his *tilma*, a poncholike cape, to show the bishop, and when he opened it he revealed the most significant miracle of all. On the inner lining was a vibrant image of the Virgin. Worn by an unlikely messenger, the tilma was immediately taken as evidence that God would smile upon those who accepted the new faith that the Spaniards had brought.

After the tilma was displayed in the local cathedral, thousands of natives of the land that would become New Spain converted to Christianity. Juan Diego's vision appealed to them not only because it had appeared to a man like him, but also because the features of its Mother of God resembled those of the people of Tepeyac. Our Lady of Guadalupe is a dark-haired, brown-skinned Virgin Mary, whom Spanish missionaries seeking to convert Indians to Christianity quickly popularized through countless reproductions, including the seventeenth-century *retablo* shown opposite.

Made circa 1698 by an anonymous artist in the region that is now New Mexico, this small devotional painting is clearly a work of Catholic art, but elements of its presentation draw on pre-Christian traditions. The cloak that the Virgin wears is blue-green, a color reserved for deities of certain native religions. Likewise, the rays of light emanating from her body may suggest the spikes of the maguey plant, from which a sacred drink used in religious rites was derived.

The bottom of the retablo also shows Juan Diego himself. With arms outstretched, he appears to be unfurling his tilma to let the world know of the visions granted to the people of the Americas. ◆

✳ *El Santuario de Chimayo*

El Santuario de Chimayo, New Mexico, built in 1816. This small church in the shadow of the Sangre de Cristo Mountains is one of the most popular Catholic pilgrimage sites in the country.

ACCORDING TO LEGEND, around 1810, a Spanish friar traveling through the desert in what is now northern New Mexico saw a mysterious light emanating from a patch of earth near the Santa Cruz River. When he dug to find its source, he discovered a rough-hewn crucifix. He cleaned it off and brought it to a nearby mission church, but the next day it was missing. Passing by the spot where it had been buried, he saw a strange light again and realized that the crucifix had returned to where he had found it. The friar erected a church there in 1816, which was later known as El Santuario de Chimayo.

A 1915 account says that this tiny Catholic shrine in the foothills of the Sangre de Cristo Mountains had been built roughly a century before, "on the spot where for long years wonderful cures had been performed by the strange virtue of the soil." From its earliest days, the church had been a place that "every day throughout the year" attracted "men, women, and children from all directions . . . all inspired with full faith in the supernatural remedial power that is here manifested."

"How and when the healing virtues of the sacred earth of this favored spot were first manifested, not even tradition tells us," the church's early chronicler wrote. All that was known was this:

> In the beginning of the nineteenth century there was a pious citizen of Chimayo on whom Providence had bestowed greater temporal prosperity than on his neighbors, and who wished to show his appreciation of his blessings in some notable way. So . . . he built a church to the glory of God. It was finished in 1816, amid general rejoicing that there should be a suitable tabernacle for worship and for the giving of thanks for the blessings of restored health and strength.

Arriving "in carriages, in wagons, on horses, on burros, or on foot," families often brought with them "some little one deformed from birth or injured by accident, whose case is beyond the curative power of the most skillful physician." They would then approach a small hole cut in the church floor—*el pocito*, the "little well," as it is called—where it was believed the legendary light-emitting crucifix was once buried. Those who made use of the powers of *el pocito* likely did not concern themselves with how these miracles began, but another legend suggests that the local Pueblo people had visited this site for much the same purpose long before the first Spanish missionaries arrived.

Today, El Santuario de Chimayo is one of the most popular pilgrimage destinations in the country. Every year during Holy Week, when Christians remember the death of Jesus Christ and celebrate his resurrection, the faithful come by the thousands, often approaching the little well where the cross was found from great distances that they travel on their knees. El Santuario's blending of folk practices with liturgical worship, and of Catholic belief with Native American traditions, is a testament to the creativity that has marked religion in America from the beginning. ◆

✳ *Junípero Serra*

A 1913 postcard depiction of Junípero Serra, the controversial leader of the California missions.

IN THE FINAL third of the eighteenth century, when the first rumblings of the War for Independence could be heard in the thirteen English colonies, another kind of revolution was already underway on the other side of the continent.

In 1769, the Franciscan priest Junípero Serra arrived in Alta California, which was the northern portion of the Province of the Californias and would become the southwest corner of the United States a century later. Serra had been working as a missionary in New Spain for a decade by that time, but he made his longest-lasting impact by establishing the first Spanish missions in what is now the state of California, which were largely responsible for spreading the Catholic faith among the Native peoples of the region. Beginning with the mission he called San Diego, Serra's efforts mapped out the cities that would be built on the church sites he established, including San Buenaventura, San Francisco, San Gabriel, and Santa Clara.

Born on the Spanish island of Majorca in 1713, Serra, like many other missionaries to the Americas, was educated by the Franciscans. He began studying for the priesthood at the age of fifteen, driven by both his religious devotion and the poverty of his farming family. At the age of thirty-six, he sailed for New Spain, where he served for two decades, including many years among the Pame people of central Mexico.

Though failing in health and of advanced age, Serra volunteered to venture into California in 1767. Following his personal motto, *Siempre adelante, nunca atrás* (Always forward, never back), he worked feverishly for fifteen years to transform the culture of the region. Not only did he play a role in the conversion of thousands; he permanently altered the lifeways he encountered by insisting that Indians who came to live in his missions take up European crafts and agricultural practices. He provided cattle and sheep for the new Christians to pasture on the small tracts of land he permitted them and, drawing on his experience as a farmer's son, also made seeds and tools available to encourage cultivation of the soil. Praised by Spanish colonizers and re-created throughout the region, Serra's missions often included conditions that amounted to slavery for those whom they were ostensibly built to serve. His motto may have implied steady progress to his fellow missionaries, but it meant incalculable loss to many others.

When the Roman Catholic Church began considering Serra for sainthood, some objected that he was no saint during his lifetime. The missions he founded are often criticized for their harsh methods of evangelism and mistreatment of indigenous people, which at times included the use of corporal punishment. His supporters counter that he is rightly remembered as the Apostle of California for bringing the Gospel to the west coast of the Americas.

Pope Francis canonized Serra as part of his visit to Washington, DC, on September 23, 2015. During the papal Mass that made this sainthood official in the eyes of the Catholic Church, the iron cross that Maryland Catholics used in the seventeenth century (page 81) was also present, momentarily uniting two distant moments in American Catholic history. ◆

❋ Yeung Wo Temple

Yeung Wo Temple, San Francisco, founded in 1852. When the first Chinese temples opened in San Francisco in the 1850s, each was affiliated with the region or town its members had left behind.

BY THE TIME it joined the Union in 1850, California had a sizable population of Chinese immigrants who had crossed the Pacific to work on the railroads and in gold mines. A small number had been in America far longer than that, including an early leader of the Chinese community in San Francisco.

Known to English speakers as Norman Assing, he had arrived in South Carolina in 1820 and then made his way west. Most of his compatriots came with the intention of working for a time and then returning home. Yet many others, such as Assing, made a new home here, in the process building places in which to practice their beliefs.

With new Chinese laborers arriving nearly every day in California in the 1840s, this immigrant community organized itself into six regional associations, or *huiguan*, which provided social support for those from the same cities or towns in China. Under the auspices of the *huiguan* known as the Yeung Wo Association, Assing set about establishing the first Chinese temple in California. Calling it a "joss house," a name derived from the Latin *deus*, newspaper accounts captured the public debut, circa 1852, of a religion new to America. The *San Francisco Whig* reported:

> Yesterday morning, the Chinese dedicated their Joss house, which is situated on the westerly side of Telegraph Hill. At sunrise, a gorgeous crimson banner . . . was hoisted on a flag staff at the corner of the house, and the Chinese began to assemble in crowds about nine o'clock. The performances commenced by placing three tablets or signs, one over the tip of the door, and the other two, upright, on either side. As soon as these were fast, fire was applied to about a thousand Chinese fire crackers. . . . Then two carved images or josses, resembling hideous owls, the presiding deities of the place, were placed on either side of the steps, and another tremendous explosion of the crackers ensued.

The term "joss house" soon became a common descriptor for Buddhist temples in the United States, but religious practitioners at the Yeung Wo Temple adhered to a mixture of Taoism and folk beliefs particular to the region of China from which they had come. Within the temple that day, priests performed a ritual formally opening the space, accompanied by a troupe of actors and a small band playing traditional Chinese instruments. "At the end of this symphony, the performers came forward, two at a time, to the front of the stage, and kneeling down, made adoration to a sacred tablet; then followed a recitation and chorus, and another band performance," the *Whig*'s correspondent noted. "These ceremonies were exceedingly novel and interesting."

Though he played no religious role in the temple dedication, Norman Assing had orchestrated it all. As a successful businessman, he helped to make San Francisco's Chinatown into a model ethnic enclave that would be replicated in cities across the country. Creating spaces where immigrants could maintain the beliefs and practices they had brought with them across the ocean, community organizers such as Assing and humble temples such as Yeung Wo allowed many temporary laborers to imagine that they could make a home for themselves in America. ◆

✳ Torah Mantle

AS NORMAN ASSING was organizing the construction of the first Chinese temple in California (page 228), a small group of Jewish merchants laid the groundwork not far away for the first California synagogue. German Jews began arriving in San Francisco in the 1840s and soon had an organization with a name befitting the Gold Rush era: the Eureka Benevolent Society. Founded to "afford aid and relief to indigent, sick, and infirm Jews; to bury the dead; and in general to relieve and aid co-religionists who might be in poverty or distress," it sponsored both communal worship ceremonies, such as the first High Holidays services west of the Mississippi, and more intimate ritual occasions, including the city's first circumcision. Such occasions were considered so novel that the *Daily Alta California* reported on them with obvious excitement, as was the case in 1850 with the celebration of the start of the month of Tamuz in the Jewish calendar, which included Hebrew blessings in remembrance of Jerusalem, the holy city of Judaism, offered in a city where immigrant Jews hoped to make a new home:

Above Congregation Emanu-El, San Francisco, founded in 1850. This temple was home to the first organized Jewish community in California.

Opposite Torah mantle, 1785. Silk. Religious items such as this German-made Torah cover traveled west with Jewish pioneers.

> Hebrew Ceremony—One of the most solemn and impressive ceremonies of the Hebrew faith was performed yesterday. . . . At the same time, we understand, a Jewish Benevolent Society was formed. As there are many enterprising and useful citizens of the Jewish persuasion in our community, we have no doubt that this society will be a large one, and that ere long we shall hear of the establishment of a synagogue in San Francisco.

Within a few years, there were in fact two more synagogues in the Bay Area, and a vibrant Jewish community was well established.

One founding father of Jewish San Francisco was a Bavarian dry-goods dealer named August Helbing. Born in Munich in 1824, he emigrated to America as a young man. Meeting many fellow Jews on his journey and in the city he soon called home, he saw that more than a few would need help. "Every arrival of steamer and sailing vessel added large numbers to the population," he said. "It became apparent to me that concerted action should be had in order to take more efficient care of Israelites landing here, broken in health or destitute of means."

The German-made silk Torah mantle shown opposite was brought to San Francisco by Jewish immigrants of Helbing's generation. Like the first men and women who prayed in its presence in America, it carried the beliefs of the country they had left behind into a land that would become home not just to "the People of the Book" but to many peoples of many books. ◆

Conclusion

IN THE SPRING OF 1831—around the time when the Cherokee people were being forced west and adopting new religious traditions along the way, the enslaved Muslim Omar ibn Said was writing the Arabic account of his life, the new religion of Mormonism was beginning to find converts, and the Second Great Awakening was nearing its end after having redrawn the spiritual map of the nation—one of the most celebrated observers of early America began to take stock of the land and its people.

"On my arrival in the United States, it was the religious aspect of the country that first struck my eye," the French historian and cultural critic Alexis de Tocqueville wrote, "and the longer I stayed there, the more I perceived the great political consequences resulting from this new state of things." In Europe, he noted, "I had almost always seen the spirit of religion and the spirit of freedom marching in opposite directions." In the United States, meanwhile, things were quite different: "But in America I found they were intimately united and that they reigned in common over the same country."

Today, some eighteen decades after Tocqueville wrote this, generations of experience with the ways in which "the spirit of religion" and "the spirit of freedom" influence each other have taught us that though they have often "reigned in common," as he described it, that situation has a volatility all its own.

In a country where religious disagreement is not only expected but seen as essential, it should come as no surprise that every person, document, house of worship, and object shown and described in the preceding pages will not resonate with the beliefs of all readers. Some will challenge, others will affirm, yet all played a role in making the nation what it is today.

"I do not know whether all the Americans have a sincere faith in their religion—for who can search the human heart?—but I am certain that they hold it to be indispensable to the maintenance of republican institutions," Tocqueville continued. "In the United States, the influence of religion is not confined to the manners, but it extends to the intelligence of the people."

According to the Pew Research Center, the ranks of religiously unaffiliated Americans have never been larger than during the first two decades of the twenty-first century, and their numbers seem to be on the rise. Yet it is unlikely that the United States will cease to be one of the most religious nations on earth any time soon. As the people, places, and things described throughout this book demonstrate, the changing roles of faith across the country have variously comforted, beguiled, and frustrated Americans from the beginning, but they have never gone away.

"In America religion is perhaps less powerful than it has been at certain periods and among certain nations," Tocqueville concluded, "but its influence is more lasting." ◆

Edward Hicks, *The Peaceable Kingdom* (detail), 1826. Oil on canvas.

Sources

INTRODUCTION

Page 1, "In their voyage": Lord Baltimore, "Instructions," November 13, 1633, National Humanities Center, http://nationalhumanitiescenter.org/pds/amerbegin/settlement/text4/BaltimoreInstructions.pdf.

Page 2, "on English-speaking American soil": "Pope Francis' Mass Includes Georgetown's 17th Century Iron Cross," September 14, 2015, Georgetown University, www.georgetown.edu/iron-cross-at-first-pope-francis-mass-in-us.

Page 4, "by far the most widely used": John Witte Jr. and Joel A. Nichols, *Religion and the American Constitutional Experiment* (Boulder, CO: Westview, 2011), 1.

NEW ENGLAND

Page 12, "If therefore the verses": Preface to *The Whole Booke of Psalmes* (Cambridge, MA: Stephen Daye, 1640), facsimile reprint (New York: Dodd, Mead, 1903), www.thefederalistpapers.org/wp-content/uploads/2013/02/The-Bay-Psalm-Book.pdf.

Page 13, "draw the natives": John Winthrop, quoted in Richard W. Cogley, *John Eliot's Mission to the Indians before King Philip's War* (Cambridge, MA: Harvard University Press, 2009), 1.

Page 13, "When I first attempted it": John Eliot, "The Letter of Mr. Eliot to T. S. Concerning the Late Work of God among the Indians," in *Tracts Relating to the Attempts to Convert to Christianity the Indians of New England*, Collections of the Massachusetts Historical Society, 3rd ser., vol. 4 (Cambridge, MA: Charles Folsom, 1834), 50.

Page 13, "some paines and teaching": John Eliot, "Much Respected and Beloved in Our Lord Jesus," in *Attempts to Convert to Christianity*, 144.

Page 14, "I told [them]": Eliot, "Letter of Mr. Eliot to T. S.," 50.

Page 15, "Indian religion": George S. Snyderman, "The Function of Wampum in Iroquois Religion," *American Philosophical Society Proceedings* 105, no. 6 (December 1961): 572.

Page 16, "the universal bonds": Ashbel Woodward, *Wampum: A Paper Presented to the Numismatic and Antiquarian Society of Philadelphia* (Albany, NY: Munsell, 1880), 21.

Page 17, "prodigious large belt": *Documents Relative to the Colonial History of the State of New-York*, vol. 7 (Albany, NY: Weed and Parsons, 1856), 56.

Page 19, "a city upon a hill": John Winthrop, "A Model of Christian Charity" (speech given aboard the *Arbella*, 1630), http://winthropsociety.com/doc.charity.php.

Page 19, "The ministers and ruling elders": Arthur B. Ellis, *History of the First Church in Boston, 1630–1880* (Boston: Hall and Whiting, 1881), 17.

Page 21, "We kept a day of thanksgiving": John Winthrop, *History of New England, 1630–1649*, vol. 1 (New York: Charles Scribner's Sons, 1895), 51.

Page 21, "Let us choose life": Winthrop, "Model of Christian Charity."

Page 23, "I have been guided": John F. Kennedy, "City upon a Hill" (speech, Boston, January 9, 1961), http://millercenter.org/president/kennedy/speeches/speech-3364.

Page 23, "The past few days": Ronald Reagan, Farewell Speech (Washington DC, January 11, 1989), www.pbs.org/wgbh/americanexperience/features/primary-resources/reagan-farewell/.

Page 23, "It was right here": Barack Obama, "University of Massachusetts at Boston Commencement Address" (June 2, 2006), http://obamaspeeches.com/074-University-of-Massachusetts-at-Boston-Commencement-Address-Obama-Speech.htm.

Page 25, "a woman of a ready wit": Winthrop, *History of New England*, 239.

Page 25, "After she had repeated": John Winthrop, *A Short Story of the Rise, Reign, and Ruine of the Antinomians, Familists and Libertines* (1644), in *The Antinomian Controversy, 1636–1638: A Documentary History*, 2nd ed., ed. David D. Hall (Durham, NC: Duke University Press, 1990), 207.

Page 25, "troubled the peace": John Winthrop, quoted in Thomas Hutchinson, *History of the Colony and Province of Massachusetts* (Boston: Thomas and John Fleet, 1767), 482.

Page 26, "the poorer sort of people": Winthrop, *History of New England*, 52.

Page 26, "a man godly and zealous": William Bradford, quoted in Eugene Aubrey Stratton, *Plymouth Colony, Its History and People, 1620–1691* (Salt Lake City: Ancestry Publishing, 1986), 42.

Page 27, "erroneous, and very dangerous": Winthrop, *History of New England*, 154.

Page 27, "First, others (and myselfe)": Roger Williams, "A Key into the Language of America" (London: Gregory Dexter, 1643), reprinted in *Collections of the Rhode-Island Historical Society*, vol. 1 (Providence: John Miller, 1827), 20.

Page 29, "From Adam and Noah that they sprang": Roger Williams, *A Key in the Language of America* (London: Gregory Dexter, 1643), 4.

Page 31, "resident strangers": Oscar Reiss, *The Jews in Colonial America* (Jefferson, NC: Mcfarland, 2004), 47.

Page 33, "been acquainted with six rabbies": *The Literary Diary of Ezra Stiles* (New York: Charles Scribner's Sons, 1901), 77.

Page 33, "express'd much concern": "Moses Seixas to Aaron Lopez," letter, May 11, 1781, in *Commerce of Rhode Island, 1726–1800*, vol. 2, *1775–1800* (Boston: Massachusetts Historical Society, 1915), 110.

Page 33, "the children of the Stock of Abraham": Moses Seixas, letter from Congregation Yeshuat Israel to George Washington, August 17, 1790, www.tourosynagogue.org/history-learning/tsf-intro-menu/slom-scholarship/85-seixas-letter.

Page 33, "It is now no more": George Washington to the Hebrew Congregation at Newport, letter, August 18, 1790, www.tourosynagogue.org/history-learning/gw-letter.

Page 36, "Some young persons": John Hale, *A Modest Enquiry into the Nature of Witchcraft* (Boston: B. Green and J. Allen, 1697), 132, http://salem.lib.virginia.edu/archives/ModestEnquiry/index.html.

Page 36, "Make a cake": Alexander Roberts, *Treatise of Witchcraft* (London: Samual Man, 1616), 53, www.gutenberg.org/ebooks/17209.

Page 36, "By these means": Samuel Parris, quoted in Charles Wentworth Upham, *Salem Witchcraft: With an Account of Salem Village, and a History* (Salem, MA: Wiggin and Lunt, 1867), 95.

Page 39, "I don't know why": Cotton Mather, quoted in George L. Kittredge, "Some Lost Works of Cotton Mather," in *Proceedings of the Massachusetts Historical Society*, vol. 45 (Boston: Massachusetts Historical Society, 1912), 430.

Page 45, "There is no want": Jonathan Edwards, "Sinners in the Hands of an Angry God: A Sermon Preached at Enfield, July 8th, 1741," http://digitalcommons.unl.edu/cgi/viewcontent.cgi?article=1053&context=etas.

Page 45, "the most brilliant": George Marsden, *Jonathan Edwards: A Life* (New Haven, CT: Yale University Press, 2004), 1.

Page 45, "Love, the Sum of All Virtues": Jonathan Edwards, "Sermon One: Love, the Sum of All Virtues," in *Works of Jonathan Edwards*, vol. 8., ed. Paul Ramsey (New Haven, CT: Yale University Press, 1989), 129–48.

Page 45, "Mt. Rushmore of Protestant American shapers": Martin Marty, "Billy Graham Taught Christians News Ways of Being in the World," September 30, 2013, Martin Marty Center for the Advanced Study of Religion, University of Chicago Divinity School, https://divinity.uchicago.edu/sightings/billy-graham-taught-christians-new-ways-being-world-martin-e-marty.

Page 47, "There is as much": J. F., "Reply to Mr. Wright," *Liberator*, July 2, 1836, 2.

Page 48, "Bell-making remained": Robert Martello, *Midnight Ride, Industrial Dawn: Paul Revere and the Growth of American Enterprise* (Baltimore: Johns Hopkins University Press, 2010), 165.

Page 48, "The sound is not clear and prolonged": Rev. William Bentley, quoted in Robert Martello, *Midnight Ride, Industrial Dawn: Paul Revere and the Growth of American Enterprise* (Baltimore: Johns Hopkins University Press, 2010), 157.

Page 50, "Mr. Revere has not yet learned": William Bentley, *The Diary of William Bentley*, vol. 3, *1803–1810* (Salem, MA: Essex Institute, 1911).

Page 50, "The Chapel Church": Henry Wilder Foote, *Annals of King's Chapel from the Puritan Age of New England to the Present Day*, vol. 2 (Boston: Little, Brown, 1896), 622.

Page 52, "One of my brothers": *Testimonies of the Life, Character, Revelations and Doctrines of Mother Ann Lee* (Albany, NY: Weed and Parsons, 1888), 42.

Page 53, "At half past seven P.M.": "Four Months among the Shakers," *Oneida Circular*, May 10, 1869, 5.

Page 55, "as if you had": *Mother Ann Lee*, 243.

Page 56, "When the late rebellion commenced": Edward Bass, quoted in Daniel Dulany Addison, *The Life and Times of Edward Bass, First Bishop of Massachusetts* (Boston: Houghton Mifflin, 1897), 175.

Page 56, "could not with safety": *Papers Relating to the History of the Church in Massachusetts, A.D. 1676–1785*, ed. William Stevens Perry (n.p.: privately printed, 1873), 696.

Page 56, "the organ-pipes": Addison, *Edward Bass*, 137.

Page 57, "The articles against me": Edward Bass, quoted in Perry, *Church in Massachusetts*, 631.

Page 58, "notorious for his extravagancies": Sidney Perley, "Lord Timothy Dexter," *Essex Antiquarian* 7, no. 3 (July 1903): 97.

Page 60, "spitfire": Anna Davis Hallowell, *James and Lucretia Mott: Life and Letters* (Boston: Houghton Mifflin, 1890), 31.

Page 60, "About the year 1825": Anna Davis Hallowell, ed., *James and Lucretia Mott: Life and Letters* (Boston: Houghton Mifflin, 1890), 86.

Page 60, "Take this, my friend": Dorothy Sterling, *Lucretia Mott* (New York: Feminist Press, 1999), 77.

Page 62, "We know this lady well": *Pittsburgh Christian Witness*, quoted in *Liberator*, July 3, 1840, 2.

Page 62, "The early Friends": Lucretia Mott, quoted in Jane E. Calvert, *Quaker Constitutionalism and the Political Thought of John Dickinson* (New York: Cambridge University Press, 2009), 322.

Page 62, "that it was time": Lucretia Mott to Elizabeth Cady Stanton, March 16, 1855, in *Selected Letters of Lucretia Coffin Mott*, ed. Beverly Wilson Palmer (Champaign: University of Illinois Press, 2002), 233.

Page 62, "I must tell you": Mariana Hopper, quoted in Sterling, *Lucretia Mott*, 216.

Page 64, "seventeen men participated": "Legend Surrounds the Building of Richmond's Old Round Church," *Bennington* (VT) *Banner*, July 23, 1966, 6.

Page 64, "It has not been occupied": Hamilton Child, *Gazetteer and Business Directory of Chittenden County, Vermont, for 1882–83* (Syracuse, NY: Journal Office, 1882), 254.

Page 65, "hooping cough": Records of the Abington Congregational Church, Pomfret, Connecticut.

Page 67, "Our sentiments are uniformly": Danbury Baptist Association to Thomas Jefferson, letter, in *The Papers of Thomas Jefferson*, vol. 35, *1 August to 30 November 1801* (Princeton, NJ: Princeton University Press, 2008), 407–9.

Page 67, "Difference of opinion": Thomas Jefferson, *Notes on the State of Virginia* (Richmond, VA: J. W. Randolph, 1853), 171–72.

Page 70, "What is the proper Business": John Adams, *The Works of John Adams, Second President of the United States*, vol. 2 (Boston: Little, Brown, 1850), 20.

Page 70, "It is the duty of all": *The Works of John Adams, Second President of the United States*, vol. 4 (Boston: Little, Brown, 1865), 221.

Page 70, "God—and a Religious President": No Infidel [pseud.], "God and a Religious President, Jefferson and No God," *Gazette of the United States* (Philadelphia), October 7, 1800, 3.

Page 71, "Twenty times": John Adams to Thomas Jefferson, letter, April 19, 1817, https://founders.archives.gov/documents/Adams/99-02-02-6744.

Page 71, "If, by religion": Thomas Jefferson to John Adams, letter, May 5, 1817, www.encyclopediavirginia.org/Letter_from_Thomas_Jefferson_to_John_Adams_May_5_1817.

Page 71, "In extracting": Thomas Jefferson to John Adams, letter, October 12, 1813, https://founders.archives.gov/documents/Jefferson/03-06-02-0431.

Page 72, "There exists": John Adams to Thomas Jefferson, letter, January 23, 1825, in *The Works of John Adams, Second President of the United States*, vol. 10 (Boston: Little, Brown, 1856), 415.

Page 73, "My Dear Waldo": *The Selected Letters of Mary Moody Emerson*, ed. Nancy Craig Simmons (Athens: University of Georgia Press, 1993), 152.

Page 73, "The pure Walden water": Henry David Thoreau, *Walden; or, Life in the Woods* (Boston: Ticknor and Fields, 1854), 319.

THE MID-ATLANTIC

Page 79, "When the old mill disappeared": *Year Book of the (Collegiate) Reformed Protestant Dutch Church* (New York: The Church, 1895), 138.

Page 80, "no scandal nor offence": Lord Baltimore, "Instructions," http://nationalhumanitiescenter.org/pds/amerbegin/settlement/text4/BaltimoreInstructions.pdf.

Page 81, "it certainly looks ancient enough": George Johnston, *History of Cecil County, Maryland* (Elkton, MD: Printed by author, 1881), 199.

Page 81, "hammered from horse-shoes": *Records of the American Catholic Historical Society of Philadelphia*, vol. 24 (Philadelphia: American Catholic Historical Society, 1913), 103.

Page 83, "Upon the whole": Andrew White, *A Relation of the Colony of the Lord Baron of Baltimore, in Maryland, near Virginia*, trans. N. C. Brooks (Baltimore: Maryland Historical Society, 1847), 23.

Page 83, "Apostle of Maryland": See, for example, Edward Devitt, "Andrew White," in *The Catholic Encyclopedia*, vol. 15 (New York: Robert Appleton, 1912), www.newadvent.org/cathen/15610b.htm.

Page 84, "From 1696 to 1786": Israel Acrelius, *A History of New Sweden; or, The Settlements on the River Delaware*, trans. William M. Reynolds, Memoirs of the Historical Society of Pennsylvania, vol. 11 (Philadelphia: McCarty and David, 1874), xix.

Page 84, "venison and corn": Johan Campanius, quoted in Emily Read, *Two Hundred Years Ago; or, Life in New Sweden* (Philadelphia: American Sunday-School Union, 1876), 53.

Page 84, "the oldest church": "Old Swedes Church," Old Swedes Foundation, Wilmington, Delaware, www.oldswedes.org/sites/.

Page 84, "Lux lucet in tenebris": Acrelius, *History of New Sweden*, 26.

Page 85, "My God will Make it": William Penn, quoted in George Patterson Donehoo, *Pennsylvania: A History*, vol. 1 (New York: Lewis Historical Publishing, 1926), 160.

Page 85, "tremble at the word": *Journal of George Fox; Being an Historical Account . . .*, 7th ed., vol. 1, ed. Wilson Armisted (London: W. and F. G. Cash, 1852), 206.

Page 86, "All persons living": William Penn, "The Frame of Government of Pennsylvania" (1682), http://avalon.law.yale.edu/17th_century/pa04.asp.

Page 91, "deemed it useful": Peter Stuyvesant, "Petition to Expel the Jews from New Amsterdam (September 22, 1654)," in *The Jew in the Modern World: A Documentary History*, eds. Paul R. Mendes-Flohr and Jehuda Reinharz (New York: Oxford University Press, 1995), 452.

Page 91, "We would have liked": Dutch West India Company, "Reply to Stuyvesant's Petition (April 26, 1655)," in Mendes-Flohr and Reinharz, *Jew in the Modern World*, 453.

Page 92, "Jews, Turks and Egyptians": Flushing Remonstrance (1657), www.thirteen.org/ dutchny/interactives/document-the-flushing-remonstrance/.

Page 93, "Patriot Rabbi of the Revolution": Howard A. Berman, "The First American Jew: A Tribute to Gershom Mendes Seixas," American Council for Judaism, spring 2007, www.acjna.org/acjna/articles_detail.aspx?id=442.

Page 93, "Gershom Seixas served": Thomas Kessner, "Gershom Mendes Seixas: His Religious 'Calling,' Outlook and Competence," *American Jewish Historical Quarterly* 58, no. 4 (June 1969): 453–54.

Page 93, "I conceive we as Jews": Gershom Mendes Seixas, Thanksgiving Day Sermon, November 26, 1789, New York, quoted in Mark I. Wolfson, "Rev. Gershom Mendes Seixas (1745–1816)," *Mikveh Israel History* (blog), June 2013, https://mikvehisraelhistory. com/2013/06/12/rev-gershom-mendes-seixas-1745-1816.

Page 94, "Rebellion to tyrants": Steven Waldman, *Founding Faith: Providence, Politics, and the Birth of Religious Freedom in America* (New York: Random House, 2008), ix.

Page 94, "my mind is my own church": Thomas Paine, *The Age of Reason* (London: H. D. Symonds, 1794), pt. 1, sec. 1.

Page 95, "A situation, similar to present": Thomas Paine, "Common Sense" (Philadelphia: R. Bell, 1776), 161.

Page 97, "One Sabbath morning": Freeborn Garrettson, quoted in William J. Shrewsbury, "British Methodism and Slavery: An Historical Review of the Influence of Methodism in Effecting the Christian Work of Emancipation," *Methodist Quarterly Review*, vol. 40 (New York: Carlton and Porter, 1858), 41–42.

Page 98, "reviler": William J. Shrewsbury, "British Methodism and Slavery," *Methodist Review* (January 1858): 42.

Page 98, "I endeavored": Ibid.

Page 98, "I saw in the visions": Freeborn Garrettson, quoted in Nathan Bangs, *The Life of the Rev. Freeborn Garrettson* (New York: J. Emory and B. Waugh, 1829), 104.

Page 98, "Once I was imprisoned": Nathan Bangs, *The Life of Freeborn Garrettson* (New York: Carlton & Lanahan, 1832), 146.

Page 99, "These religious scruples": "Freeborn Garrettson," *York* (PA) *Daily*, March 21, 1881.

Page 99, "I am going": Bangs, *The Life of Freeborn Garrettson*, 99.

Page 99, "I had a dirty floor": Ibid., 105.

Page 100, "In pointing out": Richard Allen, *The Life Experience and Gospel Labors of the Rt. Rev. Richard Allen* (1833), in *African American Religious History: A Documentary Witness*, ed. Milton C. Sernett (Durham, NC: Duke University Press, 1999), 141.

Page 103, "wholly ignorant": Jarena Lee, "A Female Preacher among the African Methodists," in Sernett, *African American Religious History*, 164.

Page 111, "children were easily": Charles Dickens Jr., "Toys, Past and Present," *All the Year Round*, October 1, 1870, 418.

Page 112, "Those of us mothers": "Mays Instead of Don'ts for Sunday," in *Babyhood: The Mother's Nursery Guide*, vol. 7, ed. Leroy M. Yale (New York: Babyhood Publishing, 1891), 129–30.

Page 114, "Deep mourning requires": E. B. Duffey, *The Ladies' and Gentlemen's Etiquette: A Complete Manual of the Manners and Dress of American Society* (Philadelphia: Porter and Coates, 1877), 295.

Page 116, "about thirty years old": Samuel Grant Zerfass, *Souvenir Book of the Ephrata Cloister: Complete History from Its Settlement in 1728 to the Present Time* (Lititz, PA: J. G. Zook, 1921), 9.

Page 119, "a flask of rum": Arthur C. Parker, *The Code of Handsome Lake, the Seneca Prophet*, New York State Museum Bulletin no. 163 (Albany: University of the State of New York, 1913), 17.

Page 120, "I am happy": Thomas Jefferson to Handsome Lake, letter, November 3, 1802, http://avalon.law.yale.edu/19th_century/jeffind2.asp.

Page 120, "When the sun goes down": Henry Whittemore, *The Abeel and Allied Families* (New York: published by the author, 1899), 8.

Page 121, "During our evening conversations": Lucy Smith, *History of the Prophet Joseph* (Salt Lake City: Improvement Era, 1902), 84.

Page 126, "licentious lewdness": *Memoirs of the Life and Religious Labors of Edward Hicks* (Philadelphia: Merrihew and Thompson, 1851), 36.

Page 127, "The facts are placed": "Separation in the West," *The Friend: A Religious and Literary Journal*, vol. 2 (Philadelphia: John Richardson, 1829), 29.

Page 127, "The lamb, the kid": *Edward Hicks*, 270.

Page 128, "Johnny's life": W. D. Haley, "Johnny Appleseed—a Pioneer Hero," *Harper's New Monthly Magazine* 43, no. 258 (November 1871): 830.

Page 129, "Toward the latter part": Ibid., 835.

Page 131, "professing to believe in Jesus Christ": "An Act Concerning Religion," September 21, 1649, http://avalon.law.yale.edu/18th_century/maryland_toleration.asp.

Page 131, "the Popish Religion": Charles Ernest Smith, *Religion under the Barons of Baltimore: Being a Sketch of Ecclesiastical Affairs* (Baltimore: E. Allen Lycett, 1899), 339.

Page 131, "A good conscience": Charles Carroll, quoted in Scott McDermott, *Charles Carroll of Carrollton: Faithful Revolutionary* (New York: Scepter, 2002), 54.

Page 132, "I can't conceive": Scott McDermott, *Charles Carroll of Carrollton: Faithful Revolutionary* (New York: Scepter, 2002), 47.

Page 132, "continues to hazard": John Adams, quoted in ibid., 143.

Page 134, "If we have the wisdom": John Carroll, quoted in Peter Guilday, *The Life and Times of John Carroll: Archbishop of Baltimore (1735–1815)* (New York: Encyclopedia Press, 1922), 126.

Page 137, "We commission": Pope Pius VI, quoted in Guilday, *John Carroll*, 360.

Page 137, "To General Bonaparte": John Carroll, quoted in Ernesto Begni, *The Catholic Church in the United States of America, Undertaken to Celebrate the Golden Jubilee of His Holiness, Pope Pius X*, vol. 3, *The Province of Baltimore and the Province of New York* (New York: Catholic Editing, 1914), 50.

Page 138, "on the very morning": *New York Evening Post*, December 2, 1820, 2.

Page 138, "the metropolis of American Catholicism": Benjamin Latrobe, *The Journal of Latrobe: Being the Notes and Sketches of an Architect, Naturalist and Traveler in the United States from 1796 to 1820* (New York: Appleton, 1905), 193.

Page 140, "The accidents of life": Elizabeth Ann Seton, quoted in Joseph I. Dirvin, *The Soul of Elizabeth Seton* (San Francisco: Ignatius, 1990), 57.

Page 140, "Elizabeth Ann Seton is a saint": Pope Paul VI, quoted in "Seton Shrine," Saint Peter's Church–Our Lady of the Rosary–Saint Joseph's Chapel website, http://spcolr.org/st-seton-shrine-1.

Page 141, "always delighted": George P. Matysek Jr., "Research Uncovers New Information about Mother Mary Lange," *Catholic Review*, February 8, 2015, www.catholicreview.org/article/home/research-uncovers-new-information-about-mother-mary-lange.

Page 144, "one of the people": Jonas Phillips, quoted in Hasia R. Diner, *The Jews of the United States, 1654 to 2000* (Berkeley: University of California Press, 2004), 54.

Page 146, "I have never witnessed": "Document 1: Rebecca Gratz," in *Women and Religion in America*, vol. 1, *The Nineteenth Century*, eds. Rosemary Radford Ruether and Rosemary Skinner Keller (San Francisco: Harper and Row, 1981), 166.

Page 146, "We all go Friday evening": Rebecca Gratz, quoted in *Jewish American Literature: A Norton Anthology*, ed. Jules Chametzky (New York: Norton, 2001), 48.

Page 146, "I claimed the privilege": *Letters of Rebecca Gratz*, ed. David Philipson (Philadelphia: Jewish Publication Society of America, 1929), 233.

Page 147, "The Religion then": James Madison, Memorial and Remonstrance against Religious Assessments (1785), www.let.rug.nl/usa/presidents/james-madison/memorial-and-remonstrance-1785.php.

Page 147, "always been in favor": James Madison to Thomas Jefferson, October 17, 1788, www.constitution.org/jm/17881017_bor.htm.

Page 147, "If we can make": James Madison, quoted in Ralph Louis Ketcham, *James Madison: A Biography* (Charlottesville: University of Virginia Press, 1990), 290.

Page 148, "The civil rights of none": James Madison, "Proposed Amendments to the Constitution, June 8, 1789," www.let.rug.nl/usa/presidents/james-madison/proposed-amendments-to-the-constitution.php.

THE SOUTH

Page 152, "Father Abraham": *Memoirs of the Life and Character of the Late Rev. George Whitefield*, ed. John Gillies, 4th ed., ed. Aaron C. Seymour (Philadelphia: Simon Probasco, 1820), 308.

Page 154, "In 1739 arriv'd": Benjamin Franklin, *The Autobiography of Benjamin Franklin* (1791; repr., New Haven, CT: Yale University Press, 2003), 175.

Page 154, "The awakeners preached": Mark Noll, *America's God: From Jonathan Edwards to Abraham Lincoln* (New York: Oxford University Press, 2002), 13.

Page 157, "All sects are mixed": *Letters from an American Farmer and Other Essays by J. Hector St. John de Crèvecoeur*, ed. Dennis D. Moor (Cambridge, MA: Harvard University Press, 2013), 36–37.

Page 158, "Whither am I going?": Francis Asbury, quoted in James Richard Joy, "Francis Asbury: A Founder of the American Nation," *Methodist Review*, vol. 105 (New York: Published by G. Lane and P. P. Sandford for the Methodist Episcopal Church, 1922), 71.

Page 159, "When I came near": Francis Asbury, *The Journal of the Rev. Francis Asbury, Bishop of the Methodist Episcopal Church* . . . (New York: N. Bangs and T. Mason, 1821), 4.

Page 161, "heathen gods": William King, *An Historical Account of the Heathen Gods and Heroes* (London: Printed for Bernard Lintott, 1750).

Page 161, "Jesus did not mean": Thomas Jefferson to William Short, letter, August 4, 1820, www.let.rug.nl/usa/presidents/thomas-jefferson/letters-of-thomas-jefferson/jefl261.php.

Page 161, "Abracadabra": Thomas Jefferson, quoted in Kevin J. Hayes, *The Road to Monticello: The Life and Mind of Thomas Jefferson* (New York: Oxford University Press, 2008), 586.

Page 161, "Dear Sir": Thomas Jefferson to Dr. Benjamin Rush, April 21, 1803, www.let.rug.nl/usa/presidents/thomas-jefferson/letters-of-thomas-jefferson/jefl153.php.

Page 163, "of a sect by myself": Thomas Jefferson to Ezra Stiles Ely, June 25, 1819, http://rotunda.upress.virginia.edu/founders/default.xqy?keys=FOEA-print-04-02-02-0542.

Page 163, "If it ends": Thomas Jefferson to Peter Carr, letter, August 10, 1787, www.let.rug.nl/usa/presidents/thomas-jefferson/letters-of-thomas-jefferson/jefl61.php.

Page 164, "Providence has reserved": George Sale, "To the Reader," preface to *The Koran, Commonly Called the Alcoran of Mohammed* (London: Printed for L. Hawes, W. Clarke, R. Collins, and T. Wilcox, 1734), v.

Page 166, "a religious ring dance": Lorenzo Dow Turner, quoted in Art Rosenbaum, *Shout Because You're Free: The African American Ring Shout Tradition in Coastal Georgia* (Athens: University of Georgia Press, 2012), 173.

Page 166, "Mohammedan parentage": Virginia Slave Act of 1682, included in John Brown Dillon, *Oddities of Colonial Legislation in America* (Indianapolis: R. Douglas, 1879), 201.

Page 166, "His principal objections": "The Unfortunate Moor," *New York Commercial Advertiser*, April 4, 1828, 1.

Page 168, "This Mohammedan": William Brown Hodgson, quoted in Ronald Judy, *(Dis)Forming the American Canon: African-Arabic Slave Narratives and the Vernacular* (Minneapolis: University of Minnesota Press, 1993), 209.

Page 168, "Mohammedan learning": Theodore Dwight, "Condition and Character of Negroes in Africa," *Methodist Quarterly Review*, vol. 46 (New York: Carlton and Porter, 1864), 78.

Page 169, "Then there came": *A Muslim American Slave: The Life of Omar ibn Said by Omar ibn Said*, ed. and trans. Ala Alryyes (Madison: University of Wisconsin Press, 2011), 89.

Page 171, "Being of a feeble constitution": "A Convert from Mohammedanism," *Boston Reporter*, September 1, 1837.

Page 171, "O people of America": Ibn Said, *A Muslim American Slave*, 71.

Page 172, "He told me": *The Narrative of the Life of Frederick Douglass* (Boston: Anti-Slavery Office, 1849), 70.

Page 173, "relics of ancient traffic": Edward Thomas Stevens, *Flint Chips: A Guide to Pre-Historic Archaeology* (London: Bell and Daldy, 1870), 474.

Page 173, "tie strings of beads": Quoted in Linda France Stine, Melanie A. Cabak, and Mark D. Groover, "Blue Beads as African-American Cultural Symbols," *Historical Archaeology* 30, no. 3 (1996): 54.

Page 173, "Osanyin, so it is believed": Robert Farris Thompson, *Flash of the Spirit: African and Afro-American Art and Philosophy* (New York: Vintage, 1984), 43.

Page 174, "My master": *The Confessions of Nat Turner, the Leader of the Late Insurrection in Southampton* (Baltimore: Thomas R. Gray, 1831), 8.

Page 176, "He stimulated his comrades": "The Insurrection," *Richmond Telegraph*, reprinted in *Liberator*, September 10, 1831, 147.

Page 176, "I venture to predict": Rev. John Holt Rice, quoted in *Liberator*, November 19, 1831, 186.

Page 177, "It appears that this was": "Particulars of the Negro Plot at Charleston," *Hagerstown* (MD) *Torch Light and Public Advertiser*, August 13, 1822, 2.

Page 178, "In the prosecution": *Niles' Weekly Register* 23 (September 7, 1822): 12.

Page 179, "Rebellion to Tyrants Is Obedience to God": http://thefederalistpapers.org/founders/franklin/rebellion-to-tyrants-is-obedience-to-god-benjamin-franklin.

Page 179, "In several instances": John Carle, "A Funeral Sermon, Preached at Rockaway, December 29, 1799, on the Much Lamented Death of General George Washington" (Morristown, NJ: Printed by Jacob Mann, 1800), 11.

Page 180, "Moses led the Israelites": Peter Folsom, quoted in James P. Byrd, *Sacred Scripture, Sacred War: The Bible and the American Revolution* (New York: Oxford University Press, 2013), 70.

Page 180, "After God had done": John H. Stevens, *The Duty of Union in a Just War: A Discourse Delivered in Stoneham (Mass.)* (Poughkeepsie, NY: C. C. Adams, 1813), 6.

Page 180, "one of the best": Mikveh Israel resolution, quoted in Isaac Markens, *Abraham Lincoln and the Jews* (New York: Printed by author, 1909), 42.

Page 182, "To further incite them": James Mooney, "The Cherokee Ball Play," *American Anthropologist* 3, no. 2 (April 1890): 107.

Page 183, "a school for the painter": George Catlin, quoted in *Southeastern Indians Life Portraits: A Catalogue of Pictures, 1564–1860*, ed. Emma Lila Fundaburk (Birmingham: University of Alabama Press, 2000), 125.

Page 183, "converted more American Indians": Jerry L. Faught II, "Jones, Evan (1788–1872)," in *Encyclopedia of Oklahoma History and Culture*, Oklahoma Historical Society, www.okhistory.org/publications/enc/entry.php?entry=JO019.

Page 184, "cast off their savage habits": Andrew Jackson, quoted in Samuel Gordon Heiskell and John Sevier, *Andrew Jackson and Early Tennessee History* (Nashville: Ambrose, 1920), 206.

Page 188, "Sir, I congratulate you": John Leland to James Madison, letter, February 15, 1789, https://founders.archives.gov/documents/Madison/01-11-02-0322.

Page 188, "mammoth cheese": J. Boehm, *Thomas Jefferson Encyclopedia* (October 1997), www.monticello.org/site/research-and-collections/mammoth-cheese.

Page 189, "When the collection plate": *New York Evening Post*, December 7, 1824, 2.

Page 190, "'Tis thus the rich man": "The Sunday Bill," *Liberator*, August 10, 1855, 128.

Page 190, "to compel a man": Thomas Jefferson, Virginia Statute for Religious Freedom (1785). For text and commentary, see *The Virginia Statute for Religious Freedom: Its Evolution and Consequences*, eds. Merrill D. Peterson and Robert C. Vaughan (New York: Cambridge University Press, 2013).

Page 190, "a contradiction": James Madison, "Memorial and Remonstrance against Religious Assessments" (1785), http://founders.archives.gov/documents/Madison/01-08-02-0163.

Page 191, "remain in the family": George Mason, quoted in Kate Mason Rowland, *The Life of George Mason, 1725–1792*, vol. 1 (New York: G. P. Putnam's Sons, 1892), 58.

Page 191, "In a society": Lauren F. Winner, *A Cheerful and Comfortable Faith: Anglican Religious Practice in the Elite Households of Eighteenth-Century Virginia* (New Haven, CT: Yale University Press, 2010), 33.

Page 192, "Religion, or the duty": George Mason, "16th Article of the Bill of Rights," in Charles Fenton James, *Documentary History of the Struggle for Religious Liberty in Virginia* (Lynchburg, VA: J. P. Bell, 1900), 62.

Page 192, "Anglicans, Roman Catholics": H. J. Eckenrode, *Separation of Church and State in Virginia: A Study in the Development of the Revolution, Special Report of the Department of Archives and History* (Richmond, VA: D. Bottom, Superintendent of Public Printing, 1910), 45.

Page 192, "For some Christian communities": Winner, *Cheerful and Comfortable Faith*, 33, 35.

Page 193, "In the National Museum": Robert Shackleton, *The Book of Washington* (Philadelphia: Penn, 1922), 332.

Page 195, "When the mind": Martha Washington to Jonathan Trumbull, letter, January 15, 1800, quoted in Harrison Clark, *All the Cloudless Glory* (Washington, DC: Regnery, 1998), 427.

Page 195, "The precepts": Martha Washington to Catherine Garrettson, letter, March 25, 1800, quoted in Abel Stevens, *Sketches from the Study of a Superannuated Itinerant* (New York: Carlton & Phillips, 1853), 255.

Page 198, "The Address of the Hebrew Congregations," in Abraham Simon Wolf Rosenbach, *Dedication of the New Synagogue of the Congregation Mikve Israel at Broad and York Streets on September 14, 1909, Elul 29, 5669* (Philadelphia: Cahan, 1909), 14–15.

Page 200, "equal to the BEST French": *South-Carolina Gazette*, August 19, 1756, quoted in Barnett Abraham Elzas, *The Jews of South Carolina: From the Earliest Times to the Present Day* (Philadelphia: J. B. Lippincott, 1905), 48.

Page 200, "It took the Jews": Elzas, *Jews of South Carolina*, 149–50.

Page 204, "beautiful, bright-eyed": "The Dead Voudou Queen," *New York Times*, June 21, 1881, 2.

Page 205, "The people met": Dr. Baxter to Dr. Alexander, letter, January 1, 1802, reprinted in "The Great Revival in Kentucky," *Presbyterian Magazine* 5, no. 3 (March 1855): 131.

Page 205, "It began": "Revivals," *Indianapolis News*, November 11, 1875, 2.

Page 205, "a guilty, wretched sinner": *Autobiography of Peter Cartwright, the Backwoods Preacher*, ed. W. P. Strickland (Cincinnati: L. Swormstedt and A. Poe for the Methodist Episcopal Church, 1859), 37.

BEYOND THE BORDERS

Page 212, "The iconography of Isis": Stephen Benko, *The Virgin Goddess: Studies in the Pagan and Christian Roots of Mariology* (New York: Brill, 1993), 212, quoted in Michael P. Duricy, "Montserrat Black Madonna/Black Madonnas: Our Lady of Montserrat," International Marian Research Institute, University of Dayton, Ohio, https://udayton.edu/imri/mary/m/montserrat-black-madonna.php.

Page 215, "pile of useless masonry": Jane Landers, *Black Society in Spanish Florida* (Champaign: University of Illinois Press, 1999), 114.

Page 215, "the oldest bells in America": "The Oldest City in the States," *Chambers's Journal* 64, no. 2 (November 19, 1887): 745.

Page 219, "Holy Infant of Atocha": Ray John De Aragón, *The Penitentes of New Mexico: Hermanos de la Luz/Brothers of the Light* (Santa Fe: Sunstone, 2006), 206.

Page 220, "skins . . . very well dressed": "Translation of the Letter from Coronado to Mendoza, August 3, 1540," in George Parker Winship, *The Coronado Expedition, 1540–1542* (Washington, DC: U.S. Government Printing Office, 1896), 560.

Page 222, "My dear little son": "Our Lady of Guadalupe," *Catholic Online*, www.catholic.org/about/guadalupe.php. For more on the Lady of Guadalupe's history, see Jody Brant Smith, *The Image of Guadalupe* (Macon, GA: Mercer University Press, 1994), 1–8.

Page 225, "on the spot": Le Baron Bradford Prince, *Spanish Mission Churches of New Mexico* (Cedar Rapids, IA: Torch, 1915), 318.

Page 229, "Yesterday morning": "Chinese Dedication," *San Francisco Whig*, reprinted in *Salem* (MA) *Register*, December 27, 1852, 2.

Page 231, "afford aid and relief": "Eureka Benevolent Society (San Francisco, Calif.) Records, 1850–1977," Magnes Collection of Jewish Art and Life, www.magnes.org/collections/archives/western-jewish-americana/eureka-benevolent-society-san-francisco-calif-records.

Page 231, "Hebrew Ceremony": *Daily Alta California*, June 14, 1850, 2.

Page 231, "Every arrival of steamer": August Helbing, quoted in "August Helbing (1824–1896)," *American Jerusalem: Jews and the Making of San Francisco*, www.americanjerusalem.com/characters/august-helbing-1824-ae-1896/22.

CONCLUSION

Page 233, "On my arrival": Alexis de Tocqueville, *Democracy in America*, trans. Henry Reeve, rev. Francis Bowen (New York: Century, 1898), 394.

Acknowledgments

Objects of Devotion would not have been possible without the support of H. Bruce McEver, whose leadership of the Foundation for Religious Literacy has benefited so many individuals and institutions. His tireless efforts to bridge the worlds of business, poetry, and faith are a model of creative engagement with diverse interests and communities.

Heartfelt thanks also to my many colleagues who contributed to the creation of the *Religion in Early America* exhibit, including David Allison, Stevan Fisher, Tanya Garner, Margaret Grandine, Katharine Klein, and Christine Klepper; to Richard Strauss and Jaclyn Nash, who provided many of the evocative photographs; and to Sarah Richards, who was kind enough to translate the German *Taufschein* text in the Fraktur section.

I am grateful as well to members of the scholarly community for their encouragement, particularly Dr. Kathryn Gin Lum and Dr. John Wigger, who reviewed the exhibit script; Dr. John Fea and Dr. S. Brent Plate, who provided helpful comments on *Objects of Devotion*; and Dr. Stephen Prothero, for his early and ongoing contributions to the discussion of religion at the National Museum of American History. Any errors that may remain are, of course, my own.

The team of editors and designers brought together by Smithsonian Books— Antonio Alcalá, Juliana Froggatt, Carolyn Gleason, Laura Harger, and Christina Wiginton—have all enhanced and improved this work.

Finally, this book and its author owe a debt of gratitude to Lilly Endowment, whose generous support has secured a permanent place for the study of religion in American history at the Smithsonian.

Index

CREDITS

Acronyms

HABS: Historic American Buildings Survey

LOC: Library of Congress

LOC, PPD: Library of Congress, Prints and Photographs Division

MIDW DAPP: PC: Miriam and Ira D. Wallach Division of Arts, Prints, and Photographs: Photograph Collection

NGA: National Gallery of Art

NMAAHC: National Museum of African American History and Culture, Smithsonian Institution

NMAH: National Museum of American History, Smithsonian Institution

NMNH: National Museum of Natural History, Smithsonian Institution

NPG: National Portrait Gallery, Smithsonian Institution

NYPL: New York Public Library

SI: Smithsonian Institution

Title pages: *ii*: courtesy Congregation Shearith Israel, New York. **Contents**: *iv–v*: NMAH, 1987.0006.02. **Foreword**: *vi*: courtesy LOC, LC-DIG-pga-04612. **Introduction**: *viii*: NMAH, lent by

Georgetown University, Washington, D.C.; *3*: photograph by George J. Vaillancourt, courtesy LOC, HABS, HABS-RI-38; *4*: Harry T. Peters "America on Stone" Lithography Collection, NMAH, DL*60.2918; *7*: on loan from the Basilica of the National Shrine of the Assumption of the Blessed Virgin Mary, Archdiocese of Baltimore, photograph by NAMH. **New England**: *8*: courtesy Mr. and Mrs. Samuel M. Nickerson Collection, The Art Institute of Chicago, 1900.558; *11*, *12*: courtesy Sotheby's; *13*: courtesy of Natick Historical Society, Natick, Massachusetts; *14*: courtesy of American Bible Society; *16*: gift of Mendel L. Peterson, National Numismatic Collection, NMAH, NU*70.80.20; *18*: photograph © 2017 Museum of Fine Arts, Boston; lent by First and Second Church in Boston; maker: "T. C.," English; *20*: from *American Architect and Building News* 1 (Boston: James R. Osgood & Co., 1876); *21*: courtesy American Antiquarian Society; *22*: Collection of the Massachusetts Historical Society; *23*: from NYPL, MIDW DAPP: PC; *24*: courtesy LOC, PPD,

LC-USZ62-53343; *26*: courtesy Rhode Island Historical Society, RHi x17.1147; *28*: courtesy of Providence City Archives; *30*: courtesy LOC, PPD; *31*: courtesy LOC, Collection of the Hebraic Section, African and Middle Eastern Division; *32*: courtesy NPG, SI, acquired as a gift to the nation through the generosity of the Donald W. Reynolds Foundation, NPG.2001.13; *34–35*: courtesy of Morris Morgenstern Foundation, National Museum of American Jewish History; *37*: from records of the Court of Oyer and Terminer, 1692, Essex County Court Archives, vol. 1, no. 31, Massachusetts Supreme Judicial Court, Judicial Archives, on deposit at James Duncan Phillips Library, Peabody Essex Museum, Salem, Massachusetts; *38*: courtesy LOC, PPD; *41–43*: NMAH, 2003.0085.01; *44*: from G. H. Hollister, *The History of Connecticut, from the First Settlement of the Colony to the Adoption of the Present Constitution* (New Haven, CT: Durrie and Peck, 1855); *46*: courtesy NMAAHC, 2012.46.46; *49*: courtesy American History Collection, gift of J. P. Stevens & Co., Inc., through

American Textile History Museum Collection; *50:* from *Massachusetts Spy*, October 28, 1804, courtesy Paul Revere Memorial Association; *51, top:* courtesy New York State Museum, Albany, New York; *51, bottom:* courtesy of Warshaw Collection of Business Americana, NMAH; *52:* detail of image, courtesy Collection of the United Society of Shakers, New Gloucester, Maine; *54, top:* gift of Mrs. Laura E. C. Crow, NMAH, TE*T15611; *54, bottom:* courtesy LOC, HABS, HABS ME-107; *55:* NMAH, MG*71.92b; *56, 57–59:* courtesy St. Paul's Church, Newburyport, Massachusetts; *61:* photograph by F. Gutekunst, courtesy LOC, Records of the National Woman's Party, Manuscript Division; *62:* gift of Lucretia Mott (Churchill) Jordan (Mrs. H. Donaldson Jordan), NMAH, CS*268643.012; *63:* courtesy of Richmond Historical Society; *65:* photograph by Bruce Hedman, Abington Congregational Church; *66:* © 2017 White House Historical Association; *68:* courtesy LOC, Thomas Jefferson Papers, Manuscript Division; *70:* courtesy NPG, SI, NPG.71.4; *73:* courtesy Houghton Library, Harvard University, MS AM 2982 (84); *74:* courtesy Concord Museum, gift of E. H. Kittredge (1942), TH0006B; *75:* courtesy of Town of Danville, New Hampshire.

The Mid-Atlantic: *76:* courtesy LOC, PPD, LC-USZC4-543; *78:* photograph by Stevan Fisher, NMAH; *80:* watercolor on paper by John Moll, n.d., courtesy of Maryland Historical Society, M1955.44.1; *81–82:* NMAH, lent by Georgetown University, Washington, D.C.; *84:* courtesy LOC, HABS, HABS DE-92; *85:* courtesy NGA, gift of Edgar William and Bernice Chrysler Garbisch, 1980.62.15; *86:* from *The Papers of William Penn*, vol. 2 (1680–1684), courtesy University of Pennsylvania; *87:* courtesy of Mount Vernon Ladies' Association; *88:* courtesy St. John's Lodge No. 1, Ancient York Masons; *90, 92:* courtesy Congregation Shearith Israel, New York; *94:* courtesy NPG, SI, NPG 69.74; *95:* courtesy LOC, American Imprint Collection, Rare Book and Special Collections Division; *96:* from Nathan Bangs, *The Life of the Rev. Freeborn Garrettson: Compiled from His Printed and Manuscript Journals, and Other Authentic Documents* (New York: T. Mason and G. Lane for the Methodist Episcopal Church, 1974); *98:* courtesy of C. Wesley Christman Archives, New York Annual Conference of the Methodist Church; *100:* courtesy NPG, SI, NPG.79.93; *101, top and bottom:* courtesy United Library at Garrett-Evangelical Theological Seminary; *103:* courtesy

LOC, PPD, LC-USZ62-42044; *105:* NMAH, TE*T293320.0700; *106:* gift of Mrs. Mary E. Lyddane, NMAH, TE*T07319; *107:* courtesy Oblate Sisters of Providence Archive; *109:* NMAH, 1987.0006.02; *110–13:* from Collection of Judy and Jim Konnerth; *115:* NMAH, CS*202946.162; *116:* courtesy LOC, HABS, HABS PA,36-EPH,1; *117:* courtesy American Folk Art Museum/Art Resource, NY; *118:* collection of New-York Historical Society, gift of Thomas Jefferson Bryan, photography © New-York Historical Society, www.nyhistory.org; *122–23, 124, bottom:* courtesy Church History Library, The Church of Jesus Christ of Latter-day Saints; *124, top:* National Numismatic Collection, NMAH, 1985.0441.2219, government transfer: US DOTT, USM; *125–26:* courtesy NGA, gift of Edgar William and Bernice Chrysler Garbisch, 1980.62.15; *128:* from W. D. Haley, "Johnny Appleseed—A Pioneer Hero," *Harper's New Monthly Magazine* 43, no. 258 (November 1871); *129:* gift of Miss Mary Maxwell, NMAH, DL*368807; *130:* on loan from the Basilica of the National Shrine of the Assumption of the Blessed Virgin Mary, Archdiocese of Baltimore, photograph by NAMH; *133:* on loan from the Basilica of the National Shrine of the Assumption of the Blessed Virgin Mary, Archdiocese of Baltimore, photograph by NAMH; *135:* NMAH, lent by Georgetown University, Washington, D.C.; *136:* courtesy of Maryland Historical Society, 1897.1.3; *138:* on loan from the Basilica of the National Shrine of the Assumption of the Blessed Virgin Mary, Archdiocese of Baltimore, photograph by NAMH.; *139:* courtesy Daughters of Charity Province of St. Louise, St. Louis, MO; *141–42:* courtesy Oblate Sisters of Providence Archive; *142:* photograph by NMAH; *143:* courtesy Library Company of Philadelphia; *145:* courtesy Rosenbach Museum and Library of the Free Library of Philadelphia, 1954.1936; *149:* courtesy NPG, SI, gift of Katie Louchheim, NPG.77.252. **The South**: *150:* image courtesy of Gibbes Museum of Art/Carolina Art Association, 1938.036.0070; *153:* private collection, photograph © Bonhams, London, UK/Bridgeman Images; *154:* courtesy Texas Baptist Historical Collection, Waco, Texas; *155, left and right:* from NYPL, MIDW DAPP: PC; *156:* courtesy World Methodist Museum; *157:* courtesy LOC, PPD, LC-USZC4-6153; *158:* courtesy Archives and History, The United Methodist Church; *159:* courtesy World Methodist Museum; *160, 162:* NMAH, PL*158231; *163:* NMAH,

PL*314048.A; *165:* courtesy LOC, Rare Book and Special Collections Division, BP109 .S3 1764; *167:* courtesy of Hargett Rare Book and Manuscript Library/University of Georgia Libraries; *170:* courtesy Randolph Linsly Simpson African-American Collection, James Weldon Johnson Memorial Collection in the Yale Collection of American Literature, Beinecke Rare Book and Manuscript Library; *172:* courtesy Louisiana Department of Culture, Recreation, and Tourism: Louisiana Division of Archaeology and Louisiana State Museum; *175:* courtesy Special Collections, University of Virginia Library; *177:* courtesy of Family of Benjamin Frazier and the Margaretta Childs Archives at Historic Charleston Foundation; *179:* NMAH, TE*T13957.000; *181:* Getty Images; *182:* Smithsonian American Art Museum, gift of Mrs. Joseph Harrison, Jr., 1985.66.428A; *183:* NMNH E383638-0; *184:* David M. Rubinstein Rare Book & Manuscript Library, Duke University; *186:* courtesy Library of Virginia; *187:* from *Writings of the Late Elder John Leland: Including Some Events In His Life* (New York: G. W. Wood, 1845); *189:* courtesy Virginia Baptist Historical Society; *191:* courtesy Board of Regents, Gunston Hall; *193:* NMAH, PL*001175; *194:* NPG, SI, NPG.70.3; *195:* courtesy Mount Vernon Ladies' Association; *197:* courtesy of Special Collections, College of Charleston Libraries; *201:* Ursuline Convent Collection, Archives and Museum of New Orleans; *202:* photograph in Carol M. Highsmith Archive, LOC, PPD, LC-HS503-1380; *203:* courtesy Louisiana State Museum; *205:* photograph by Charles E. Peterson, courtesy LOC, HABS, HABS-KY-20-8. **Beyond the Borders**: *206:* NMAH, 1986.0639.0320; *209, 210, 213:* gifts of Teodoro Vidal, NMAH, 1997.0097.0785, 1997.0097.0901, 1997.0097.0721; *214:* from NYPL, MIDW DAPP: PC; *217:* courtesy Architect of the Capitol; *218:* gift of Mrs. W. C. F. Robards, NMAH, CL*67.806; *221:* gift of Dr. J. Walter Fewkes, NMAH, CL*176402; *223:* NMAH, CL*200826; *224:* photograph by Richard L. Rieckenberg; *226:* from NYPL, MIDW DAPP: PC; *228:* courtesy Huntington Library, San Marino, California, California Letter Sheets, RB 48052:069; *230:* gift of Congregation Emanu-El (San Francisco), 1987, NMAH, 1988.0183.001; *231:* from NYPL, MIDW DAPP: PC.

Conclusion: *232:* courtesy NGA, gift of Edgar William and Bernice Chrysler Garbisch, 1980.62.15.

This book may be purchased for educational, business, or sales promotional use. For information, please write: Special Markets Department, Smithsonian Books, P.O. Box 37012, MRC 513, Washington, DC 20013

Published by Smithsonian Books
Director: Carolyn Gleason
Managing Editor: Christina Wiginton
Production Editor: Laura Harger
Editorial Assistant: Jaime Schwender
Edited by Juliana Froggatt
Designed by Antonio Alcalá, Ricky Altizer / Studio A
Indexed by Scribe, Inc.

Library of Congress Cataloging-in-Publication Data
Names: Manseau, Peter, author.
Title: Objects of devotion : religion in early America / Peter Manseau.
Description: Washington, DC : Smithsonian Books, 2017. | Includes bibliographical references and index.
Identifiers: LCCN 2016038040 | ISBN 9781588345929 (hardcover)
Subjects: LCSH: United States—Church history. | United States—Religion—History. | Material culture—United States. | Material culture—Religious aspects—Christianity. | Material culture—Religious aspects.
Classification: LCC BR520 .M3628 2017 | DDC 277.3/07—dc23
LC record available at https://lccn.loc.gov/2016038040

Manufactured in China, not at government expense

21 20 19 18 17   5 4 3 2 1